DENIS JOHNSTON: A RETROSPECTIVE

IRISH LITERARY STUDIES

DENIS JOHNSTON:
A RETROSPECTIVE

edited by
Joseph Ronsley

Irish Literary Studies 8

COLIN SMYTHE
Gerrards Cross, 1981

BARNES AND NOBLE BOOKS
Totowa, New Jersey

This collection first published in 1981
by Colin Smythe Limited, Gerrards Cross, Buckinghamshire

British Library Cataloguing in Publication Data

Denis Johnston: a retrospective.
– (Irish literary studies; 8 ISSN 0140-895X).
1. Johnson, Denis, *b. 1901* – Addresses,
essays, lectures
I. Ronsley, Joseph   II. Series
822'.9'14   PR6019.0397Z/

ISBN 0-86140-078-X

First published in 1981 by Barnes & Noble Books,
81 Adams Drive, Totowa, N.J.07512

Library of Congress Cataloging in Publication Data

Denis Johnston, a retrospective.
(Irish literary studies, ISSN 0140-895X; 8)
"Check-list of Denis Johnston's writings. Joseph
Ronsley": p.
Includes index.
1. Johnston, Denis, 1901–   – Criticism and
interpretation – Addresses, essays, lectures.
I. Johnston, Denis, 1901–   .   II. Ronsley,
Joseph.   III. Series: Irish literary studies; 8.
PR6019.0397Z63 1981   822'.912   81-7983
ISBN 0-389-20233-9

Typeset by Inforum Ltd, Portsmouth
Printed in Great Britain by
Billing and Sons, London, Guildford and Worcester

CONTENTS

INTRODUCTION

Readers of this book may know Denis Johnston in any of a variety of ways, because during the course of his life, so far, Johnston has been a barrister, an actor, a theatre director, a playwright, and a film director. He has been a script writer, producer, and commentator in radio, a script writer, playwright, and producer for television, and a BBC war correspondent. He has been an essayist and historian, a book reviewer and drama critic. He has been an opera librettist, teacher and literary scholar, a public lecturer, an autobiographer, and a philosopher. He has had a vast international range of personal relationships. Nevertheless, he disappointed his father by not continuing to practise the law; 'we all disappoint our fathers' he has said. And he is convinced that Yeats had him personally in mind when he spoke of 'Base-born products of base beds.' He has complained, or more properly announced, that he was not found acceptable, at different periods in his life, to be a member either of the I.R.A. or the Royal Irish Academy. He has been a member of the Irish Academy of Letters since 1950, however, and has received the Order of the British Empire for service as a B.B.C. war correspondent, and more recently 'a couple of medals from Tito's Partisans', also in the late 1970s the Annual Award for Literature from the Allied Irish Banks and an honorary Doctor of Literature from the New University of Ulster. But, he says, 'what I prize most of all was the fact that we were both (his wife Betty and himself) elected Class Honoraries by three separate Classes at Mount Holyoke! This was something one really had to earn!'

Johnston has remarked that O'Casey may just possibly be remembered more for his autobiography than for his plays, a comment which, again just possibly, may make a veiled comparison with his own artful, autobiographical *Nine Rivers from Jordan*; but I am convinced that Johnston's plays will be the most important legacy of all his work. This though I have heard *Nine Rivers from Jordan* praised as one of very few authoritative books about war as seen from the perspective of the journalist reporting it, and referred to as the 'Bible' for a former CBS Viet Nam correspondent who carried the book with him constantly, reading it over and over in the field during his tour of duty. Moreover, it is a beautiful, perhaps a great book, on its own terms, as Vivian Mercier more than suggests in this volume. A more recent non-dramatic, partly autobiographical work, *The Brazen Horn,* is complex and abstruse, and still too new for full assessment. It is safe to say, however, that it will have a more limited general appeal than *Nine Rivers from Jordan. In Search of Swift,* on the other hand, a fine piece of original scholarly research, reads like a good mystery story. But Johnston has written five, perhaps six, successful, important, full-length plays, another that is superb and exciting but just misses success as a finished work of art, and several minor, partially successful dramatic works. Very few Irish playwrights to date can claim as much.

Furthermore, probably none can claim so wide a range of different modes. Johnston has received both praise for his versatility and condemnation for his failure to develop further any one method. Given the complaints on this score, it is easy to imagine Hilton Edwards's disappointment in Johnston's shifting not only modes of drama, but careers – a terribly frustrating dispersal of talent, implied Edwards writing in *The Bell* some forty years ago: 'Everything he has touched has proved his talent; has proved that he has something to give; but he has only touched it long enough to get fun from it; to show what he could do – never long enough to give us of his best with it.' Edwards' view commonly prevails. Certainly the eighteen years Johnston spent almost hidden away in New England college towns removed him both from his dramatic stimuli and from the limelight in whih he had basked during the 30s. Though he did write two plays during the period, it may be that we are thus deprived of a larger portion of Johnston's most valuable work; it is difficult to tell. But Hilton Edwards recognized that dismay over Johnston's departure from the precincts of the Gate and the Abbey does not take into account the other very real artistic and intellectual contributions he has made, or the richness the variety of experience has given to his own life, and undoubtedly to his later writings.

A source of impatience among Johnston's admirers is his compulsion to revise. In most cases the revisions effect improvement, perhaps even the final polish the author wishes to see on the plays – though personally I prefer both *A Bride for the Unicorn* and *The Golden Cuckoo* as they appeared previous to the 1977-79 *Dramatic Works.* In any case, I suppose most of us, agreeing with Vivian Mercier, would prefer that he turn his attention to writing a new play.

Unfortunately, I have not been able to obtain for this volume essays on all aspects of Johnston's multifarious career. He made a 16mm film version of Frank O'Connor's 'Guests of the Nation' in 1933, for instance, featuring Barry Fitzgerald, Cyril Cusack, Dudley Walsh, Hilton Edwards, and Fred Johnson. He has also written a satiric ballet, 'The Indiscreet Goat', which got him into trouble for his own indiscretions with the more 'respectable' and 'devout' elements of the Dublin audience, and the libretto for an opera version of Pirandello's *Six Characters in Search of an Author*. The most glaring omission is probably his broadcast work, both in radio and television. This is a pity since, especially in television, Johnston's work was central in pioneering techniques in a brand new medium. After serving as Features Writer/Director for BBC Radio in Northern Ireland, he was made a Director in BBC Television in 1938. (Most North Americans, I believe, were totally unfamiliar with television other than in experimental forms before World War II, whereas in fact regular programme service was begun in 1936 by the BBC.) Johnston returned to television after the war, and remained until he moved to the United States in 1947. During this time he was Head of Programmes, and explored such basic problems as where to place the cameras, how to shift scenes, and the use of cuts instead of mixes (which he got the technicians to do only by suggesting that they were not able to). There was no video tape at the time, thus no cutting room, no chance for retakes and editing. Television, Johnston has pointed out, is akin neither to the theatre nor to the movies, but is a development from sound broadcasting, radio. Sound, he says, is the essential element in television, vision in the movies. There must be someone around who was associated with Johnston during his broadcasting days, and can write about it, but I was unable to find him. Whoever he is, I hope he will write something on his own.

While this book appears at the time of Denis Johnston's eightieth birthday, it is not a book of tributes. It is true that all the contributors admire Johnston's work; otherwise they would not be inclined to give their time and energy to the study of his writings as they have done. For some, the admiration is very deep indeed, and not only for the work but for the man as well. But it is clear that none of the contributors engages in idolatry, that none, in fact, admires Johnston's work uncritically. Some have important reservations, and all prefer certain works to others, the range of assessment, by implication or direct statement, being from outright failure to brilliant success. Critical comments or attacks, disagreements or expressions of frustration and outrage, nevertheless, do not lower the value of Johnston's artistic and intellectual achievement, but in the seriousness and intensity of the responses serve to recognize it more fully. Controversy has accompanied nearly everything Johnston has produced, and he has thrived on it. By being essays of scholarship and outspoken criticism rather than of unqualified praise. The contents of this book assume both a seriousness and usefulness, to say nothing of honesty, that will make them of lasting value. They are not only written for contemplation by Denis Johnston, after all, but for his audience. By discussing Johnston's plays and other writings with critical and scholarly detachment, then, by exploring his ideas and sensibilities, and by providing candid glimpses into his character and his extraordinary life experience, this book is meant to be itself the best tribute we are able to make, and the best way we can say 'thank you,' and 'Happy Birthday, Denis.'

Joseph Ronsley
Montreal

ACKNOWLEDGMENTS

I have had considerable help in the production of this book, mainly with the bibliographical checklist but in other ways as well. To Colin Smythe, Ann Saddlemyer, David R. Clark, Mary Cannon, F. J. E. Hurst who is Librarian at The New University of Ulster, his assistant Margaret Vowles, Christine St. Peter and Sr. Veronica O'Reilly, Don Kennedy, Jim McAllister and Barbara Durack of Radio Telefis Eireann, Jacqueline Kavanagh of the BBC Written Archives Centre, Alan Reid of BBC Belfast, my wife Joanne, my daughter Jill, and Denis Johnston himself, I extend my sincere thanks.

I am also grateful to the Social Sciences and Humanities Research Council of Canada, and the McGill University Faculty of Graduate Studies and Research, who have supported the costs of editing this book.

I am most grateful to the BBC for permission to use photographs of *The Unthinking Lobster* (*A Fourth for Bridge*) and *Weep for the Cyclops* (*The Dreaming Dust*), to the BBC's Written Archive Centre for providing details of the casts of these plays, to Mme. C. Wandersleb-Herz for making available the picture of Cyril Cusack and to Denis Johnston for providing the rest of the pictures.

Joseph Ronsley

ILLUSTRATIONS

between pages 148 and 149

1. Denis Johnston.
2. Micheál MacLiammóir and Meriel Moore in *The Old Lady Says 'No!'*, 1929.
3 and 4. *The Old Lady Says 'No!'*, 1934.
5. *The Golden Cuckoo*, 1939.
6. *The Golden Cuckoo*, 1950.
7. *The Golden Cuckoo,* 1956.
8. *Weep for the Cyclops*, 1947.
9 to 13. *A Bride for the Unicorn*, 1936.
14 to 18. Some of the cast of *The Moon in the Yellow River*, 1931.
19. Cyril Cusack as Mr. Dotheright.
20. Denis Johnston with Winston Churchill.
21. *The Scythe and the Sunset*, 1958.
22. *The Unthinking Lobster,* 1948.
23. A dress rehearsal of *The Táin*, 1956.

AN APPRECIATION

HILTON EDWARDS

Did you ever have an enigma as a friend? I have. Its name is Denis Johnston and he is eighty this year and I write this to celebrate the occasion.

Denis had a delightful father who was from the north of Ireland and was a judge. He himself was, I believe, born in Dublin and received his early education there, so he may be said to straddle the North and South of Ireland.

He was further educated at Cambridge University in England and at Harvard University in the United States. He became a barrister, was called to the Irish Bar and later to the English Bar. Having achieved all this as a very young man, he becomes a playwright and his very first work, *The Old Lady says 'No!'*, is a masterpiece, which, incidentally, provided me with one of the most interesting productions I have ever tackled, and my late beloved partner, Micheál MacLiammóir, with one of his greatest roles: the Speaker who plays the part of Robert Emmet. There is often a misunderstanding about this term 'masterpiece'. It is, I suggest, not necessarily an artist's finest work, but that achievement that makes him acceptable as a master craftsman in his own right. For Denis to have attained this with his very first play strikes me as remarkable.

Denis Johnston then goes on to write a round dozen or so of plays, every one of which is worthy of production and revival. Far reaching in their themes, they tackle the simplest matters or those of the greatest complexity in a clear, precise and limpid English, with more than a hint of a poet's gift, that is never confused and is understandable by anyone who knows the language. He has a scalpel-like wit and an almost boyish sense of humour, and it goes with a good deal of charm thinly masked by an attitude of severity.

He proves himself to be a master in several areas: of irony; of a keen humour that cuts to the bone and yet is never offensive; of romance, which is never sentimental; of nostalgia, as in the Trinity student and his girl in *The Old Lady Says 'No!'* and the young lovers in *A Bride for the Unicorn*. He could write a scene of uproarious low comedy: Katie and Lizzy and the Speaker in *The Old Lady Says 'No!'*. He could rise to thunderous soul-shattering heights in his

1

massive orchestration of his credo in the same play. There seems to be no facet of the dramatic scene that he cannot handle with skill and to tremendous effect.

Unlike the great poet Yeats, he possesses and uses, when required, the common touch, without ever descending to vulgarity. His imagination sweeps across a tapestry of Irish history and Greek mythology to almost contemporary conflict. He plunges courageously into the heart of another enigma, the mystery of Dean Swift and his relations with Stella and Vanessa, and unravels a tangled skein and finds a plausible solution to the mystery of their relationships. He does this not only in a series of radio plays but, in a fine stage play, *The Dreaming Dust*. And he goes further and publishes the whole thesis in prose form. He enters the lists with O'Casey and emerges triumphantly with a play about the 'troubles' in Dublin – *The Scythe and the Sunset*. He has been produced with constant success by us at the Gate, and the Abbey Theatre has been equally successful with his *The Moon in the Yellow River*.

Having produced a considerable opus, he tends to rewrite almost as often as he creates. An obvious perfectionist, he seems to grow easily dissatisfied with his work and recasts it again and again, always to good effect, and each time revealing another facet of his theme. But for this tendency – unusual, I think, in playwrights – his output of works would have been far greater.

But Dublin is, or was, too small to satisfy the needs of such a talent. He attended the accouchement of television at the Alexandra Palace, became a producer of the BBC and later their war correspondent in the Middle East and Europe, and the result was a fine volume, *Nine Rivers from Jordan*. He found time to sit with us upon our Board of Directors at the Gate Theatre for a brief period, then off with him to America, where he had yet another career, that of a lecturer and producer in one of America's most prestigious colleges.

He once told me that he thought that Ireland and particularly Dublin was the finest place in the world to be born in and to which to retire; implying, I presume, that it was less suitable to live and work in.

This indeed may be the answer to the enigma which can be fairly stated: Why, why, with all these unquestionable talents, does Denis Johnston stand nobly and with certainty a giant upon the periphery of the Irish dramatic scene instead of being at its heart. I think that I am as much to blame as anyone for this, for not producing him more

2

widely and more often. Why have I not done so? I pause guiltily, unable to find an answer. He is undoubtedly one of the finest Theatre Craftsmen that Ireland has ever produced and has created a rich mine of tremendous variety in which to delve.

He is in my mind, without question, one of the four first dramatists of the Irish Theatre, and possibly one of the three finest still living. We do not perform him enough. *Mea Culpa*. It is not that he is too highbrow. Although intellectual content is always present in his plays, he never commits the fault of writing primarily for the intellect but has always struck principally and truly, as every good playwright should, at gut reaction and to the heart. Yet he gives his audience enough cerebral satisfaction for them to leave the theatre not feeling that they have indulged in just another evening of mere entertainment.

On this, the occasion of his eightieth year, I salute his contribution to the Theatre, I rejoice in the possession of his friendship and hold in my mind his image as a prodigy in the Irish Theatre, to whom, for some reason which remains a puzzlement to me, we have always given appreciation (I cannot remember him having a failure in the Theatre) but never accorded to him his just due. At least let me here acknowledge our debt to him and salute him on this occasion with my personal awareness of his true quality.

Since writing the above I have had the opportunity to read Denis's latest book, *The Brazen Horn*. I found it fascinating but difficult to understand partly because for much of it one requires a knowledge of mathematical formulae beyond my capacity to grasp. The book seems to embody a fairly comprehensive philosophic concept based upon dimensions in time, but, even though it is written in its decoded form *'en pleine'* as it were, I found it gripping and fascinating, but mystifying. *The Brazen Horn* reveals Denis in an aspect previously only hinted at in his work.

Yet, this aspect of Denis Johnston should have been no surprise to one who has many times produced his first play, *The Old Lady Says 'No!'*, a play in which the protagonist is invaded by the personality he is playing, and experiences almost a lifetime of events in a few seconds; in a passage through time and space, in the time it takes for a doctor to step off stage, pick up a rug with which he returns and covers the stunned body of the actor who plays Robert Emmet.

ON *THE OLD LADY SAYS 'NO!'*

MICHEÁL MACLIAMMÓIR

The second Peacock season looked an exciting one, though its financial aspect in that little place was, with our growing ambitions and hatred of tawdriness on the stage, a little rocky. Hilton and I often took a taxi because we hadn't the money for a tram, which sounds absurd if you don't know the beautiful trustfulness of Dublin taximen. They knew, like Tessie Martin, that we would pay them some day, and none of them, I hasten to add, was disappointed. In fact they were often paid sooner than they expected because on a Friday night, when we drew our small salaries, we would feel so gay at having some money in our pockets that we would decide on a taxi to the Plaza or some late-houred restaurant, and the driver would almost inevitably be one to whom we owed two or three fares. So then we would pay him altogether, and have only a little left again. People who were making money used to tell us we were crazy to work so hard for no return. 'You'll find yourselves in the soup some day,' they said, wagging their fingers. But we saw what we wanted to do and we believed that we could do it. Besides, we had discovered an amazing secretary-manager, a Mrs. Isa Hughes, who seemed convinced of our ultimate success and loudly urged us forward, and also a couple of new artists – Dorothy Casey, a character actress, and Edward Lexy, whose comedy gift found its way years later on to the films. The plays, too, looked exciting, and with Coralie's help – for she is an invaluable play-picker – we had chosen them carefully.

We had done *Powers of Darkness, The Unknown Warrior,* Capek's *R.U.R.*, a triple bill from Galsworthy, Evreinov, and An Philibin, a delicate lyric poet, and Elmer Rice's *Adding Machine*. We produced, too, a play about a gunman called *Juggernaut*, by David Sears. It had been rejected by the Abbey but we liked it and so, it seemed, did our small but growing audience, and it gave the signal for that inevitable attack on the National Theatre by all those people in Dublin who had a grudge against it for no better reason than that it was an established institution that had had the impertinence not to fall into decay and disappear. 'The Abbey's dead,' people would say to us gleefully, knowing quite well it was nothing of the kind, and letters to the newspapers on the subject

4

became a fashion. We at the Gate were seized upon in this campaign as a stick to beat the old traditional horse, and that we were neither flattered by this move nor willing to be so used counted little, and a few enemies were made for us in the senior theatre – a silly, distressing business it all was that should never have begun.

But as the spring days passed, paint-splashed and work-worn, into summer and the hawthorn broke into flower over the railings of Stephen's Green, a new excitement had arrived and we were too absorbed to notice anything else. Denis Johnston offered us his first play, *The Old Lady Says 'No!'*, and with it a subsidy towards its production of fifteen pounds by the Abbey. The figure sounds incredible but it is correct, and it is correct too to say that we welcomed it. More still, we welcomed the play which was altogether remarkable and precisely the sort of Irish play we had been hoping for. It was described by the author as a Romantic Play with Choral Interludes, and it dealt with an actor playing the part of Robert Emmet, the rebel leader who was executed in 1803, and with his search for Sarah Curran, for the Ireland of his imagination, and for his own self. With its majestic vocal orchestration, its deadly malice, its influence of Toller and Joyce, its dream-like atmosphere, its flashes of low comedy, its looming chaotic background of Dante's purgatory, and its Sitwellian feeling for the Irish pastorales of the nineteenth century, it read, as Hilton remarked, like a railway guide and played like *Tristan and Isolde*. It gave at least two magnificent acting parts, and the chance of a lifetime to the sort of producer Hilton was rapidly becoming, a producer who can handle choral speaking, rhythmical movement, metrical climax, and a magnificence of massed effect with the precision of a ballet-master.

I was to play the Emmet part: it remains the most musically exhilarating experience I have had on the stage, for it gives one the sense of being a soloist in some gigantic concerto, ping on the note, and away you go and keep going until the orchestra crashes about you and then is silent again for your next big attack, and all in a dazzle of green light and black, blinding shadow.

But the trouble was with the leading women. It was not a part for Coralie, demanding as it did an Irish actress for its double role of the romantic Sarah Curran, not as yet Far from the Land for the play opens on the night of Emmet's arrest, and the bloodthirsty drab which was Denis's pleasing conception of Yeats's Cathleen Ni Houlihan, 'that Ireland for whose sake so many have lain down their lives,' the old Dublin flower-woman who haunts the nightmare reaches of College Green selling, instead of flowers, her 'four beautiful green fields' which she offers at a penny a bunch.

'Oh, God, he's a terror,' I said for the twentieth time, poring over the script; 'listen to this.' And I read aloud: 'Aw, very well, very well, all me sons is again' me. But it won't be the cough'll have the stiffening of him, not if I lay a hold of him. If once I get me hands on your dirty puss I'll leave me mark on you, never fear.' Then after the boy has died for her and a government minister's wife approaches with a funeral wreath: 'Ah, come in, lady, come in; ah, he was me favourite of them all, lady, never a bitter word, never a harsh glance; ah, God, aren't ye the kind-hearted government and isn't them the gorgeous flowers!'

'Oh, shut up!' said the producer, looking up from a chaotic casting list; 'who's going to play her? That's what I want to know.'

'May Craig?' I suggested.

'Abbey can't release her.'

'Shelah Richards?'

'Abbey.'

'Ria Mooney?'

'America still. Renewed her contract with Eva le Gallienne.'

'Any chance of Allgood?'

'In London. It's hopeless. City the size of a flea-bite. No bloody actresses. In London you could just –'

'What about Maire O'Neill? She's the finest Irish actress –'

'Doing films at Elstree.'

'Oh, well.'

We took a tram to Lansdowne Road and called on Denis. He was sitting hunched up in a chair, a colossal young man with thick coal-black hair, a long gloomy good-natured face and long gloomy good-natured feet in carpet slippers.

'Hullo.'

He got up and switched off the gramophone that was playing 'Rhapsody in Blue'.

'Now look here, Denis, we've got to find her. What are we going to do?'

'Come to supper to-morrow. You'll meet somebody you might like.' His accent, in spite of his Dublin birth and a series of universities, still reminded one of the North of Ireland. So did the brief, emphatic use of words, everything pared down to the bone.

'Is she a good actress?'

'She might be.'

6

'Do you know her?'

'Known her for years.'

'Irish?'

'Dublin. That's what you want, isn't it?'

'Any experience?'

'Couple of shows here. Like every one else. Then she got a few jobs. She's back from a tour with Seymour Hicks. Have some tea?'

'Hicks? That sounds like musical —'

'Well, just meet her.'

'What's her name?'

'Meriel Moore.'

And that night we met her. Very charming she looked, brown-haired and blue-eyed, cool and poised as a tight-rope walker, and with a smooth, varying contralto, long sensitive hands, and an eloquent and easy flow of speech. She talked things over with us that night, gave an audition next morning, and on the following day rehearsals for the *Old Lady* began.

*

We were nearly mad. All day long, until our quiet triple bill performance in the evenings came like an oasis of restful convalescence, though in reality it was strenuous enough, all day long the drum was beating. For the bulk of the action of the *Old Lady* passes in the delirium of the actor playing Robert Emmet, who has met with a blow on the head causing concussion, and Denis had introduced for his 'Choral Interlude' a host of shadows, figures of the fevered imagination of the injured man, who formed the background to many of the principal scenes. His stage directions, like Shakespeare's, were of the briefest and left unlimited scope to the producer, and Hilton had discovered a seemingly unconscious rhythm in the lines spoken by the shadows and had introduced them with a pulsation of light and the notes of a drum beaten with varying *tempi*. The effect he achieved was in performance overwhelmingly exciting, but the mastery of its technique led all of us to the threshold of sheer lunacy. One or two of the shadows dropped out exhausted, some of them wept, others departed with determined expressions and were not seen again. But most of them stuck loyally to it and, swaying their bodies, their faces gleaming with sweat, they moved silently to and fro under his beckoning hand, advancing and retreating, bending their knees and straightening their backs,

7

revolving in circles, in semicircles, breaking up into small groups and forming big wedge-shaped battalions on the tiny stage while they whispered and shouted their lines with the fervour of negro revivalists, and all to the incessant throb-throb of the drum, while a frenzied stage-manager tried to imprison the order of their positions in the prompt-book.

Art O'Murnaghan wielded the drumsticks with untiring devotion and a rapt expression like a Druid at some sacred rite. He was an elderly saint who worshipped Angus and Lù and the ancient gods of Ireland and who had a miraculous flair for all the known arts, from the loveliest Gaelic illumination in the manner of the fifth-century monks to the making of properties, the writing of music, the research of ancient lore, the management of a stage, and the playing of character parts – his acting as Firs in our production of *The Cherry Orchard* many years later was of the rarest beauty and distinction. There he sat on these days of incessant rehearsal for the chorus of Denis Johnston's play, beating rhythmically on the drums, his thoughts in God-knew-what dim regions of mist and mistletoe, but his grey eyes faithfully fixed for the cue to stop or change the rhythm on the restless figure of Hilton, enveloped in clouds of tobacco smoke, darting backwards and forwards between stage and stalls, leaping to and fro between the players to push them into the patterns he desired, racing to the back of the auditorium to watch the effect, and beating out the time with both hands like a conductor directing an orchestra.

'Now, you Shadows,' he would shout, 'we'll go back to the third move. Hold that drum, Art. Take it easy, Meriel. Coralie, this doesn't affect you for the moment. Come and watch it with me. No, sit this side. I want to dodge about and get it from every angle. All right, Art, tap tap – *pianissimo* first, please. Now – come on, you cows, its got to start in a whisper and grow to thunder. Now . . .'

And the poor bedraggled things began all over again.

*

Well, it was worth it. There were thunders of applause, showers of praise and abuse, the usual accusations that the author had 'flung mud and dirt at the Irish people' – a comment neatly anticipated in the play – and one obscure but learned charge of blasphemy, not of language, but of symbolism. But Hilton and I were happy as we sat among strawberries and champagne in the house of Denis's parents

8

after the first night, for this was the end of our shop-window days, and we knew it. Things could not go on at the Peacock for ever, but our work was growing and there was, it seemed, a place for it. Our new actress had played beautifully and had said she wanted to remain with us. She and Coralie were perfectly balanced. Our new author had all the qualities we were seeking; he was vigorous, sensitive, and alert, and he meant what he said. What was more important still, he meant what he wrote. We went home from the party on foot, refusing lifts from a dozen people – what need to hurry to bed on a night that ought to have gone on for ever? – and walked slowly through the long brightening streets that smelt of hawthorn and wet blue slate. It was dawn by the time we stood at Tessie's door in Pembroke Street, and a cart was jolting down Fitzwilliam Square.

The play had a prolonged run and the theatre was booked out every night. That was the end of the season, and the summer sun poured out its gold on the battered, dawdling, friendly, malicious city.

Strumpet city in the sunset, Denis had made Emmet say at the end of the play:

Suckling the bastard brats of Scot, of Englishry, or Huguenot,
Brave sons breaking from the womb,
Wild sons fleeing from their mother,
Wistful city of savage dreamers,
So old, so sick with memories.
Old mother,
Some, they say, are damned.
But you, I think, one day shall walk the streets of paradise,
Head high and unashamed.
   'There. Now let my epitaph be written.'

The play was launched: it might serve as a model for what we were seeking, who knew? But it had been born: the day of our anxious midwifery had dawned and died. What were we going to do now?

THE OLD LADY: IN PRINCIPIO

CHRISTINE ST. PETER

Denis Johnston's *The Old Lady Says 'No!'* seems to have been conceived around 1925-26. This conception is recorded in the second half of a 2d notebook which bears the appropriate trade-name, 'The Monster'. The first half of this notebook records questions and practice answers on Constitutional Law, an early example of Johnston's lifelong tendency to straddle more than one professional world at a time. Of the twenty-four pages devoted to the play, eleven include explicit descriptions of his plans for and his desired emphasis in this first full-length play. He wrote no dates in the notebook, but the law questions were written during his year in London while devilling for admission to the English Bar. This gives us a *terminus a quo,* at least, for the *The Old Lady*'s beginnings.

To the reader who knows *The Old Lady* only in its 1977 Colin Smythe version or now out-of-print 1960 Jonathan Cape version, the play envisaged in the notebook may seem somewhat unfamiliar. But then it is only the proto-version of a play which was to be rewritten several times over the next fifty years. By examining the notebook and the subsequent versions, we can trace the development of an immature young writer to a fully-formed successful dramatist. Limitations of space make it impossible to explore this development systematically through all two hundred pages of revisions here. I intend only to point to some of the characteristic and particularly interesting revisions.[1]

As Johnston has grown older he has wished to disengage himself from the play's original focus – the violent, visionary ideal of the hero, Emmet. Instead he has increasingly favoured the cool, rational irony of the hero's foil, the statue Henry Grattan. Thus, he remarked in a letter of 1977:

> The parts of the present play that seemed most up-to-date in the last production [1977] were Grattan's lines and those of the Blind Man [orating on the folly of dreams].[2]

Yet Emmet and the ideal for which he stands continue to fascinate Johnston. In an interview in 1976 he remarked:

10

As an old man, I would opt for a realistic ending . . . But perhaps in spite of myself Emmet took over the end of the play and I felt I had to let him . . .[3]

Johnston is referring here to two possible and opposing interpretations of the play. If the Grattan view of Emmet is to predominate, the end of the play simply shows the hallucinations of a maddened visionary engulfed by his hopes and out of touch with reality. If, however, Emmet 'took over the end of the play', then his dying vision declares the redemption of Dublin wrought by the strength of his own creative powers. However unpalatable such a conclusion may seem to the rationalist, when we examine the notebook we shall see how important this emphasis was to Johnston when he first planned the play.

That Johnston's attitudes should have changed is scarcely unusual; dramatists must frequently feel that their earlier works no longer express their complete understanding. What is unusual is Johnston's decision to return to his earlier works at various times, to modify them according to his changed ideas. As his publishers and critics know to their dismay, for Johnston, a play is never complete. It must remain, rather, part of an unfolding process, subject to constant revision as his perceptions change. His entire career is a search. But, like the protagonist of *A Bride for the Unicorn*, Johnston is not certain of the nature of that for which he is searching. He does not have a complete and consistent vision to communicate. Writing – and rewriting – is for him a way of knowing. In 1946 Hilton Edwards was unwilling to admit the essential honesty of this approach and spoke disparagingly of the rapidity with which Johnston's titles, views, and opinions changed:

Denis will never find his feet; Denis will never settle down; Denis does not want to settle down, he does not want to find his feet. He is a Sphinx in search of a secret, he is going to try everything twice, and when he has found what he wants he won't want it any longer. Meanwhile the search goes on . . . Denis Johnston is a born dilettante – yet he does things well; but not, I think, for long enough. To profess is to lose impartiality, to cut off a way of retreat – to commit.[4]

But a great part of Johnston's appeal resides precisely in his willingness to change, to rethink his positions, and to rewrite his

11

works. It is only necessary for us to acknowledge that a play of Johnston's is a play with multiple texts, each of which must be examined if we are to understand the play fully.

Eight extant versions of *The Old Lady* remain, excluding the notebook.[5] Although I intend to return to the notebook to examine Johnston's original plans, I should here designate the different versions to which I shall make reference:

1. The first version, eventually called *Alpha* by the author, has the title *Shadowdance* on its title page. This unpublished typescript, still in the author's possession, numbers 72 leaves. A reader, perhaps Lennox Robinson, has written marginal notes objecting to the play's length.

2. The second version, also called *Shadowdance*, was renamed *Beta*. This typescript is a radical recasting of the two-act *Alpha*. Among other changes, Johnston shrank the play to a one-act version of 54 leaves. This version was read and closely edited by W.B.Yeats.[6] We shall return to these first two versions later.

3. The third version, written after Yeats and Lady Gregory had rejected the *Beta* for either the first or second time, was a nearly total recasting of the entire play. Here the two-act structure reappears, but more tightly orchestrated. The 54 leaves of *Beta* become 68 leaves, nearly its original length. *Delta*, for this is the name of this typescript, was the version used by Hilton Edwards for the play's original production at the Dublin Gate Theatre in July 1929. The typescript, with Edwards's notes in the margin, remains in Johnston's possession.

4. The fourth version, the first published one, is the Jonathan Cape edition of 1932, which closely resembles *Delta*.

5. The fifth version, also in Johnston's private papers, is his own recasting of the play as a radio drama for Radio Eireann, which was broadcast on 23 October 1955.

6. In 1960 Jonathan Cape published a revised *Old Lady*. The changes are extensive, but, in general, involve the modernizing of the dialogue and the topical allusions; these all reflect Johnston's desire to keep the play as contemporary as possible.

7. The most recent version is in the 1977 Colin Smythe *Dramatic Works of Denis Johnston, Volume One*. As we shall see the changes here are small but significant.

8. The eighth version does not deserve to be considered as part of the play's development, as it was rewritten without Johnston's help. I mention it only because it had a wide audience and might be the

only version seen by many British audiences. It was rewritten for BBC production on 13 March 1964. The producer made basic errors in interpretation; for example, he cast two different actresses as Sarah Curran and the Old Flower Woman instead of one actress playing a character with two different faces.

* * *

The very first page of Johnston's notebook jottings lists a bibliography with a note by Johnston that he must read the books listed:

1. Memoirs of the Life and Times of the Rt. Hon. H. Grattan (5 Vols.).
2. History of the First [Irish] Rebellion in 1798 – W.H. Maxwell.
3. Curran and His Contemporaries: Charles Phillips.
4. Life of Curran: W.H. Curran.

The selection is as suggestive in its exclusions as in its inclusions, as it includes no study of Robert Emmet, although several were available. But Johnston's plan was to work from the popular romanticised version of Emmet's story. The notebook makes his intentions explicit: he would open his play with a short parody of a 'Macardle Drama', typical Abbey fare. Page 8 includes stage directions for the meeting of the lovers Emmet and Sarah at Rathfarnham: 'The Abbey is acting an Irish Patriotic Play and doing it badly.' By means of this parody, Johnston hoped to raise certain kinds of false, sentimental expectations in his audience which he would then summarily dash when the Redcoats club Emmet. The rest of the play would be Johnston's re-education of his audience and his hero as he took Emmet into a Strindberg-like dream play from which he would emerge purified and more truly heroic.

As the bibliography shows, Johnston felt the need to present an historically accurate picture of Grattan and Curran. In writing the play Johnston was careful to make the picture of Grattan's rationally calculated parliamentarianism appealing. Because of his ability to embrace both ends of the political spectrum, Johnston had no difficulty in making Grattan attractive. But it is Emmet who is given the role of the national Messiah. In none of the books cited in the bibliography is Emmet treated as a hero. The Charles Phillips book, for example, treats Emmet as a 'melancholy and romantic' dreamer whose rebellion destroyed the much-admired work of Grattan. But this study obliquely furnishes a picture of Emmet very like the one that Johnston presents in the last moments of the play. Phillips quotes from a paper written by Emmet about his political dreams and left in one of his ammunition depots:

> . . . if my hopes are without foundation – if a precipice is opening under my feet, from which duty will not suffer me to run back, I am grateful for that sanguine disposition which leads me to the brink and throws me down, while my eyes are still raised to that vision of happiness which my fancy formed in the air.[6]

To an audience raised on the saccharine popular version of Emmet *qua* lover, this solitary and single-minded revolutionary leader comes as a surprise.

Johnston's notebook reveals that he had originally intended to exploit various possible historical references. Five of the twenty-four pages were devoted to working out lines for specific statue-characters. Although by *Alpha* Johnston had cut the statues down to the one of Grattan, in the notebook he had Gratton, William III, Nelson, and O'Connell. But he stated on page 19 of the notebook that 'the Statues each represent a warring sentiment in the Auditor's [Emmet's title in the notebook] brain and not historical characters.' By eliminating the extra statues, Johnston brought the central tension in the play – Emmet's ideal opposed to Grattan's – into sharp focus.

The 'warring sentiments' in Emmet's brain are given dramatic form in a variety of ways. Hence the dream play structure is invaluable as it cuts the play free from any of the structures of logical connected realism. Thus, when Emmet loses Rathfarnham in the opening playlet, the author could present him with a dizzying variety of other forms of his 'Land o' Heart's Desire'. On page 19 Johnston made a note about Emmet's visits to various sacred Dublin institutions: 'He enters the Dail, etc., thinking it is Rathfarnham.'[8] Seen in this light, the entire play is the process whereby Emmet seeks the Rathfarnham he lost in the opening playlet. Only in the slum scene at the end of the play does he realize that Sarah's Rathfarnham and the romance it symbolizes is a false goal, just as the political, social and cultural 'Rathfarnhams' offered by post Civil War Dublin in the course of the play are false. Instead, he must create his own. We find these explanations in the notebook on page 11 under notes for the slum scene (the italics are mine):

> Triumph of mind over circumstances
> *'I will create the substance of my dreams'*
> cries the Auditor
> *'This is Rathfarnham'* and lo, it is. 'I have been carried along too
> long. I will take the earth in both my hands and mould it nearer to
> my heart's desire.'

On pages 21-22, we find further reference to this scene:

> Voices
> Poet (on death bed) oh where is Rathfarnham
> [Poet] dies
> *Auditor creates*
> *The Metamorphosis*
> The moon comes through
> Sarah. Victory Victory
> *He doesn't want her now.*
> He calls the company around him
> 'Old Mother Dublin'
> ....
> *He creates a new world* – but the Audience do not see any
> difference and wonder are they intended to. But he is quite
> satisfied.

Another reference, this one on page 20, stresses the same point:

> Auditor marches crisis by crisis to his ebb tide in the slum. There
> he triumphs over adversity and the perversity of his fellows by
> creative genius. The Metamorphosis of the Slum.

I have reproduced these passages at length to show where the
play's primary emphasis lay in the notebook stage. The ironic
treatment of Dublin which now seems the play's hallmark is
sketched out in the notebook, but this irony is secondary to the
focus on the hero as creative visionary.

We see this emphasis worked out unsuccessfully in the first two
versions of the play, *Alpha* and *Beta*. In these Johnston composed
an original dock speech for Emmet when he appears as Shadow in
the final scene. In *Alpha*, Emmet's dock speech, written in poetic
verse, numbers 156 lines; in *Beta*, Johnston discarded the poetic

form and 39 lines. Even in this shorter form, Yeats found 42 lines of the speech superfluous and badly written, so crossed them out with the devastating marginal comment 'rubbish'.

As every reader of any of the published versions of the play knows, the dock speech in its final form became a powerfully effective composite of quotation from a variety of authors, including Dante, Rabelais and Blake, as well as Biblical paraphrase and a modified version of the Anglican Commination service. It took this form in the *Delta* typescript and remains essentially unchanged from *Delta* to the 1977 Colin Smythe edition.

The *Alpha* dock speech, which contains some of Johnston's earliest dramatic writing, is worth examining because it shows him attempting to write poetic drama, something which he essentially never tried to do again. It is also notably less competent than is the writing of *Delta*. Because it is otherwise unavailable I have taken the opportunity of quoting it at some length here:

> I stand here as Robert Emmet, posturing upon the stage, playing
> my precious part here in sight of all, and unashamed.
> I stand here as Robert Emmet
> Alone
> Facing the scudding shades that cluster round my path and seek to
>   bar the way.
> I am Robert Emmet
> Weaving the ever widening warp and woof of
> That incarnate heritage that fools call Fate
> Rythms [sic] of the pregnant earth.
> High harmonies that wake to life
> The slumbering memories of God.
> And send the mists [afloating?] from around his throne.
> ....
> I am Robert Emmet
> Wandering in the crazy twilight of my time
> Crying aloud the twisting terrors of my heart
> Singing the songs of my passionate longing
> Under the roofs of the great, out in the alleys of the poor
> And I am mocked, I am mocked.
> And [?] am unashamed.
> For I have solved the riddle of the Sphinx
> Now I have torn aside the veil
> And found the secret of my mother's destiny.[9]
> ....

16

The world is very weak and wan and sad
But I must prize her as she is until I make
A new and a better world, to bear the flame
    of my desire.

(Alpha, leaves 136-37)

One is tempted to dismiss the fulsome, alliterative style, but, in fact, Johnston was attempting a most difficult thing; as the best poets of the century, T.S. Eliot and Yeats, knew well, modern public speech cannot easily be transformed into great dramatic poetry. The following statement which Johnston made in 1946 stresses how displeased he was even with his final composite dock speech. Once again we are reminded of the visionary importance Johnston gave this final scene in his notebook:

> [*The Old Lady*] is a spontaneous reaction, following an age of false, romantic values and rancid political clichés, and it was bound to have been written by somebody. But what a pity it was not written by a Poet instead of a Half-Coherent who, whenever he finds himself staggered by the gigantic issues he has raised, has nothing better to do than to fall back upon Dante and Holy Writ! It is true that these issues are fundamentally religious ones, but what they cry out for is to be restated in the language of great verse, rather than in that of a revivalist meeting.[10]

The entire final section of the play has continued to trouble Johnston throughout all his versions of the play. Part of his worry is that the play is so long that the audience will be too tired to concentrate by the time it arrives. This difficulty began in his original conception of the play. Interested in experimenting with Expressionist theatrical devices, he seems to have decided initially to make the Shadowdance section one of the main parts of the play. In this sequence, grotesquely enlarged, lighted figures dance behind a gauze curtain, quoting lines from great Irish writers. They thus provide a verbal bridge between the empty banality of the Dublin vernacular spoken by the other characters and the dock speech of the apotheosized Shadow-Emmet with his own version of literary truth *cum* religious ritual. Yeats disliked the Shadowdance effect, writing the following on leaf 48 of *Beta*:

17

> I feel great doubt about these Shadows. If done as proposed they
> will be ineffective unless they are recognizable forms – I think
> they should be all people like Swift, Parnell, etc. and speak
> recognizable words.

Johnston has always kept the dance 'as proposed', but in successive
versions the number of Shadows has shrunk. On page 2 of the
notebook, he lists thirteen Shadows: O'Casey, Shaw, Wilde, Yeats,
Sheridan, Synge, Mangan, Moore, A.E., P. Colum, Goldsmith,
James Joyce, Charles Lever, and an unnamed extra simply called
'An other'. By the time Johnston revised the play for publication in
1977, only four Shadows remained: Yeats, Joyce, Wilde and Shaw.
This smaller grouping probably suggests Johnston's final decision
about his private Pantheon of Irish writers but he cut the number for
structural reasons. Describing the changes he made for the 1977
Abbey production of *The Old Lady,* Johnston wrote me the
following:

> . . . so far as I was concerned I did not fiddle with the text apart
> from cutting down the number of Shadows at the end in order to
> shorten the interminable conclusion. I wanted them down to four,
> but the director [Tomas MacAnna] insisted on five.[11]

The example above of Johnston's ignoring the specific advice of
Yeats is the young man's characteristic response to most of Yeats's
suggestions. That is not to say that Johnston did not take the spirit of
Yeats's advice seriously; certainly none of his dramatic writings
subsequent to *Alpha* and *Beta* would ever resemble those early,
florid efforts. A close examination of the *Beta* annotations reveals
that Yeats was not teaching the young dramatist what play to write,
but simply how to write. For one thing, Yeats seems to have read the
typescript very carefully, which suggests a flattering interest; all this
criticisms or suggested deletions were directed against the over-
written speeches of Emmet. The following is a typical example. For
Johnston's

> I, the poor hunted fox: broken, driven to the hills, lying panting in
> the bracken and stealing out only when night creeps down from
> the east to cloak my nakedness,

Yeats suggests simply: 'I am as homeless as the fox.'

But Yeats's criticisms were substantial. He crossed out 260 lines of the play, approximately one tenth of the typescript, and he questioned other passages. As Johnston ruefully observed many years later:

Whatever O'Casey may have said to the contrary, to have had a script parsed and caustically annotated by Yeats was an experience that no aspiring writer can profitably forget.[12]

Since Johnston seems to have shortened the *Alpha* version to please some or other Abbey reader, Yeats's harsh treatment of *Beta* must have been extremely disappointing. The young dramatist, who had already produced several plays for the Dublin Drama League, hoped to have his first play produced by the Abbey Theatre. In fact, across the top of page 3 of the notebook he had written in inch-high letters the hopeful epithet, 'The Abbey Theatre.'

It is difficult to reconstruct the exact dates of the play's rejections. From notes made on *Alpha* by the Abbey actress Kate Curling, it seems certain that Johnston was revising *Alpha* into its *Beta* form while he was devilling in London. That puts the date of the composition of *Alpha* before the end of 1926. When the *Beta* version was completed and then read and rejected by the Abbey Board to whom Johnston presented the script is impossible to determine. What is certain is that Lady Gregory and W.B. Yeats rejected the play twice, the final rejection taking place in August, 1928, just four months after they had rejected Sean O'Casey's Expressionist play, *The Silver Tassie*. Whether they rejected *Alpha* and *Beta* or *Beta* and *Delta* remains an open question in the absence of further information. My own conclusion, based largely on the passage from Lady Gregory's *Journals* quoted below, is that *Alpha* and *Beta* were the two versions they saw and rejected. Lady Gregory refers to revisions to the 'early part.' This would refer to Johnston's excision of the long Dail scene, most of Act I, and his replacement of it with the street scene of the Phibs girls, whose dialogue was in part supplied by Kate Curling. But Lady Gregory says: 'I still like the beginning, it set the mind wandering through romantic historical alleys. . .' The beginning, the opening playlet, remains the same in *Alpha* and *Beta* and is entirely recast in *Delta*. Had she read *Beta* and *Delta*, she would have noticed the change – and heartily disliked the pointed irony of *Delta*'s playlet.

But the most important thing the passage reveals is that both

Yeats and Lady Gregory (not just Lady Gregory) were responsible for the rejection and that they both disliked the Expressionist form of the play and, furthermore, did not understand the genre which Johnston and O'Casey were experimenting with at that time:

[14 August 1928] . . . And then after dinner, Yeats still breathing threatenings and slaughters against him [a visiting German who lunched with them and whose heroes were Charlie Chaplin, Ernst Toller and Upton Sinclair] and against A.E. for sending him, and Toller, C.C. and Co. I spoke of Denis Johnson's [sic] play, and he said he wanted to hear it after its rewriting, and I read it, from 9 o'c to near midnight, with some interruptions for criticism. I have just written to L.R. [Lennox Robinson] – what I think –: 'I read the Emmet play and liked it – thought all the early part much better than before, and that as the author would be producing it, it would be possible. I got tired when half through, and thought it was going into jazz, and that if Yeats had liked it we might put it on, so I sealed it up – with five seals – in an envelope and addressed it to you. But Yeats said he hadn't read it since alterations, and last evening I read it straight through. I still like the beginning, it set the mind wandering through romantic historical alleys, but the later part seemed really bad – poor – not worth putting on our stage. But I didn't say so nor read it badly. I gave it every chance. I do not think it should be produced at the Abbey, I am sorry, for the early part sent the mind wandering – (mine permanently it seems!)'

Yeats had said 'I told G.B.S. the other day I perhaps ought not to judge plays but give place to someone else as I don't know much about impressionism,' and he said 'There is nothing in it, in impressionism'.

I asked Yeats then 'What is impressionism?' and he said 'No law' – and I said 'all jaw'. And he said 'Just so.' And that certainly describes the play.[13]

If, as Lady Gregory reported, Yeats had qualms about judging 'impressionism', they were obviously momentary; his dismissive 'no law' reveals what we shall see to be his most serious reservation about this sort of drama and Johnston's play in particular – its apparent formlessness.

Lady Gregory's reactions would appear to have been less sophisticated; the 'beginning' of the play and the only part that she admired was the sentimental love scene, between Emmet and Sarah Curran intended as a parody of the 'Macardle drama'. Here is a short section of the original playlet:

SARAH: Oh Robert, Robert, why have you ventured down. You are in danger. The soldiers are everywhere.

SPEAKER: The soldiers! Have they been searching for me here?

SARAH: Last night they ransacked the house. They even broke into my boudoir.

SPEAKER: (his eyes blazing) God!

SARAH: They will come back again . . . You must go, dearest, quickly, back to the mountains.

SPEAKER: Oh, if there was a sword in every Irish hand! If there was a flame in every Irish heart to put an end to slavery and shame! Oh, I would end these things!

SARAH: It is too late. Your men have melted away into the mist of the night. Robert, dear one, you must fly.

SPEAKER: How can I fly? Where can I fly? The mountains are full of a wild singing, and the streets are throbbing with the rush of feet and the crying of angry voices. I have lit such a flame in my heart that all the waters of the Erne could never quench – a flame that burns and tortures me with everlasting anguish. I cannot rest. I cannot sleep. Last night the winds were sighing 'Erin, Erin, Erin' in my ears. To-night, it is the trees that whisper soft the blessed name of 'Sarah Curran'.

(*Alpha*, 11. 1-2, *Beta* 11. 4-5)

When Lady Gregory and even Yeats missed the parody quality of this section, Johnston recast it into an unmistakably satiric pastiche of sentimental eighteenth- and nineteenth-century verse from the *Dublin Book of Irish Verse*. In this version, even an audience totally unfamiliar with Irish poetry would recognize that its collective leg was being pulled when they heard such dialogue as:

SPEAKER: Let them come! A million a decade! Let me be

21

> persuaded that my springing soul may meet the eagle on the hills, and I am free.

SARAH: Ah, go, forget me. Why should sorrow o'er that brow a shadow fling?

SPEAKER: My strong ones have fallen from the bright eye of day. Their graves are red, but their souls are with God in glory.

If the Abbey Board to whom the fledgling dramatist was submitting his play thought highly enough of Dorothy Macardle's plays to produce three of them between 1918 and 1925, writing a parody of her work does not seem the most judicious means of winning their approval. But the young Johnston was nothing if not intrepid. Consider, for example, the following letter he had published in *The Irish Statesman* on 5 February 1927:

> ... the Directors of the Abbey are undoubtedly in competition with the younger and less-established playwrights of the city, and however honest their motives there will always be the tendency so long as the present system continues to put on such plays as 'The Big House' and 'Oedipus Rex' in preference to the work of Mr. [F.J.] O'Hare and his friends. It is not, I repeat, conscious unfairness. It is merely human nature.

This *ad hominem* attack on Dublin's most influential theatre figures at the very period in which they were considering his play, gives a good sense of Johnston's mettle. And it is with this spirit in mind that I turn to the most recent version of the play, the 1977 Colin Smythe edition.

Johnston has made many small, delightful changes like the replacement of the respectful maid in the tea party scene by an insolent modern maid who serves tea in unwashed cups. He has made some interpretative changes too, as, for example, when he has Grattan refer to Ireland's 'spurious moral courage' instead of the earlier 'pitiless moral courage'.[14] But the most interesting change of all in this last version is the introduction of the title 'Partisan' for Emmet. This anachronistic reference to Tito's Partisan movement, which Johnston describes with such admiration in *Nine Rivers from Jordan,* reminds us of Johnston's ambivalent feelings about his hero.

22

While on the one hand, he now says he favours Grattan's rational control, the fascination of the revolutionary ideal continues. If *The Old Lady Says 'No!'* is a young man's play, the young man lives still in the older and wiser dramatist.

NOTES

1   For the fuller treatment of this question see my 1979 Doctoral Dissertation for the University of Toronto, 'Denis Johnston's *The Old Lady Says 'No!'*: The Gloriable Nationvoice'.

2   Letter from Denis Johnston to the author, 3 June 1977.

3   Interview with Denis Johnston, Toronto, 8 March 1976.

4   'Denis Johnston', *The Bell,* Vol. 13, No. 1 (October 1946), p. 9.

5   Harold Ferrar erroneously reports that 'there are three extant versions of the play', the *Beta* and the two published Jonathan Cape versions. *Denis Johnston's Irish Theatre* (Dublin: Dolmen Press, 1973), p. 22.

6   Logically, a *Gamma* should follow *Beta*. If such a typescript once existed it now seems to be lost. But no essential step has been lost, as the revisions in the margins and on the verso leaves of *Beta* are almost identical to the *Delta* script.

   A xeroxed copy of *Beta* is available from the University of Victoria, British Columbia, which now owns the typescript.

7   *Curran and His Contemporaries* (New York: Harper and Brothers, 1851), p. 271.

8   The Dail scene sketched out in the notebook and written out on seventeen leaves in *Alpha* is one of the casualties of the cuts for *Beta*. It is a brilliant bit of comic writing which unfortunately remains unpublished.

9   This line is Johnston's second thought. The first, modestly discarded, is 'And seen my Mother in her nakedness'. One is reminded how small the Dublin theatre world is; Joseph Holloway records in his diary that Johnston's parents and W.B. Yeats were at the opening night of the first production. *Impressions of a Dublin Playgoer,* July-September 1927, Vol. 1, Ms. 1927, National Library, Dublin, Ireland, p. 15.

10   'Drama: Dublin and Balfast', *The Bell,* Vol. 3, No. 5 (February 1946), pp. 359–60.

11   Letter to the author, 3 June 1977. Tomas MacAnna's selection of Shadows was the following: Shaw, O'Casey, Wilde, Yeats, James Clarence Mangan.

12   'What Has Happened to the Irish?' *Theatre Arts*, Vol. 43, (July 1959), p. 72.

13   Lady Gregory, an unpublished passage from her Journals, Vol. 38, p. 62. Reproduced by permission of Colin Smythe Ltd., publishers of the Coole Edition of Lady Gregory's works. Published in North America by Oxford University Press. I am grateful to Dr. Mary FitzGerald for bringing this passage to my attention.

14   *The Dramatic Works of Denis Johnston*, Vol. 1 (Gerrards Cross, Bucks.: Colin Smythe, Ltd., 1977), p. 34.

WAITING FOR EMMET

D.E.S. MAXWELL

(i)

There is no disagreement that in the nineteen-forties and -fifties the Abbey Theatre was not, to speak charitably, at its best. In 1953, W. Bridges Adams, who had perhaps indulgent praise for the enthusiasm and discrimination of the Dublin public, regretted the persistence of the 'genre-drama of Irish provincial life . . . When Pegeen Mike has a radio and a plug-in kettle from the E.S.B.'[1]

Adams's viewpoint had had plenty of support over the previous decade. Gabriel Fallon had deplored the Abbey's shortcomings, particularly its entrenched realism. It had secured that ground against enterprising possibilities in the late nineteen-twenties with its rejection of Denis Johnston's *Shadowdance (The Old Lady Says 'No!')* and Sean O'Casey's *The Silver Tassie*.[2] John Alldridge's 'What's Wrong with the Abbey Theatre'[3] arose from Val Iremonger's and Roger McHugh's protest, during a 1947 performance of *The Plough and the Stars,* against 'the incompetent artistic policy' of the Abbey management.[4] Paul Vincent Carroll joined in the dispute that followed. He alleged 'indifferent acting, and slipshod production' in 'an ordinary barnyard theatre of poor plays'. In 1943, Richard Watts, reviewing Myles na gCopaleen's *Faustus Kelly*, remarked that in producing it the Abbey was 'justifying its existence.' He added, however, 'that the most celebrated of Irish theatres is in need of some new talents . . . this is not one of its epic periods.'[5]

The chronicle of outrage is a venerable one.[6] Critics accepted early, if restively, that the Abbey would have its vacant inter-lunar phases. Two articles[7] in Volume I of *The Irish Review* advance the proposition in the configurations it had then. Walter Mennloch sees Yeats and Synge as 'the two "explosions" that carried the Irish theatre so far up the hill.' Of the two Synge was without doubt dramatically the greater. Mennloch acknowledges a greatness in Yeats's plays but has reservations about the transparency of his characters and predicts that he will make no new explosion – though one might now see *The Words Upon the Window Pane* and

24

Purgatory as more of a bang than a whimper. 'There is need of another,' Mennloch concludes, to 'clear the theatre of its impeding lumber of dead conventions and traditions.'

G. Hamilton Gunning would have agreed that the Abbey was thus lumbered. The next as yet unknown explosion in store was to be Sean O'Casey. Gunning's essay argues that the decline apparent to him in 1912 has some hope of such a sequel. It is bad in such garish ways that it must provoke its own arrest. Gunning categorises its playwrights – his exemplars are Lennox Robinson (*Harvest* and *The Clancy Name*); St. John Ervine (*Mixed Marriage*); T.C. Murray (*Birthright*) – as 'the gunshot school of drama', attaining their resolutions in 'a loud and stirring gunshot'. Their achievement is to have 'vulgarized the sources of inspiration of the first dramatists' and delighted 'the sporting editor of our daily papers, who in Ireland is frequently the dramatic critic also.' The consequence must be that 'no serious writer can venture to present a peasant in literature for the next ten years.' Yeats, looking back from 1919, concurred: 'we did not set out to create this sort of theatre, and its success has been to me a discouragement and a defeat.'[8] Yeats esteemed the peasant – as Yeats envisaged him – but not as he appeared in 'social-realist' plays.

From these interrogations – 1901-1958 – we can derive a sense both of the Abbey's (Yeats's) early intentions and of the actual course of events. The former wanted 'to bring again the theatre of Shakespeare or rather perhaps of Sophocles'[9] and large audiences. Yeats for a time evaded the recognition that even when there were such audiences they did not attend the kind of play he favoured. Acknowledging this later he opted for 'an audience of fifty, a room worthy of it (some great dining-room or drawing-room)'.[10]

The Abbey's critics have been, essentially, in agreement with its founder's disenchantment. There is, particularly after the Second World War, 'technical' complaint: insecure production and acting, theatrical *laisser-faire* (no 'workshop', a cloistered repertoire). The central grievance, however, turns upon faults of managerial imagination and the mediocrity of the plays themselves: ill-judged rejections, indifference to new work, insularity, plays homogenised from a restricted diet of realities. Yet it is not entirely clear what is the model which the critics saw its inheritors as debasing, nor in precisely what their fault lay. Gunning lumped together as 'literary plays' (approved) the works of Yeats, Synge, and Colum, the 'three dramatists of genius' who opened the Abbey.

The three have little in common. They all wrote about 'peasants', but in utterly dissimilar ways. The poetry of Yeats's language is not that of Synge's. Synge was 'realist' but in an individual and eccentric way. Yeats saw this. He said that Synge's characters were not replicas of Irish country people. The person in the audience seeing them 'has added to his being, not to his knowledge'.[11] Other dramatists arrived at this effect from a closer documentary fidelity, and in less figured and elaborate speech. Colum is in the latter category, circumstantial, plainer-spoken, starker. In his tradition William Boyle and T.C. Murray, first produced in 1905 and 1909.

There was a variety of styles, subjects, attitudes. The early Abbey seemed to open up a range of possibilities. The appearance was illusory. Yeats did not achieve his ambition to make a theatre for poetry. The Abbey has not fostered a poetic drama – nor, at least in Yeats's sense, has anywhere else – in a century uncongenial to it. The only heir to the younger Yeats has been the older Yeats.[12] Synge's language was appropriate to peculiar and transient circumstances, dispersing as he wrote. There is an unconsciously ironic application in Pegeen Mike's last words, 'I've lost the only playboy of the western world.' The transformations of twentieth-century life were taking hold.

The complaints, finally, were against the dominion of realism and against a poverty of talent, let alone genius, in its practitioners. Boyle, Murray, Ervine, Robinson corroborated Colum's initiative and established the voice which has since been clearest – and most popular with audiences – in Abbey dramatists. From 1921 George Shiels – who is not to be disprized – consolidated it further with his long series of immensely successful plays. O'Casey's Dublin trilogy was Mennloch's third 'explosion'. For all its novelty, it was perfectly compatible with the dramatic – not always the political and moral – orthodoxies of the Abbey. It added an urban duncher to the realist wardrobe. By the nineteen-twenties, in short, the Abbey had settled its character and had financial insurance in the box office appeal of Shiels, O'Casey, and Brinsley MacNamara (*The Rebellion in Ballycullen*, 1919; *The Glorious Uncertainty*, 1923).

It was a period for the Abbey of – rather misplaced – self-confidence. O'Casey – and the controversy over *The Plough and the Stars* – gave the appearance of a comprehensive originality and daringness. So did O'Casey's next dispute, with the Abbey itself over its rejection of *The Silver Tassie* in 1928. According to Joseph Holloway – not a friend of the *avant-garde*[13] but an invaluable chronicler – the event supplied the Dublin intelligentsia with debate throughout 1928 and 1929. Holloway himself vacillated. He said at first that the play was turned down 'because it was a poor one, and for no other reason'. A few days later he thought that the Directors had 'made a big mistake,'then proposed to read the play before taking sides. When he did read it his instincts/prejudices triumphed: 'coarse expressions, ugly words, and ugly situations. Sex is over all.'[14] The Directors were right. Right or wrong, they were not venturesome. Their theatre was living essentially on revivals and replications of the past.

Micheál MacLiammóir recalls the time with some affection:

> The Abbey was, as it had been for so many years, interestingly on its last legs. But of course it wasn't on its last legs . . . Until the discovery of O'Casey it did seem to be falling on evil ways. It had not attained the poetic, rhapsodic beauty that Yeats had hoped for, and the miracle of John Millington Synge was short-lived. I think the most important persons at the time were Lennox Robinson, T.C. Murray, and that much overlooked man who wrote *The Dandy Dolls* – what's his name, my God – George Fitzmaurice . . . there were the old plays, the old William Boyles and the Lady Gregorys – those charming comedies . . . I often used to wonder what people meant in the early twenties when they said the Abbey had gone to the dogs.[15]

It was certainly a livelier time than any in the next thirty years, whatever one may think of O'Casey nowadays. The Abbey Theatre, by any reputable standards, was still limping, but as Brendan Behan used to say, 'Every cripple has his own way of dancing.' A kinder – though selective and rather euphoric – view of the period than the one offered here is possible. Harold Ferrar writes: '. . . the Dublin Theatre was more lively than it had been for twenty years: the Abbey was doing Ibsen and a controversial Shakespeare [Denis Johnston's production of *Lear*]; the Drama League had vastly broadened the scope of the Irish stage; and the Gate was on its way.'[16] Yeats, too, was beckoning to unfamiliar routes, but between 1919 and 1929 the Abbey produced no new work of his, largely, no doubt, because of his own change of mind about the sort of audience he wanted.

This account of the condition, and the origins of the condition, of Irish theatre in the nineteen-twenties concerns the Abbey. The

Abbey was, as to a great extent it still is, Irish theatre. The tentative beginnings of the Gate Theatre Studio under Hilton Edwards and MacLiammóir, entered alternative directions. Their aim, says MacLiammóir, was 'a new sort of theatre in Ireland . . . something more than a national theatre which interpreted but a portion of the national life.' As they hoped to correct 'the lack of visual sensibility of a nation whose ears had always been its strongest point of aesthetic perception', so they would contribute to 'methods of acting, production, design and lighting.' The material for these endeavours was to come not from the nurturing of new writers, but from 'ancient and modern plays from all sorts of places':[17] a corrective emphasis on acting and stage techniques and on cosmopolitanism.

The Gate opened successfully at the Peacock Theatre on 14 October 1928 with *Peer Gynt*. It played there for two seasons before inaugurating its own theatre on 17 February 1930 with *Faust*. The Gate put on, among others, Farquhar, Austin Clarke, Shaw, T.C. Murray (*A Flutter of Wings*, rejected by the Abbey), St. John Ervine (*The Lady of Belmont,* a sequel to *The Merchant of Venice*), Congreve, Wilde, Sheridan; and a number of new, but hardly 'explosive', Irish writers: the Earl of Longford, the Countess of Longford, David Sears, Mary Manning. It is not a prospectus for wild revolution, though the range of plays invites a greater variety of production and acting than the Abbey repertoire.

There was in addition some representation of expressionist drama: in 1927 *The Emperor Jones*; in 1928 *The Hairy Ape*; and in 1929 *The Adding Machine*; in 1931 a local version of a favourite expressionist form, the revue, *The Dublin Review*, devised mainly by Denis Johnston, Frank O'Connor, and Tom Purefoy, caused hostility. According to Holloway, 'it just suited the dungminded, well-dressed patrons of the Gate . . . I hissed quite heartily.'[18] The Gate did then, entertain a new mode – 'Since then,' says MacLiammoir of Expressionism, 'little completely new has been stated'[19]; and found a native exponent of it in Denis Johnston – the nearest, in MacLiammóir's opinion, to 'the unique dramatist' whom the Gate had in mind but never discovered.[20] The Gate presented his *The Old Lady Says 'No!'* on 3 July 1929. It displeased Joseph Holloway – 'a madhouse play' – though he allowed some merit to the acting and production and thought that 'MacLiammóir looked very like "Emmet".'[21] He also acknowledges contrary views, as that of David Sears, who reviewed the play favourably for *The Irish Independent*.

The Gate Theatre had had its harbingers. The Dublin Drama League, founded by Yeats and Lennox Robinson in 1918, and the New Players had already given plays by Continental and American Expressionists. The enterprise of these companies is part of the *biographia literaria* of Denis Johnston. He had become interested in theatre while reading law at Harvard in 1924. He read Shaw's *Prefaces* and attended all the Boston little theatres he could find, such as Catherine Huntington's on Beacon Hill. This interest persisted. Around 1925, with Sean O'Casey, he saw Claude Rains in Kaiser's *From Morn to Midnight* at the London Gate Theatre; in 1928 he saw in Munich a production of *Lear* which influenced his own interpretation. In Ireland he worked, while a practising barrister, with the Drama League. He acted in Pirandello (1927), Strindberg (1928), and O'Neill (1928); and produced *From Morn to Midnight* (New Players, 1927) and Toller's *Hoppla* (Drama League, 1929). During these years, from about 1926, he was writing *The Old Lady*.

It was unquestionably the utterance of an eloquent and attractive new voice. On the whole, the critics gave it a good, some of them an enthusiastic, hearing. But there was also loud complaint, verbal and written, for the usual Irish reasons. The play was seen to be anti-Catholic, anti-National; and seamy. To re-phrase the ground of complaint: the play is satirising the rigidities and mawkishness which dogma can produce; and it recognises that human discourse accommodates, 'you'll do the hell of a lot, ma . . . in me eye!' as well as 'Was ever light of beauty shed on loveliness like thine!'[22] The satiric intent and the designing of the language are inseparable. The characteristically modernist device of parody, linguistic burlesque, realises and embodies the satiric attitudes. *The Old Lady* is a remarkably effective blending of invention which looks to cosmopolitan sources and a content which is parochial. The parochial, unlike the provincial, has an assured sense of its identity, and latent universal implications readier to be delivered. As Johnston himself has observed:

> The theme of the Romantic temperament seeking for an environment in which to express himself is a universal one, but everybody cannot be expected to know about Robert Emmet. When an old lady appears upon the stage and maunders about her four beautiful green fields, it is too much to expect of a London audience that it will recognise the traditional figure of romantic

29

Nationalism for whom Mangan and Pearse sighed. It is only in the Free State that the O'Donovan Rossa speech and Committee Room 15 (where Parnell was betrayed) can be relied upon to call up any recollections without the aid of a footnote.[23]

A similar judgement might be passed on *The Waste Land*'s grander larcenies, but the poem does – as, I would argue, does *The Old Lady* – carry itself. For all its innovativeness, it is in a way the most 'Irish' of plays.[24] Unlike its ancestral *casus belli (The Playboy of the Western World, The Plough and the Stars), The Old Lady* offended not just by subverting received Irishryness. It was out to domesticate novel forms of statement. The new voice was Irish, but with, so to speak, a Continental accent. *The Old Lady* was shocking in its reversals of orthodox sentiment. It also, in ways more manifest than Synge's ritualisation of language, took up with a strange dramaturgy, and made the stage itself an alien scene.

Some of Johnston's own statements on the play suggest a natural impatience about having it unequivocally docketed by kind. There is something curt and dismissive about docketing. So in the Preface to the 1960 Cape edition of his plays, Johnston refers to one of them, presumably *The Old Lady,* as 'an expressionist gesture of dissent'. His Introduction to the play speaks of 'its expressionist tricks'. But the 'Note on what happened' (1929) includes a firm disclaimer: '*The Old Lady Says 'No!'* is not an expressionist play and ought never to have been mistaken for one.'[25] Johnston has also claimed that the play's 'actual foster parents are neither Evreinov, O'Neill nor Georg Kaiser . . . The two plays to which this experiment does owe something are, first, Kaufman and Connelly's *Beggar on Horseback* – a superb piece of American expressionism that I have always admired – and secondly, a Continental satire called *The Land of Many Names'* by Josef Capek.'[26]

It is possible to reconcile the apparent contradictions. A play drawing on 'expressionist tricks' need not be a thorough-going expressionist play. *The Old Lady* is so charged with expressionist contrivances that the distinction may seem something of a quibble. The technicalities of expressionist presentation, too, were more than a strictly methodological sabotage of conventional stagecraft. Like Joyce's and Eliot's underminings of traditional forms, they enacted the disjunctions, elisions, *dérèglements* of consciousness; and politically were 'symbolic of the revolution against the bourgeoisie'.[27] But these were also purely theatrical procedures, amenable to other imaginative dispositions. It is thus, it seems to me, that Johnston takes them. *The Old Lady* imitates the fluidities, the disruptions, the intricacies of lighting effects, the phantasmal 'dissolves' of the expressionist stage: supplanting plot and sequential narrative. Johnston transposes these to an unmistakably localised Dublin, far different from the indeterminate settings of expressionism. His real divergence is from the generally rather oppressive solemnity of the Ur-expressionists.

Johnston's renunciation of his imputed foster parents comes out of these disparities. One would need an imaginative ear to pick up, in *The Old Lady,* even remote echoes from *From Morn to Midnight.* Kaiser's play, like Johnston's, does indeed turn upon a journey, undertaken by a clerk who has stolen money from the bank where he works. Without discernible wit, scenes at a racetrack, a private room in a cabaret, a snowy field (with a tree that becomes a skeleton), satirise a decadent, rapacious, fragmented society. The clerk dies (apparently) in the last scene, the lights go out, and the play ends with the no doubt metaphorical line, 'There must be a short circuit in the main.'

Despite Johnston's acknowledgement, *Beggar on Horseback,* a comedy with some not exactly tigerish satire, is no more likely a forebear. As most of *The Old Lady* may be taken to be the actor's/Speaker's/Emmet's hallucinations, so a large part of *Beggar on Horseback* is the hero's dream. But the Kaufman/Connelly play works on a fairly standard Broadway plot: struggling young composer finally gets the right girl. The elaborately staged dream anticipates the 'dream sequences' of innumerable Hollywood musicals; and has about as much substance. *Beggar on Horseback* is a straight 'romantic comedy' which its authors have dolled up with a battery of, it is fair to say, 'expressionist tricks'. Johnston's achievement in *The Old Lady* is to have secured a ground between Kaiser's stodginess and Kaufman/Connelly's froth. In *The Old Lady,* comic deflation, rather than earnest *Angst,* identifies and reduces extravagances of serious concern.

(ii)

These generalities call for confirmation from the play itself. Johnston claims for it, and might properly claim more, that at the time of writing it was 'a fairly original play'.[28] Its structure, shuffling

31

various intimations of reality, severely tested the theatrical anti-
cipations of its first audiences. Yet the apparently random fusions
and ruptures of times and places are in fact under firm imaginative
control. The structure, though intricate, is lucidly articulated
Associations of mood and theme, a consort of antiphonal forms of
speech, a complex apparatus of stage design, replace naturalistic
sequence or narrative. The reassurance of the more or less solid and
identifiable properties in the opening scene recede into expanses of
light and shade, gauze, drumbeats, fugitive sounds and settings.

The Old Lady opens with a sequence, put together by Denis
Johnston from romantic fragments of Mangan, Moore, Ferguson,
and others of that sort. The language, inflated in itself, should be
hammed in delivery. It is part of a non-existent melodrama about
Robert Emmet, his love for Sarah Curran and his nationalist zeal.
Major Sirr, the villain, enters to arrest Emmet, who is accidentally
knocked out. When we are admitted into what is going on in his still
unconscious mind, the play proper begins. The Emmet-figure, now
called the Speaker, makes a progress through twentieth-century
Dublin. He is variously an actor – 'Perhaps he acts for the Civil
Service Dramatics'; an actor who knows that he is cast as Emmet – 'I
can't even remember my lines'; and believing that he is Emmet –
'We know only one definition of freedom. It is Tone's definition; it
is Mitchell's definition; it is Rossa's definition.'

The rôles are not rigidly segmented. When, for instance, the
Speaker sees the death of the young man he has shot, and says, 'I am
only a play-actor,' he is commenting in a sense on the 'real' Emmet
that he is merely posturing over ideals and their violent execution.
Acting and the stage become a metaphor of self-indulgent politics
exploited for its histrionic satisfactions. Not even the illusions/de-
lusions are reliably stable:

OLDER MAN: This chap says he's Robert Emmet.

SPEAKER: I am.

OLDER MAN: Oh, you are, are you?

SPEAKER: I am.

OLDER MAN: Well answer me this then. *What's happened to your
             boots?*

VOICES: Ah-ha!
             Look!
             What about his boots?

32

OLDER MAN: He comes here and says he's Robert Emmet, and where are his boots? . . .

SPEAKER: I don't know . . . I thought they were . . . I see your point . . . I . . .

VOICES: Well?

SPEAKER: Perhaps I had better explain. You see . . . someone took them from me when I was playing Robert Emmet and . . .

OLDER MAN: *(with heavy sarcasm).*
Oh so you were *playing* Robert Emmet. A play-actor are you? Some of this high-brow stuff I suppose?

Absurdities multiply as the parody-quester encounters the banalities of 'liberated Ireland'. It presents both indifference to and debasements of his own ideals. The platitudes of modish life occupy a Flapper and her boy-friend: 'Do you like my nails this shade? Heart's Despair it's called' – compare, 'my heart bleeding for my country's woes'. All the talk of Bernadette and Carmel, in the accents of plebeian Dublin, is of 'the fellas'. The Flower Woman drinks, brawls, and obliquely pimps. Kathleen ni Houlihan is broken down into images of futility. The Minister for Arts and Crafts degrades imagination to the Deserving Artists' (Support) Bill, No. 65 of 1926: 'it helps to keep an eye on the sort of stuff that's turned out, you understand.' The statue of Grattan (played by Major Sirr) is frustrated by the life he sees from his pedestal in College Green. He tests his own diction, because it now expresses his disenchantment; and in an O'Casey-like tenement room, a young man still declaims, 'Up the Republic!'

This swirling collage does not represent Glorious Past versus squalid present, though there is perhaps a note of lament for squandered innocence, self-deception uncovered. The play dramatises an instance of history's trick of repeating itself in an unprecedented, unforeseen idiom. The following excerpt epitomises something of the method:

SPEAKER: *(commencing to act again, at the top of his voice).*
Their graves are red but their souls are with God in glory. A dark chain of silence is thrown o'er the deep.

33

> Silence . . silence I say. O Ireland, Ireland, it is still
> unriven, that clanking chain . . . still unriven. O
> Ireland, Ireland, no streak of dawning is in the sky.
> (*As he has been declaiming the crowd breaks up and
> passes to and fro as in the street. The gauze parts.
> Headlights of motor cars. A policeman with a white
> baton is directing traffic, while behind him upon a
> pedestal stands* GRATTAN *with arm outstretched. He
> has the face of* MAJOR SIRR.)

SPEAKER: (*now in the midst of the traffic*).
> Men of Eire, awake to be blest! Do you hear? (*He
> fiercely accosts a* PASSER-BY.) Do you hear? Awake!

PASSER-BY: (*politely disengaging himself*).
> Sorry. The banks close at half two.

The passer-by's – quite worthy – pursuit is entirely at odds with
Emmet's ardour; as their manners of speech are at odds. *The Old
Lady* is testing the mettle of Manganese. The audience needs no
intimate acquaintanceship with its practitioners. While the more
peculiar allusions Johnston refers to are local lore, Manganese is
regulation nineteenth-century versifying; and the opening playlet,
in any case, fully demonstrates it. The subsequent action punctures
it with demotic Dublinese, though that is not being held up as a
model either. The play, in one formulation, is setting rhetorics
against one another as a means of enquiry into the sentiments they
are used to express.

Imitations of genuine argots occupy the stage. But some of
Johnston's imitations are of other literary imitations. The Blind
Man picks up his speech from Synge: 'Asking the way of an old dark
fiddler, and him tip-tappin' over the cold sets day in and day out
with never sight nor sign of the blessed sun above.' The tenement
room houses the dialect of Boyles and Joxers. Johnston has this to
say about the *Old Lady*:

> It was Plato who first told us that if we don't like our environment
> it is up to us to alter it for ourselves. If the Emmets in particular or
> if intransigent Irish Republicanism in general are to be taken as
> having made any contribution to the world of applied philosophy
> I feel that it is this characteristic attitude of mind. 'The Republic
> still lives' is not the expression of a pious hope, but in is itself a
> creative act, as England knows to her cost.[29]

The play poises us between the Older Man's, 'bloody words. You can't change the world by words'; and the Younger Man's, 'What other way can you change it? I tell you, we can make this country – this world – whatever we want it to be by saying so, and saying so again.' As it began, the play ends with borrowed words, spoken by the Shadows, from 'some of Dublin's greatest contributors to the World's knowledge of itself'[30]; and, in its final speech, from Emmet's speech from the dock, the resurrection thesis of the Litany, and the Commination service of the Anglican church. Words have the last word, but they gesture towards positions rather than fix the play in a stance.

Dublin waited long for this particular Emmet. It is a brilliant *tour de force,* putting a richly comic imagination to the service of feeling and intelligence, commanding the local into the general, calling on a theatrical cartography which surprises new contours in familiar scenes. Harold Ferrar describes *The Old Lady* as a 'landmark in the story of the Irish theatre – at once a summing up of the advances of the decade and a herald of future possibilities.'[31]

The fact is that *The Old Lady was* the advance; and that it was a herald to whose call no Irish poet or dramatist much attended. There was to be no Eliot with *Sweeney Agonistes*; no Auden with *The Dance of Death, The Dog Beneath the Skin*; no MacNeice with *Out of the Picture;* no Spender with *Trial of a Judge.* Nor did the Dublin Gate Theatre import any of these. Their merits – which can at least bear comparison with the staple of Irish theatre in the period – are not the issue. Irish horizons closed in again. The Abbey shut the kitchen door. The Gate's 'new sort of theatre' defaulted. *The Old Lady Says 'No!'* speaks with undiminished assurance beyond its period. Its period's promise deceived.

NOTES

1   'A National Theatre', *Drama* 51, Winter 1958, pp. 27–30.
2   'The Future of the Irish Theatre', *Studies* XLIV, Spring 1955, pp. 92–100.
3   *The Irish Digest,* February 1948, pp. 17–19.
4   Another Abbey shindy, recalled by Liam Miller in 'Eden and After: The Irish Theatre 1945–66', *Studies* LV, Autumn 1966, pp. 231–5.
5   'Guest Critic', *The Bell* V, 6 March 1943, pp. 482–7.
6   It in fact ante-dates the Abbey. In 1901, *Irial* (Frederick Ryan) was dealing in *The United Irishman* with the question, 'Has the Irish Literary Theatre Failed?' (VI, No. 141, 9 November, p. 3).
7   Walter Mennloch, 'Dramatic Values,' *The Irish Review* I, 1911-12, September 1911, pp. 325–9; G. Hamilton Gunning, 'The Decline of the Abbey Theatre Drama', February 1912, pp. 606–9.

Denis Johnston: a retrospective

8 *Explorations*, p. 250.
9 Ibid, p. 252.
10 Ibid, p. 255.
11 *Synge and the Ireland of His Time* (Dublin: Cuala Press, 1911), p. 36.
12 One can argue correspondences between Yeats's Theatre and Beckett's, but the differences outweigh them. See Thomas Kilroy 'Two Playwrights: Yeats and Beckett' in J. Ronsley (ed.) *Myth and Reality in Irish Literature* (Waterloo: Wilfrid Laurier Press, 1977), pp. 183–195.
13 Yeats had this to say about Antheil's score for *Fighting the Waves:* 'exciting dramatic music' (*Explorations*, p. 371). Holloway considered it 'harsh, discordant notes . . . braying . . . this riot of discords.' (*Joseph Holloway's Irish Theatre*. ed. Robert Hogan and Michael J. O'Neill; Dixon: Proscenium Press, 1968, Vol. I, pp. 50–51). There might be some sympathy for Holloway's judgement, 'when I heard that Yeats liked the music that was enough for me – as he has no ear for sound!'
14 op. cit., pp. 34–6.
15 Hilton Edwards and Micheál MacLiammóir, 'We Must Be Talking . . .' in Des Hickey and Gus Smith, *A Paler Shade of Green* (London: Leslie Frewin, 1972), pp. 80–1.
16 *Denis Johnston's Irish Theatre* (Dublin: The Dolmen Press, 1973), p. 14.
17 Micheál MacLiammóir, *Theatre in Ireland* (Dublin: The Three Candles, 1964) pp. 23–4, 28.
18 op cit., p. 74.
19 *A Paler Shade of Green*, p. 74.
20 *Theatre in Ireland*, p. 37. As a footnote to MacLiammóir's judgment on Denis Johnston, the latter has remarked, 'The trouble with the Gate, although it did brilliant work, was that it was run by actors for actors.' (Denis Johnston, 'Did you know Yeats? And did you lunch with Shaw?,' *A Paler Shade of Green*, p. 69.)
21 op. cit., pp. 48–51.
22 Denis Johnston recalls, in 'Did you know Yeats?', that Yeats objected to the line, 'I have written my name in letters of fire across the page of history.' He proposed to substitute, 'I shall be remembered.' It is a curious failure in Yeats to miss the need for Emmet's outworn grandiloquence.
23 *The Dramatic Works of Denis Johnston* (Gerrards Cross: Colin Smythe Ltd., 1977), p. 80.
24 Johnston has said that since writing *The Old Lady,* 'I have had no further complexes or heart-burnings about Ireland or her damned politics, because, in that play, I had given public expression to all I had to say on the subject. It acted upon me like a sort of jail delivery -- a catharsis – and that's all of that, so far as I'm concerned.' (*The Journal of Irish Literature*, May-September 1973, pp. 30–44). Yet he in fact did return to the subject, in a more naturalistic way, in *The Moon in the Yellow River* (1931) and *The Scythe and the Sunset* (1958).
25 *The Dramatic Works*, p. 79.
26 Ibid, pp. 17–18.
27 Christopher Innes, *Piscator's Political Theatre* (Cambridge: Cambridge University Press, 1972), p. 20. On expressionist staging, Innes quotes the Bauhaus architects' concept of 'a great keyboard for light and space . . . a flexible building capable of transforming and refreshing the mind by its spatial impact alone . . . The playhouse itself, made to dissolve into the shifting, illusionary space of the imagination, would become the scene of action itself.' (p. 162).

28   *Dramatic Works,* p. 17.
29   Ibid, p. 80.
30   Ibid, p. 81.
31   op. cit., p. 15.

A NOTE ON THE NATURE OF EXPRESSIONISM AND DENIS JOHNSTON'S PLAYS*

CURTIS CANFIELD

The distance the Irish Drama has travelled away from the conventional realism of the peasant play, picturesque and vital though much of it was, is nowhere more strikingly marked than in the works of a young revolutionary playwright, Denis Johnston. He is not a rebel in the political sense but an artist, striving to liberate the drama from forms and subjects which in his estimation are now stereotyped and outmoded. With this aim in view it was fitting that he should turn first to the persuasive force of James Joyce's *Ulysses*, and then to continental European sources for inspiration, to *Faust, Peer Gynt,* and especially to the experimental dramas of August Strindberg. There is little doubt that the Irish drama needed the literary revitalization which this master of iconoclasm could provide. Strindberg's arrival in Ireland was tardy but nonetheless timely considering the transitional state of the Drama. *The Old Lady Says 'No!'*, antedating Sean O'Casey's *The Silver Tassie* by two years, was the first convincing sign that the break away from traditional forms was at hand.

The Old Lady Says 'No!' (1926) follows the structural pattern of Strindberg's *A Dream Play* (1902) by placing the action within the subconscious mind of the leading character. We look on Dublin life through the refracted vision of a stunned actor, and it is a nightmare. Since this reflecting mind through which impressions of the natural world are filtered is temporarily incapable of systematic thought and deprived of rational guideposts, the form of the drama attempting to record these impressions is not orderly in the conventional theatrical sense. For example, no limitations of time, space, or action are imposed on the playwright. He is completely free from demands for logical causation, inevitable effects, and responsible sequences. His drama is at the mercy of a Will on a rampage.

* Reprinted from Curtis Canfield, ed., *Plays of Changing Ireland,* New York, The Macmillan Company, 1936, with the kind permission of Curtis Canfield.

A note on the nature of Expressionism

Nevertheless this does not mean that Expressionism is wholly lacking in design, a meaningless jumble of incoherent ideas. Nor does it mean that it is concerned primarily with Freudian psychoanalysis, nor with tracing certain mystical thought-processes. Far from it. Expressionism usually shows us a mind in chaos, but it is purposeful chaos whose pattern is based on the principles of the musical composition rather than on the rules of conventional dramaturgy. To understand it we must first forget Scribe and remember Beethoven, forget exigencies of plot, systematic scene-arrangements, individual characterization, and all the paraphernalia of the well-made play school in order to be more fully aware of rhythmic movement, recurring thematic ideas, exaggerated contrasts and antitheses, contrapuntal effects, discords, and ultimate harmonies. Expressionism is commonly a fusion of music, poetry, dancing, symbols, and subjective action. As such it demands a new set of critical standards enlarged by the presence in the plays of these several contributory art-forms.

Surface realism, working with more or less normal aspects of characters whose believable actions take place in natural surroundings, presents a straightforward picture of concrete and particular cases. The idea behind Expressionism is to give us this surface realism in synthesis. Instead of moving from the particular to the universal under our own power, as we are permitted to do by the realist, the expressionist asks that we focus on abstract meaning immediately. He does this by distilling universal significance from specific cases at the very beginning of his play. In other words he emphasizes the forest by suppressing individual trees. Each character in an expressionistic play is less an individual and more a general type or, as in the medieval Morality, the symbol of an idea or an attitude, or a representative of a larger group or class.

Hence, in *The Old Lady Says 'No!'*, the leading figure, Robert Emmet, symbolizes the ideals of patriotism and self-sacrifice set in conflict with the collective personality and the general character of the whole city of Dublin. The large conception of the theme is enhanced and its philosophical implications made clearer by the author's selection of characters who are readily proportioned for exaggeration into satirical types. Robert Emmet is the generic patriot, speaking not only his own historic lines but also those of Padraic Pearse, martyred leader of the 1916 rebellion, and Charles Stewart Parnell. Grattan ceases to be important as a person in comparison to his value as a representation of the qualities of

39

balance, reasonable action, and mature wisdom. The bystander, Joe, as Grattan explains, is the symbol of Irish genius dying gracefully; while the Old Woman who says 'No' to Emmet is a caustic vision of modern Ireland, a degraded Kathleen ni Houlihan.

The musical basis of the composition of *The Old Lady Says 'No!'* is indicated by the description of it as 'a romantic play with choral interludes'. After the introductory movement of the Prologue which establishes the romantic theme, the play might be described as a two-part Nocturne. The first part is made up of a series of kaleidoscopic street-scenes ending with the climactic wounding of Joe. Then a grotesque cadenza introduces the second part with an entertaining digression from the main story. This departure from the plot, like the Aristophanic parabasis in Greek Comedy, ridicules contemporary figures in letters, art, and politics. The principal theme of Part II has to do with the strange transformation of Sarah Curran and the death of the poetic Joe. These are developed in turn in two contrasting interior scenes, the fashionable salon and the filthy tenement, emblematic of the extremes of Irish society. So Robert Emmet, in his rambling, takes in a representative cross-section of Dublin life.

The playlet which sends the action off in the numbed brain of the Actor-Emmet character should be regarded as more than an arbitrary trick. It is a theatrical *coup*. The hero is immediately established as a puppet in the operatic tradition by being made to speak a romantico-patriotic poem fashioned from separate lines from well-known, fervid 18th and 19th century authors. He and Sarah Curran are revealed in all the trappings of grandiose artificiality with which the legend-makers have burdened their memories. The hero's stagy posturing and his excessive rhetoric foreshadow his future development as the essence of tragic and sententious irresponsibility. By reincarnating Emmet in the person of a play-actor, the author cuts still deeper into the romantic view of his leading character. The playlet further provides important thematic lines, and the repetition of these key-phrases throughout the play helps to bind the whole together in coherent form. Thus the Prologue establishes the mode and sets the tone for the main work but in addition serves as a natural beginning. The blow the Speaker receives on his head should be convincing explanation, even to the over-skeptical, for the chaos and unreality of subsequent scenes. It is a more original and dramatic start than Neil McRae's dream in *Beggar on Horseback*.

A note on the nature of Expressionism

Out of the welter of the play's confusion – the tinny jargon of the streets, the bedlam of newsboys and shouted catchwords, the snatches of political bromides and romantic fustian – the larger meaning of the drama gradually takes shape. It shows how inept idealism, nourished by the inflammable poetry which sentimentalizes the tragic mistakes of the past, can destroy all that is good in the youth of the nation. One may conclude from the play that the survival of a patriotic ideal which demands that life be sacrificed for a cause is not only retrogressive in effect but wasteful and ridiculous. The Blind Man, an ever-present figure in Irish literature, represents those who live on the ashes and rotten bones of the past. He is left, ironically enough, as Emmet's lone sympathizer, while Joe, though dimly and obliquely outlined as the symbol of youth and life, is destroyed by the bungling jingoist. The Emmet-type of patriot is highly dangerous because his savage ignorance is coupled with a belief in his own high destiny which neither mockery nor insult is able to shake.

Mr. Johnston's sharp blade, swung with all the *saeva indignatio* of a modern Swift, cuts two ways. His satire seems to attack not only the harmful influence of demagogues but goes further in concluding from the illustration of the Old Flower Woman's character that Ireland herself is unworthy to be saved by sacrifice. William Butler Yeats's beatific vision of Kathleen ni Houlihan, the spirit of Ireland for whom Irishmen went smiling to death in the field or on the gallows, has changed here to a drunken hag who curses her son as he dies for her. It is a savage and bitter conception that strikes at the heart of sentimental idolatry, and is, of course, a complete inversion of Mr. Yeats's view of Kathleen.

It will be observed that the action of *The Old Lady Says 'No!'* takes place in the few seconds required by the Doctor to fetch a rug for the prostrate Actor. This same freedom from conventional restrictions applies to the treatment of certain characters who are transformed or merged into others. Not being fixed in the determining mind they dissolve and change, fade and reappear as pictures in a dream. This usage is again characteristic of Strindbergian Expressionism. In *A Dream Play* the Officer becomes the Lawyer, Poet, Teacher, Pupil, Scholar, and Dullard in turn in order to express the multiple personality of the author himself. Our American expressionistic comedy, *Beggar on Horseback*, shows the irrepressible Mr. Cady haunting the mind of Neil McRae as widget manufacturer, murder-victim, judge, and

41

slave-driver. It seems not unnatural then that the people in the Prologue of *The Old Lady Says 'No!'*, since they are uppermost in The Speaker's mind at the moment when he loses consciousness, should persist in distorted guise after that moment. Mr. Johnston's selection of these extra-personal identities seems most fortunate in view of the fact that each is a satirical exaggeration of the original character. Sarah Curran's transformation into Kathleen ni Houlihan is a readily understandable confusion but Kathleen into the Old Flower Woman is an inevitable development if the significance of Part II is to be made clear. Again, Emmet, the Speaker, tells us that the animated statue of Grattan has the face and voice of Major Sirr. I suspect the author has done this deliberately, not merely for the purpose of bridging the gap between Prologue and Play nor to remind us of the vague but persistent continuity between the Speaker's conscious and unconscious states, but more importantly because Grattan stands in the same dramatic relationship to Robert Emmet as Major Sirr does. Both are symbols of the opposition. Grattan is the sensible statesman to whose intelligence Emmet's hare-brained schemes are as repugnant as Emmet's presence was to Major Sirr. Emmet is naturally inimical to both. Furthermore the choice of Grattan as Emmet's opponent makes for scenes of fine contrast. They strike fire at many places, the reasonable man against the emotional, the calm against the reckless, the preserver against the destroyer, the wise against the foolish.

Other changes of identity involve minor characters and are made primarily for comic purposes. The awkward soldier in the opening scene has evidently fulfilled all the requirements for military promotion when we see him later as a singing Free State General; and the Minister for Arts and Crafts, who 'bears a strong resemblance to the Stage Hand', has obviously been appointed because of his prowess in scene-shifting and faithful attendance at his Irish class. The skilful purpose behind these selections calls attention again to the carefully arranged inner design which is so much a part of Mr. Johnston's work. Just as in this play, some of the more trivial incidents of his next, *The Moon in the Yellow River*, assume large proportions when related to the completed pattern of meaning.

The Old Lady Says 'No!' is an outstanding example of a form which uses the resources of stage setting in dynamic fashion. The stage settings as well as the characters are made to melt away and reappear in changed form, thus preserving still further the feeling that the action passes in a dream, – 'the walls of the room seem to fade apart as the crowd draws aside' and 'the black curtains close behind the Speaker blotting out the room, and the voices fade away.' Thus the settings are not static backgrounds against which the actor alone presents the play's ideas but, with the lighting, function in active collaboration with the actor by changing and moving freely in accordance with his changing moods and circumstances. Their job is to interpret and reflect his fluctuating mental states. The Speaker's effort to regain consciousness is vividly suggested by showing him actually struggling against the enveloping folds of the black curtain, while in an earlier scene the pulsating light on the figure of the stricken actor, accompanied by a measured drum-beat, pictures in colour and sound the resumption of the actor's normal heart action. This bold handling of theatrical materials with its forceful pictorial representation of the actor's inner condition and mental attitude is possible only in such a form as Expressionism, where the illusion of reality does not have to be maintained.

Expressionism has been criticised on the grounds that it makes life too easy for the playwright. By releasing him from the salutary pain and drudgery of making his situations natural, his dialogue logical and connected, and from all the other rules of 19th century dramaturgy, Expressionism, it is argued, leads the dramatist toward a lazy, slipshod technique. It is all a question of the individual playwright of course, but I cannot agree that art is valuable only in proportion to the artist's creative agony. Even if this were so, there is to my mind wholly as much or more scientific dramaturgic craftsmanship in the structural design of *The Old Lady Says 'No!'* in its present form as would be required were it re-written as a well-articulated realistic play. Consider the rhythmic contrasts between the poetic speeches of Grattan and the vulgar phrases of the Old Woman which are set against them; the arrangement of contrapuntal effects in the lines of the Speaker, the General, and O'Cooney in the salon scene, all scored for rhythmic effect; and finally the sharp conflict of opposites repeated both in scene (salon to tenement) and action (the death of Joe amid the clamour of an absurd political debate). The opening playlet is in itself a fine combination of literary research and dramatic virtuosity. The rules for writing an expressionistic play are no less exacting than those for realism. They are simply different rules.

Part II of *The Old Lady Says 'No!'* moves from the good-natured satire of its opening digression to savage denunciation at the play's end. It may be contended that the implications of the satire in the salon scene are too parochial in interest and comedic appeal for an audience outside Dublin. This may be true to a certain extent, but to conclude further that the satire can be understood only by spectators familiar with the individuals involved or with every topical allusion made is contrary to all theatre practice. If, for example, we fail to recognize Phrynichus by name when the Chorus Leader mentions him in the parabasis of 'The Frogs,' we can still deduce from the context and the very tone of voice in which he is named the reason for his being brought into the play. And we can look him up later! The specific meaning of the satire need not be immediately grasped to be enjoyed provided some emotional effect is produced on the listener. We can agree that any play that fails to whet intellectual curiosity in one way or another is not worth its salt as dramatic literature and, conversely, no play is to be dismissed because an effort is required before its whole meaning is revealed. Since its art is based on rhythmic as well as literary principles, we should approach this new drama in the same way we approach great music. It asks to be seen and studied again and again, as a symphony must be heard many times before the student reaches a point of comprehension where full appreciation is possible. Expressionism more than any other dramatic genre points emphatically to two needed reforms in the theatre, first the establishment of permanent repertory systems wherein plays are presented for several seasons at a low admission price and second, an increase in the use and distribution of printed plays.

The nub of meaning in *The Old Lady Says 'No!'*, that youth is forever to be broken on the wheel of romantic folly and patriotic jingoism unless some kind of rational balance in weighing the worth of 'causes' is maintained, is surely not insular in application. American history may not supply us with a character exactly like Robert Emmet, although we have some parallel figures in John Brown, George Armstrong Custer, and Daniel Shays. But the general type is recognizable anywhere as the man whose noble motives and personal magnetism are joined with ineffectuality in action and lack of vision, the divine blunderer who paves his own and his fellows' way to Hell with the best intentions.

I, for one, cannot look on Mr. Johnston's rebel with much sympathy, as a splendid hero from a glamorous past whose high-mindedness is unjustly scorned by the ignoble citizenry of modern

Dublin. Some echo of the idealized past and the wretched present is inevitable owing to the play's arrangement, but the author's pen, truly an 'Ithuriel Spear', stabs vindictively into both. Ireland suffers under the delusion that it can cure its present ills by invoking the dead past. If I interpret it correctly, the play expresses the hope that the dead past may be buried so deep that lovers of life and beauty may prevail over the worshippers of death. Life is more precious than any ideal which demands that it be forsaken. Life is. Compared with this all other truths are insignificant. The fierce indignation against needless waste of life, and Ireland's complacency with its own destruction, burns again in *The Moon in the Yellow River*.

Robert Emmet's curse at the drama's close is proof enough for me that he is a destructive agency. Yet the play cannot be interpreted as a strictly pacifistic document except by those who side with Grattan. And in Ireland today these are in the minority. Emmet's final, 'I will take this earth in both my hands and batter it into the semblance of my heart's desire,' sums up all for which he stands, a creative force moving not by reason but by emotion, remaking the world in the only way he knows how.

The author attempts to give 'the devil his due' in this final scene, and he finds something to say for the Speaker's free, wild, poetic spirit. But as an artist Mr. Johnston takes sides neither with Grattan or Emmet, nor with either of the Old Flower Woman's sons, the respective spokesmen for Status Quo and Republican sentiments. The voices of Dublin's great which echo from the dancing shadows fail, on the whole, to affirm the Patriot's view, although they may have been introduced for this purpose. It would be difficult to reconcile Shaw's socialistic evangelism, Swift's intellect, or Sheridan's conceits with Emmet's impassioned Nihilism.

The reasonable man cannot help hoping that there will be a future for Ireland wherein 'those who build but do not destroy' will survive the Speaker's curse. But whatever the future, the hero of this play goes to the shades unregenerate and unashamed, a slippered Dante baffled but unbowed in a Dublin Inferno. He is a tragic figure because of the immensity of his ignorance, and a pathetic one because he cannot see the bitter joke on himself, nor the irony of his confident, 'Ah, I was so right to go on!' But perhaps it is kinder to let him depart thus, proud and sure of everything except the enormity of his own self-deception.

The Moon in the Yellow River grows directly out of the thesis developed in *The Old Lady Says 'No!'* and is, in fact, a deeper sequel to it. . . . The two plays need to be examined together. They are alike in that they are based on Ireland's final renunciation of those idealists who would sacrifice life for her, whether the zealots are engaged in struggle against Major Sirr, the symbol of British tyranny, or against Herr Tausch, the symbol of modern machinery. Both enemies may be regarded as obstacles thrown in the way of Irish peace and freedom. We may endorse Ireland's disavowal of Emmet's legend as a necessity for the country's future well-being, but, though Blake's ideal is as nihilistic in principle as Emmet's, there is more to be said for it in this play where the issues are not as clearly outlined as they were in *The Old Lady Says 'No!'*. Whether Ireland eventually gains or loses by Blake's death is a question the author does not attempt to answer, but he considers the whole subject with profound understanding and insight in the final Act.

The gulf of time and temperament separates Darrell Blake from Robert Emmet but the ideal of freedom through destruction is their common possession. Robert Emmet was an old-fashioned patriot in the sentimental tradition; Darrell Blake is a modern intellectual revolutionary, a cynical classicist who conjoins in his nature daring recklessness in action and the charm of a poetic visionary. There are further likenesses in their histories. Blake's failure to blow up the Works, due in the main to the stupidity and ineptitude of his followers, recalls the series of tragi-comic accidents which marred Emmet's rebellion in 1803. Chief among these was the explosion in the Patrick Street storehouse of a large cache of powder and bullets, a noisy blunder which must have given the whole game away to the vigilant British authorities.

Mr. Johnston has deepened the meaning of *The Moon in the Yellow River* beyond the topical pertinence of the preceding play by placing Darrell Blake's motives above the immediacy of political conviction. Blake is far more than an agitator for the Republican cause, and we have his own word that he does not believe in spilling blood for the 'colouring on maps'. He fights, rather, for a way of life in which Ireland shall stand in the place of Nirvana, a country offering dreamers like himself seclusion from a world grown too busy and embittered, a haven of isolation and peace such as Hilton's Conway found at Shangri-La. The trouble with Darrell Blake is that he can envision this Lipovian paradise but is imperfectly adjusted to it in temperament. The combination of Erin and China is at best a compromise, and this miscegenation in Blake is at the root of his tragedy. His youth and saturnine sense of humour stand in the way of complete detachment just as Dobelle's moods of impatience and irritability stand in the way of his. However successfully Blake may delude himself, we feel that a call for vigorous action or the chance to lead a night sortie would forever be interrupting the hours which the true initiate would devote to bland contemplations of his navel. Here is the essence of Blake's romanticism. Perhaps it is too much to interpret Blake's declaration that there is nothing cruel about Death as proof of his kinship with those Oriental philosophers who regard Death as a comparatively unimportant step in the liberation of the soul from the causal nexus, but it does seem to place Blake dangerously near the worshippers of death who were so soundly flayed in *The Old Lady Says 'No!'*. Tausch's guess that Dobelle must have lived in China as well as the Gran Chaco is to the point here because Dobelle, too, has felt the pull of Eastern philosophy. But whereas he, with his toy trains and his books, has succeeded in removing himself from life almost as completely as any Lama or Buddhist monk, he is unlike Blake in his unwillingness to fight against inroads on his meditations. This Oriental influence runs in undertone through the thinking of these two characters and its significance is aptly caught in the play's title.

Like its predecessor, *The Moon in the Yellow River* moves darkly along the shores of Cocytus and Phlegethon but, unlike it, tempers the bitterness of its conclusion with the forecast that its people will come forth at last, like Dante, 'once more to rebehold the stars.'

The play's principal struggle transpires from two conflicting notions about the nature of progress as these are enunciated by Herr Tausch and Darrell Blake. The German would have us believe that his machinery, by releasing those who control and serve it to pursue the things of the spirit where they will, is part of a great purpose for the world's good. Darrell Blake, on the other hand, sees the machine as an emblem of enslavement and misery. He forthwith takes steps to remove its latest encroachment on his domain by the straightforward expedient of blowing up the foreigner's Power House. The argument between them is amiable, even amusing, until Commandant Lanigan's shot brings it down from the plane of abstract speculation to the reality of blood and death. The sentimental German, seeing his enemy so ruthlessly destroyed, executes an about-face and denounces Lanigan as a murderer. In the final scene of summation the playwright penetrates with great skill into the heart of his mystery by showing Tausch his own guilt in the killing. Commandant Lanigan, according to the sentient

Dobelle, is merely Tausch's instrument, carrying the fight to the cruelly logical conclusion which the German's good-nature did not permit him to foresee or comprehend. That end from which Tausch's sensibilities shrank in horror, projected with unemotional finality by the Free State gunman, was the monstrous revelation of self that Dobelle told Tausch he was destined to see in the mists.

The Works are ultimately destroyed by accident and thus both antagonists are defeated. The wasteful, blundering Land, as if conscious of its superiority to the foreigner and at the same time disdainful of the sacrifice which the Byronic Blake had made in order to help Ireland do something it could accomplish with ease alone, is the final victor. Resistance to change is seen to be no man's personal prerogative. Ireland can take care of herself. Unchanged, unchanging, she looks serenely down on a new day as a ship hoots merrily in the yet-unsullied Shannon; and out of her immensity she gives a new life as if to prove that Blake's was as nothing compared to her abundance. Agnes, the old Mother, the symbol of Ireland again, contradicts Dobelle's gloomy prophecy about Death and Darkness by announcing the birth of the latest Mulpeter and by letting the light stream in through the window.

Beginning with this masterful conception of an important theme, Denis Johnston has gone on to weave into his plot a gallery of characters so original in outlook and so varied in personality as to enliven the whole texture of the play. The composition in which these characters are held, and the excellence of the play's construction, make *The Moon in the Yellow River* a work of exceptional distinction.

Denis Johnston, by virtue of these two rich and mature plays, is the spearhead of the new Irish Drama. At this stage of his career he may be a little surer of his material than he is about his method of treating it, having given the impression, by following each experimental play with one in conventional form, that he is trying to ride the two horses of Expressionism and Realism at once. His writing is informed with deep conviction and fearlessness; and if his future evolution fulfils the promise of these early plays, his classical background and training should help him toward that unity of form and subject matter so necessary for great drama. In him, more than in any other Irish playwright of the present time, the hope of the literary drama lies.

THE MOON IN THE YELLOW RIVER:
DENIS JOHNSTON'S SHAVIANISM

THOMAS KILROY

The Moon in the Yellow River is a highly rational comedy about the nature of power under several of its guises, the technological, the political, the familial. Indeed, about the only such arena omitted is the sexual, if one discounts the puppy-love of the teen-aged heroine, Blanaid for the IRA man Darrell Blake. Its more subtle passages are to be found, as one might expect, where Johnston deals with the most ambiguous and beguiling of all flights from reason, that which we associate with human emotion and its various kinds of romanticism. Denis Johnston has carried out a personal engagement with romantic attitudes throughout the whole of his writing life, worrying the subject with the kind of zeal which suggests a deep romantic urge within the man himself. One of the successes of *The Moon in the Yellow River* is that this conflict is given a precise focus and a dramatic form, a context that enriches and illuminates it.

The idea of the play (and it is a 'problem' play in this sense) is set within a solid, naturalistic structure. The element of surprise is confined to its wit, to stylistic twists and turns in the dialogue and to one or two unpredictable moments in an otherwise linear plot. As an audience of this play we are being invited to attend to the working out of a cluster of ideas surrounding the one idea of power and the essential dramatic form is that of a series of debates between antagonists, one in each of the three acts. The setting is that of an eccentric household, presided over by an eccentric father-figure. A grave political situation exists without but this is reflected within the inner world of the play (and, therefore, to a degree, is neutralized) in terms of farce, ironical distortion. In the end, the values which the household represents are seen to transcend the merely political, standing, as they do, for a beleagured civilization in a difficult period of a difficult century. Finally, these values are given emotional expression in the diminuendo of the last act and the Prospero-Miranda-like contact between father and daughter.

Now all of this is strikingly reminiscent of *Heartbreak House* (a point which has been made more than once, before[1]) not just of

49

Shaw, then, but of the Shaw who was responding in his own way to the London productions of Chekhov in 1913 and the experience of the First World War. This comparison is worth rehearsing once more, partly because it has not been exhausted, partly because it helps us to locate Denis Johnston among Anglo-Irish playwrights.

Johnston has described himself as 'a good Shavian of the generation whose processes of thought were largely formed by Shaw.'[2] When, later in the same radio programme, he goes on to specify this Shavianism he does so, as follows: 'I learnt from Shaw the same scepticism of greatness and a profound dislike of anything that savours of magic.'[3] He might almost have been consciously thinking of Yeats and of Yeats's idea of an Irish theatre which would celebrate the heroic in the Irish tradition and the native genius for transcending the ordinary, the mundane, through the imagination. Certainly Johnston stands apart from the main thrust of Irish drama in the first half of this century; the theatre which he represents, a comic theatre of ideas, has never really taken hold in Ireland. Thirty years ago, Thomas Hogan attempted to deal with this issue in *Envoy*. His essay is contentious but its presentation of Johnston's isolation is, I think, accurate: an intellectual in a theatre given to emotionalism, an Anglo-Irishman of the kind who never really seems at ease with the native. Johnston had no antecedents in the local theatrical scene and has had no influence on those who followed him. One may take Hogan's view of this, that Johnston is the 'last of the Anglo-Irish', as unnecessarily grave but there is a ring of truth to his grim, final remark: 'It is not possible to be an Anglo-Irish writer any more. The old blind fiddler, with his mysterious ways and his dark traditions, has moved in.'[4]

It is arguable that of the three early plays, *A Bride for the Unicorn* is the only one which demonstrates an entirely personal form, the kind of play of which we say this has to be the work of this writer and of no other. It was a failure, both in the theatre and in the life of Johnston in that it did not seem to free him, creatively.[5] In both *The Old Lady Says 'No!'* and *The Moon in the Yellow River,* on the other hand, we are constantly reminded of other influences, other presences behind Johnston, even though both plays are virtually flawless, technical achievements of their own kind. Neither play had any impact upon the development of the Irish drama; each is an example of technique borrowed to fit the particular purpose of the playwright of that moment and is then discarded. The Shavianism of *The Moon in the Yellow River*, then, is a remarkable exercise, but one of the major reservations which one must have of the play is that Shaw does the same thing better in *Heartbreak House* and on a more ambitious scale.

Both plays have this mixture of conventional, mechanical domestic comedy of late Victorian theatre and a kind of visionary, apocalyptic writing, a forward looking consciousness which is, however, in both plays, deeply cynical about contemporary progress. In this way, the worthwhile in both is expressed in a refined helplessness, a civilized lunacy, a mild pathos which is the English-speaking theatre's reading of Chekhovian atmosphere, of Chekhov's treatment of a doomed, leisured, civilized class before the horrors of modernity. As with Shaw, Johnston's specific concern is the dangerous absurdity of a situation where 'power and culture are in separate compartments.'[6] The England of 1913 (and Shaw would claim it represented Europe) and the Ireland of the late twenties had this, at least, in common: both were threatened by violence and this violence was associated by both playwrights with a progressive materialism. The principal victim of this inhumane force in both plays is romanticism. It is typical of both Shaw and Johnston that while they see this fate as deserved, the romantic as an obsolete figure, it nevertheless allows them to concede a degree of guarded affection towards the romantic, however absurd he, Hector Hushabye or Darrell Blake, may be. What survives in both plays is a little community of inspired lunacy, people with a marvellous capacity to simply ignore or deflate the movement of power across their path. Observers of all this are Shotover and Dobelle, masters of the central rhetoric of the plays which is made up of scepticism, even misanthropy, plain-speaking and paradox and a vision which transcends the squalid present. It is an important part of the action of both plays that each man is reached, touched, restored by a figure of virginal girlhood.

Now we know what Captain Shotover's crazy house stands for in *Heartbreak House* and even if we should miss it, Shaw informs us in the first sentences of the Preface:

> Heartbreak House is not merely the name of the play which follows this preface. It is cultured, leisured Europe before the war.[7]

We do not know the religion, the affiliations of Dobelle in *The Moon in the Yellow River*, although the playwright has made sly reference to this.[8] Nevertheless, it seems clear, at least to an Irish audience, that Dobelle's world is Johnston's own Anglo-Irish world faced with a new, potentially savage and soulless Ireland struggling into being. The world of Dobelle is cut off from the Ireland outside and is presented as a place of immense, cultivated charm and lethargy, its great skills atrophied or turned into childish games, its rich, cultural stock shelved like books to be taken down from time to time to support wit and debate. It is easy to extrapolate wider meaning from the story of Dobelle, the retired engineer with his life lopped off and the perspective which it offers on the emerging Ireland is unmistakably that of a class, once ascendant but now trying to find itself in the sometimes extremely distasteful elements around it. The native Irish in the play are represented, in turn, by Agnes, the maternal, garrulous, ham-fisted, good-natured maid; her son, the absurd IRA volunteer, Willie; Blake, the romantic, intellectual Republican and Lanigan the pedestrian but highly effective Free State officer-killer. Between them and Dobelle's household stands Tausch, the German engineer in charge of the Power Station. The action of the play moves between these three centres and they, in turn, provide a kind of model of the whole state in the years immediately after Independence.

The play opens, like *Heartbreak House,* with a visitor arriving into a strange house which manages to upset every normal expectation of any normal visitor. In such a way and in the Shavian detail of the stage-directions describing the curious architecture, we are alerted to the fact that this is no ordinary house and no ordinary household. Tausch is a complete outsider but he has arrived in a house which itself is outside that Ireland which is to be the source of puzzlement and torment to the German over the following three acts. Tausch is introduced to that Ireland by the household of Dobelle and the education of Tausch provides one of the main lines of the play. He claims to have been attracted to Ireland because of a kitsch romanticism:

> It is the call of the west wind. One grows tired of those places where everything has been done already. Then one day comes the call of romance. I answer. You understand.[9]

The action of the play is a stripping away of those absurd notions and replacing them with some concrete reality. But, again like Shaw, Johnston does not offer us any simple overweighing of one character by another. All of the main antagonists are subject to the sceptical criticism which is the principal point of view in the play. There is sympathy for the bluff, honest anger of Tausch and it is he who provides the most telling insight into Dobelle's malaise, the 'satiric neurosis'[10] which has left the man acutely aware but morally impotent before events at large and before the pathetic need of his own child.

The principal comic technique which Johnston acquired from Shaw is the creation of the eccentric group through which all the issues and ideas of the play are filtered. As in *Heartbreak House,* this circle is characterized by its unpredictability in thought and speech, its insulation from the mundane, ordinary concerns of daily life and its espousal, at all times, of individualism, however outrageous. Within the English tradition, comedy has always tended to promote such a privileged circle and the discriminations of the comedy have often to do with why certain persons are admitted and certain excluded. Even more than Shaw's, Johnston's group is chiefly marked by that kind of dottiness in which both playwrights found a kind of wisdom before the more lethal absurdities of the world outside. Indeed when Johnston's comedy becomes tiresome it is due to an excessive trust in the charm of the eccentric, a kind of facetiousness which mars *The Golden Cuckoo,* for instance.

Aunt Columba with her paranoia and her bicycle, honest George, the friendly gun-maker, Blanaid, the child, and, of course, Dobelle himself make up this circle, this inner family of the play. George (along with his side-kick, Potts) is the most difficult to place but they both reflect an Ireland now passed away, Greystones and Malahide, boarding-houses and Palm Court hotels, retired military and navy men, old Imperial servants, pottering around between the garden, the pub and the sea-front. All of the circle to one degree or another share that relentless, unnerving logic which characterizes the select few of Shavian comedy, even if the premise, as in the case of Aunt Columba, be bizarre or original motive for action, as in the case of George, be casual when the proposal is to fire his gun at the Power House. Each is unshockable and shocking: while Tausch trembles and perspires during the central action involving the IRA, the family proceeds as if mayhem and arson, shooting and all the rest of it were part of the everyday. The dottiness, then, is a way of surviving when all power has passed to the brutally efficient, the engineers and the gunmen. In the case of Dobelle, however, there is something more. What is whimsical in the others is elevated in

Dobelle to an elaborate style, self-protective to the point of nearly destroying his instincts as a father but enormously witty and provocative as well. He enunciates the crucial paradox of the play which, like its Shavian equivalent, is intended to shake conventional moral assumptions. Like the Shavian formula it attempts to hold contraries, contradictions, the problematical elements in life, in some kind of coherent, sane balance. What is sometimes in Johnston mere verbal flair is here a matter of intense feeling expressed through the intelligence:

> I am against their rightness. It is right that a woman should die so that a child's immortal soul should be saved from Limbo, therefore I say that I am against right. It is right that men should murder each other for the safety of progress. I admit it. That is why I am against right and believe in wrong. When I look back over my life, it's as plain as a pikestaff to me. It is always evil that seems to have made life worthwhile, and always righteousness that has blasted it. And now I solemnly say that I believe in wrong. I believe in evil and in pain and in decay and, above all, in the misery that makes man so much greater than the angels.[11]

It is a speech worthy of an Undershaft and like Undershaft Dobelle has looked into the abyss and has retained his sanity through an unsentimental clarity of mind and a command of the language to articulate it.

It seems to me that Johnston is much less happy with the three locals who have a place within this charmed circle: Agnes, the housekeeper, her son Willie, the hopeless gunman, and Darrell Blake, the IRA dreamer and intellectual. The mother-and-son pair hardly matter that much and one can accept the rough farce for what it is. Blake, however, is crucial: he is the romantic, doomed revolutionary, dashing, poetic, inefficient, humane, and like the figure of Emmet he arouses that mixture of response in Johnston which makes his work both stimulating and difficult: an attraction to romantic excess and a determination to show how it cannot survive in this world. In order to suggest the bond between Blake and the household of Dobelle, Johnston invests him with some of the leisurely, somewhat barmy intellectualism of his host and the effect is quite difficult to accept.

The structure of *The Moon in the Yellow River* is that of the debate: in point of fact, each of the three acts is constructed about a particular argument. In Act One, the antagonists are Tausch and Dobelle, in Act Two we have an orchestrated debate, officiated by Blake and involving, virtually, all the characters in the play. In Act Three, the issue is that of Lanigan's shooting of Blake: it brings Tausch and Lanigan, representing the two forces of active power in the play, into direct confrontation. Dobelle stands as a kind of referee between them.

The debate of Act One, which is based upon the device of a foreigner and an estranged Irishman talking about Ireland, allows Johnston the kind of ironical distancing and repartee in which he delights, and across some of the recurring topics of the play: politics and revolution, progress and technology and the dangerous magic of emotionalism and superstition:

TAUSCH: Come, come, Mr. Dobelle.

DOBELLE: And in the mists that creep down from the mountains you will meet monsters that glare back at you with your own face.

TAUSCH: Ah now, Mr. Dobelle, you cannot frighten me with parables. You forget that I am a German, and what you say only convinces me how much you really need my work.

DOBELLE: I know that nobody will ever listen to me; but remember, I have warned you.

TAUSCH: I think, if I may say so, that you are a little afraid of life and that is why you live here. But we are not like that in Germany. There we still have the virile youth of a new nation: hope, courage, and the ability to rise again. Put Germany in the saddle and you will find that she can ride.[12]

After Dobelle's bogey-men and Tausch's preposterous and chilling hymn to organization the debate is broken by the arrival of Willie, the useless gunman, in a beautifully timed piece of melodrama. It is the first of several melodramatic moments of the play, each one used by Johnston with great precision.

The second debate, that of Act Two, is the typical trial scene with which we are familiar throughout Johnston's plays. In somewhat contrived fashion and as part of an elaborate jest, Tausch and his

Power House are placed on trial before the household with Aunt Columba in charge of the minutes. The incidentals of the scene are delightful and intellectually interesting: the problem is in the contrivance of the event, not its working-out.

However, the scene represents the climax of the play in which conventional action and conventional ideas about achievement in the world are opposed by the alternative, anarchistic views of Dobelle's household and the romantic, Luddite attitudes of Darrell Blake. In spite of Tausch's discomfiture the whole thing is seen to be a jest and the alternative values offered against Tausch are doomed; he is, after all, the victor. The debate of Act Two, again, ends with a second and much more powerful melodramatic intervention when Darrell Blake is shot dead by Lanigan.

There is much that is admirable in the play up to this point but it is the quality of Act Three which raises it to the complexity of art. The final debate concerns Lanigan and his action, specifically the way in which Tausch dementedly tries to disown the Law and the Order which he has invited in in the first place. Lanigan is that quintessentially modern figure, the professional butcher with a naive, stubborn and, in the end, terrifying belief in the rightness of his actions, however brutal. In the subsequent discussions, no longer whimsical but touched now by an element of terror and hysteria, Johnston writes a prescient tract for the times. The banal, pathetic gunman and the hysterical technocrat wander in and out umbilically attached to one another in a kind of grotesque comedy quite unlike anything else in the play.

Seen in this way *The Moon in the Yellow River* is a fine example of that kind of drama of ideas which Shaw describes in *The Quintessence of Ibsenism*:

> An interesting play cannot in the nature of things mean anything but a play in which problems of conduct and character of personal importance to the audience are raised and suggestively discussed.[13]

There is no doubt about the contemporary force of the problems in *The Moon in the Yellow River*: the hydro-electrification of the new state, the republican subversion of the new government, the capacity of that government to act outside the conventional moral code, if necessary, to suppress subversion. Indeed, the problems are

56

not confined to the twenties but have a resonance in the Ireland of the present day.

What really distinguishes the play, however, is that Johnston, like Shaw, has found a form where the mechanized plot and system of ideas in the play are leavened by a delicate, touching movement in feeling. Both Shaw and Johnston display a reserve, a mockery, even a sense of distaste before excessive emotion. Their work is armoured against excess of this kind. Consequently the expression of simple, naked feeling has to be hard-earned in a play by Shaw or one by Denis Johnston. When it is, it is all the more moving on that account. The portrait of Blanaid, the child aching for love, is one of the finest of its kind in the modern theatre. The scenes in which Johnston handles this intensely private drama, below or behind the clatter of discussion, are some of the finest in the play. Even Aunt Columba emerges out of the fog of unreality when faced with the predicament of Blanaid while the final scene between father and daughter provides not a schematic resolution but the simple meeting of exchanged love.

In 1971, in an Author's Note for the programme of the play's revival at the Abbey Theatre, Denis Johnston expressed the belief:

> that with the passage of time the play has become not less but more up to date. Its concern is what is now not an Irish but a universal problem – Industrialization versus The Human Race.

While this is undeniable, what really seems of lasting worth in the play is less its treatment of social ideas than the way in which the old Ibsenite formula is layered with a less public and truly universal life of feeling. *The Moon in the Yellow River* and *Heartbreak House* are both demonstrations of the limitation of the form which rests solely upon the dramatic treatment of conflicting ideas.

NOTES

1 See, in particular, George A. Barnett *Denis Johnston,* Twayne Publishers, Boston 1978, pp. 42 ff.
2 W.R. Rogers, edit. *Irish Literary Portraits,* BBC Publication, London 1972, p. 116.
3 Ibid. p. 117.
4 *Envoy,* Vol. 3, No. 9, August 1950, p. 46.
5 See Harold Ferrar, *Denis Johnston's Irish Theatre.* The Dolmen Press, Dublin, 1973, p. 75 ff.
6 Bernard Shaw, *Heartbreak House,* Penguin Books, Harmondsworth, 1968, p. 10.

7 Ibid. p. 7.
8 Denis Johnston, *Dramatic Works* Vol. 2, Colin Smythe, Gerrards Cross, 1979, p. 81.
9 Ibid. p. 100.
10 Ibid. p. 154.
11 Ibid. p. 146.
12 Ibid. P. 109.
13 Bernard Shaw, *The Quintessence of Ibsenism,* Constable, London, 1913, p. 190.

DENIS JOHNSTON'S HORSE LAUGH

ROBERT HOGAN

Denis Johnston has usually spoken about his plays with a kind of diffident ambivalence – even, one might say, with a kind of defeated chagrin. When, for instance, *The Moon in the Yellow River* was revived Off-Broadway in 1961, Johnston pointed to an anecdote in the play, about how a man accidentally shoots the horse he is riding in the head, and remarked how different audiences had reacted differently to it:

> I have noticed with interest that in Dublin and in Paris this passage gets an immediate explosion of mirth. In London, after a moment of uncomfortable hesitation, there follows a strange delayed reaction that builds into a laugh lasting for almost half a minute, and which usually interferes with the following dialogue. On the other hand, when performed in the Polish or in the German tongues, I am informed that there is no response whatsoever. I am not certain what conclusions can be drawn from this data, but I am quite insistent that such a story – even among horse lovers – is a good example of what might be described as an authentic Irish joke, a fact that in itself may be one of the real things that is funny about the Irish.[1]

There is an engaging lack of swank and ego here, but I suspect that it disguises a hedging against failure or even against a stupid kind of success. In actuality, it is difficult to read Johnston's plays without perceiving that he knows precisely what he is doing and precisely how to get his effects. He has paid the most meticulous attention to the most minute detail. So if audiences, whether Irish or American or Polish, do not react appropriately, I should say that usually something is wrong with the production, occasionally something could be wrong with the audience, but only rarely is something wrong with the dramaturgy.

Still, Johnston's plays do take some living with, both because of their general high quality and because of their diversity of styles. During his active career, critics found him an uncomfortable writer. He was hard to pigeonhole, for his work was sometimes complex in statement and usually unpredictable in technique. Only now, at the end of his career, is his work finally being intelligently assessed and assimilated. Two thoughtful books and a few probing essays have been written, and now there is this welcome collection of papers.

I should imagine that the critical appraisal of Johnston will go on for some years. When, however, the pundits have had their say, I would put my money on two of his plays, *The Moon in the Yellow River* and *The Scythe and the Sunset*, as finishing by a nose in a dead-heat. His first and possibly best-known play, *The Old Lady Says 'No!'*, will, I think, fade in the stretch. Johnston has never been properly credited for his originality in this play of adapting the allusive technique of Eliot and Joyce to the drama. However, many of his allusions elude even Irish audiences; and in the recent adequate, but hardly inspired Abbey Theatre revival, even this strongpoint appeared weakish. The texture of the dialogue was thinner than one had supposed, and much of the bright young satiric 1920s banter now appeared more clever-clever than witty.

Johnston's own favorite play, *A Bride for the Unicorn*, could have had, with a little luck, the success of a Cocteau or, later, a Beckett play. However, at this late date, it does seem, if not the work of a clever-clever satirist à la *The Old Lady*, at least the work of a clever-clever intellectual. It would take an elaborate staging to do the piece consummately, and so it is probably as unrevivable as Colum's *Balloon*, O'Casey's *Within the Gates* or O'Neill's *The Great God Brown*.

The rest of Johnston's work seems highly revivable, and I am not sufficiently the prophetic punter to say which play could break out of the pack to place or to show in the home stretch. The trial play, *A Strange Occurrence on Ireland's Eye,* must probably be preferred over its original, *Blind Man's Buff*, and as a thoughtful courtroom melodrama must rank among the best of that usually brainless genre. The Swift play, *The Dreaming Dust,* has fine possibilities for actors and surpasses the half-dozen other Swift plays almost as much as *The Old Lady* surpasses the two dozen other Emmet plays. Still, the structure of the piece is overly schematic, and could – as I have remarked somewhere – illustrate not so much the Seven Deadly Sins as the seven deadly scenes. If *Strange Occurrence*, however, is a thoughtful courtroom melodrama, *The Golden Cuckoo* is that even rarer bird, a thoughtful farce, and a unique small gem.

So far I have been stressing how unique Johnston is, but it is the uniqueness of the consummate adaptor. His works are really adaptations of standard forms: the gloss on the medieval morality in *The Dreaming Dust*, on the patriotic melodrama in *The Old Lady*, on the broad farce in the *Cuckoo*. I mean this statement in no pejorative sense, for, as Eric Bentley has pointed out, most of Bernard Shaw's early plays made similar use of traditional forms and turned out utterly individually.

Johnston has distinctly disassociated himself from Shaw, whom he has called the 'Good Old Wenceslaus of Ayot St. Lawrence – a monarch who was always a pleasure to read, a headache to listen to, and utter confusion to agree with.' Despite that disclaimer, his plays are full of Shavian reverberations; *The Golden Cuckoo* almost seems a variation of *Saint Joan,* and *The Moon* has its obligatory discussion scene.

Johnston is most Shavian, however, in his mastery of the traditional tricks of the trade. Shaw too was a unique phenomenon, but the uniqueness had deep roots in the usual. The freewheeling and relatively ignored late plays (such as *In Good King Charles' Golden Days* or *Too True To Be Good* or *The Apple Cart*), as well as the middle masterpieces (such as *Heartbreak House* and *Saint Joan* and *Back to Methuselah*), all came out of the anti-melodrama of *The Devil's Disciple,* the anti-romance of *Arms and the Man,* the anti-pantomime of *Androcles and the Lion,* the modern version of the chronicle play of *Caesar and Cleopatra,* and the neo-Ibsenism of *Widowers' Houses, The Philanderer* and *Mrs. Warren's Profession.* All of these early pieces derived a basic strength from variations of the forms and techniques of Shakespeare, Boucicault, Planché, Ibsen and a dozen other veteran practitioners of conventional stagecraft.

In this respect, Johnston is thoroughly Shavian, and so any analysis of his technique must not begin with his own clever contributions to technique in *The Old Lady* or *The Bride* or *The Dreaming Dust,* but in his mastery of timeworn and traditional devices.

I

I propose to illustrate my point by *The Moon in the Yellow River* because it is one of Johnston's best and best-known plays, and because its conventional plotting, characterization, dialogue and spectacle brilliantly support a most unconventional theme. On the stage, the play has never been entirely successful, but it should have been. With conventional audiences and commentators, the play failed; with more urbane audiences and commentators, it achieved a limited success. With really perceptive audiences and commentators, it still, I think, might triumph. A recent English production of Granville Barker's *The Madras House* was something of a much belated vindication of that extraordinary masterpiece; *The Moon in the Yellow River* deserves a similar production and a similar vindication.

Before considering the effects of Johnston's dramaturgy, we might instructively glance at how that dramaturgy has worked upon its most notable audiences.

The Moon was first produced by the Abbey Theatre on 27 April, 1931, and was apparently an attempt to write a play that would fit the Abbey stock company. (Lest this remark be construed as a criticism of the artist prostituting his values, it might be pointed out that Shakespeare, Molière and innumerable other dramatists have traditionally written plays for particular actors.) There was a Maureen Delany part, an Eileen Crowe part, and a part that was inevitable for F. J. McCormick. Yet Johnston was not really an Abbey dramatist, particularly in those heydays of George Shiels, Brinsley MacNamara and the great comic eccentrics of O'Casey. Johnston was obviously Anglo-Irish, nominally avante garde, and had made his local reputation with the Gate – hardly the kind of person to endear himself to the lower-middle class Abbey actors and the predominantly bourgeois Abbey audience.

About this production, Johnston wrote:

> It was gently sabotaged by most of its original Abbey cast who until 1938 played it with that subtle air of distaste with which experienced actors can dissociate themselves from the sentiments expressed in their parts.[2] On its first night it had one of those very mixed receptions that usually presage a riot on the second. However, this never quite materialized, although I waited in some apprehension in the green room for another of those summonses to the stage that have nothing to do with a curtain call. All that it got was a rough deal from the newspapers, which complained that its humour was feeble, that it had no visible plot, and that it 'introduced some coarse levity on the subject of childbirth.'[3]

The conventional reaction of audience and critics might be

Denis Johnston's horse laugh

suggested by Joseph Holloway's résumé:

> 'Thank God!' rang out from Mr. Campbell all over the house when Arthur Shields announced that the author wasn't in the house. It was the best line of the evening, and it echoed the sentiment of most present who had been thoroughly bored by an undramatic play that was a sneer from start to finish of everything one holds dear in Ireland and of the Catholic faith. The last act had a very uneasy passage, one felt it in the air, and had the author had the courage to face the audience I am sure hisses would have been plentiful. The play was talky, undramatic rubbish laden with untruths. What it was all about was a puzzle to the world.[4]

On 28 February, 1932, the play opened in New York, produced by the Theatre Guild, with Claude Rains as apparently a superb Dobelle and with Henry Hull as a very American Darrell Blake.[5] *The New York Times* reported:

> It was not, in many ways and for a number of reasons, a thoroughly satisfactory evening, but it was one which stimulated the imagination – in itself an unusual achievement for the current theatre – and provided several fine and absorbing moments. 'Provocative' is a word which may partially, if somewhat inadequately, cover the situation.
>
> *The Moon in the Yellow River* is certainly not a literal and explicit play. It is beclouded with symbolic references which, on this side of the Atlantic, are obscure to those not thoroughly acquainted with Irish Free State history and politics. It rambles conversationally along a good deal of the time, discussing poetically and philosophically a variety of topics. It lacks the dramatic effectiveness of an O'Casey play, or the rich warm flavour of an Irish folk piece. It follows autochthonous moments with moments of vagueness and generalization and then breaks out in some rather explosive melodrama. In short, by rule of thumb measurements, Denis Johnston has not written a good play. But he has written one you are likely to remember after many admittedly good plays have run their course.
>
> . . . Much of what he has to say is interesting, but some of it is not so interesting in the theatre, where action still rules. 'This is not a country; it is a debating society,' is, in substance, the remark of one of the characters. That also holds true for Mr. Johnston's discursive play . . .[6]

In his long Sunday review, the *Times'* Brooks Atkinson, a generally sound critic somewhat given to gush, wrote:

> Unlike Li Po, who was drowned in the attempt, Denis Johnston has succeeded in embracing 'The Moon in the Yellow River.' He has imprisoned the most vital part of Ireland, within the three acts of a bouncing drama. Not being a literal play with a single, concrete story and a literal argument, it deceives the expectations of ordinary theatre-going. Like *The Lower Depths,* it is discursive on the surface. But it is sound and searching underneath, and it is heavily freighted with the truth of character. No other recent Irish play has contributed so much to an understanding of Ireland. Mr. Johnston does not explain; he irradiates.[7]

Part of this description seems more appropriate for J. Hartley Manners than Denis Johnston; however, Atkinson goes blithely but confusingly along to suggest that the play has lots of story, but that the story 'is only a fluttering incident in an ebullient drama. What makes *The Moon* . . . such a vital play is its racy, full-blooded characterizations . . .' Then, after developing his point about characterization, he concludes with a typically lyrical peroration:

> When a native Irish playwright gives us a beautiful, poignant drama steeped in the spirit of his own country it behooves the plodding theatregoer to pull himself up by his bootstraps. For an understanding of contemporary Ireland, *The Moon* . . . is better than Synge or Yeats and better than the urbanized O'Casey. Mr. Johnston has captured a vital part of Ireland.

In 1934, the play was produced at the Malvern Festival and then brought to London for a limited engagement. *The Times* remarked:

> Mr. Denis Johnston's tragi-comedy . . . suffers from a surfeit of ideas. It is a rare fault in the theatre, and easy in this instance to condone, so supple and revealing is the dialogue, so unstrained and abundant the underlying comic inventiveness. Because the author's study of Irish playboyism carries him over too many tricky currents of thought – the conflicting ideals of the visionary Republic and the existing Free State, peasant resentment of industrial progress, philosophic Nihilism and its painful resolution – his play loses direction and ends on the shoals of

sentiment; but the comic episodes are delightful, and the analysis of character is shrewd and diverting . . . Altogether, a play of rare quality and excusable faults, which, even in its difficult ending, bears the impress of an original and engaging mind.[8]

With some cast changes, the play transferred to the Haymarket and went on to a run of about two hundred performances. Again *The Times* remarked:

> It would have been a pity, indeed it would have been a reflection on the London theatre, if this play had vanished from sight at the end of its limited run . . . it has the structural fault of ending twice – once when a power house, symbol of industrialism in the Irish Arcady, is accidentally wrecked . . . and again when a morose neurotic realizes that there lives again in his hated daughter the mother who died giving her birth; but these are by no means ruinous flaws upon a play of rare theatrical vitality . . . But as it is presented the play – its structural faults forgotten – triumphs as a group of fantastic portraits, each with an intense theatrical validity of its own, given life by imaginative and satiric dialogue which is as stimulating as it is amusing.[9]

The play was revived Off-Broadway in 1961, on which occasion Howard Taubman wrote in *The New York Times*:

> Mr. Johnston's story about Ireland in 1927 is not all of a piece, either in mood or toughness of fibre. But it is the stimulating work of a man with a rousing aptitude for the theatre and with a joyous relish of the wonderful diversity and crustiness of the human species. In a season tinged heavily with mediocrity it is heartening to encounter a literate playwright . . .
>
> They are a pleasure, these Irish, as they blather, philosophize, bicker and bumble. There is only a trace of the stage comedian in them, for Mr. Johnston has seen them freshly . . .
>
> *The Moon* . . . has lost something in immediacy in the thirty years since its appearance. But it is still saturated by the Irish gift for mocking and mourning the contradictions of Ireland.[10]

After being once rescued by an infusion of money from a backer, the production limped on for a total of forty-eight performances.

The play has had quite a few other productions, but these are probably the important ones, and their reviews interestingly run the gamut from curt dismissal to rapturous admiration. The plot has been sometimes thought clever and at other times faulty or even non-existent. The characterization has been called realistic and been called theatrical. The theme has been thought pro-Irish and anti-Irish, as well as trenchant and muddled. Obviously, either the playwright is hopelessly confusing, or his audiences are innately confused. I should like to suggest that the fault is not primarily the playwright's.

II

Many commentators have been troubled by both the plot and the theme of *The Moon in the Yellow River*. The plot has often seemed a group of discursive conversations interrupted by explosions of melodrama or eruptions of sentiment. The theme has often seemed more an anthology of the author's diverse pre-occupations than the coherent statement about a single topic that one finds in most plays. Johnston's theme, however, rises out of his plot, and in discussing the play it is difficult and unnecessary to divorce the two.

The plotting of Act I is both highly craftsmanlike and highly conventional. It broadly works like this: an outsider, Tausch, is introduced into an eccentric Irish household; and, as he is the voice of reason, common sense, industry and courtesy, we see initially through his eyes and we judge by his judgements. However, by the end of the act, the procession of fey Irish eccentrics has so engaged our sympathies that we have grown tolerant of their humorous naturalness and a little critical of Tausch's stiff correctness. The audience, in other words, has become inclined toward a tolerance of their lawless and anti-civilized but apparently harmless behaviour, and toward an intolerance of Tausch's lawful, civilized but possibly harmful behaviour.

Most of the act is concerned, as most first acts in any play, in introducing, identifying and describing these characters. And at the end of the act, in the best Horatian, Jonsonian and Drydenian fashion, an entry is made into the actual action: that is, Blake announces his intention to blow up the powerhouse, and Tausch begins the counter-action by secretly phoning the police. Most of the intellectual content of Act I is not, nevertheless, the play's real theme. It is an introductory theme, and no more than the old

Shavian topic of the difference between the Irish and the rest of the world.

This contrast between civilization as embodied in Tausch and anarchy as embodied in the varieties of Irishmen is consistently made by jokes and witty juxtapositions, so that the bulk of the act is comic in effect. Even the most portentous action, the plan to destroy the powerhouse, is made by a comic, although not ridiculous statement. All of this is quite Shavian; as in Shaw's early plays, comic actions and illustrative jokes are made to emphasize an alternative truth to the conventional one that the audience entered the theatre with. As Shaw's Broadbent comes to seem to the audience the romantic rather than the practical man, so also are we made to see in Johnston's play a truer truth than the usual theatrical platitude. In making us tolerant of his charming, anarchical Irish, Johnston has pushed us to see the truth behind the paradox and the lie behind the platitude.

This theme of Irish anarchy versus world civilization may be seen, then, not as the false theme of a comic prologue, but as a conditioning to accept the real, if paradoxical, truths of the major theme which is developed in Act II. (Some years ago, during a production of *The Dreaming Dust,* Johnston told me that it was impossible to implant in an audience's mind something that it did not already believe. *The Moon* and, of course, practically all of Shaw are just such attempts; and Johnston's remark may possibly be taken not only as a repudiation of Shaw but also of his own early work. As substantiation of this disillusionment with audiences, I might cite another remark that Johnston made at the same time. His main character in *The Dreaming Dust,* Jonathan Swift, made a remark which said, in effect, well, I must go out and write *Gulliver's Travels* now. As this seemed to me an exceptionally bald line, I suggested that we cut it, but Johnston replied that it had to stay in because three-fourths of the audience would not know that Swift had written *Gulliver's Travels.*)

The centre of Act II is a Shavian discussion scene in which the characters sit down and give their votes and their reasons, yea or nay, for blowing up the powerhouse. In *The Quintessence of Ibsenism,* Shaw wrote that the discussion was going to be the most vital part of the new drama. For once, Shaw seems to have been wrong, and the drama has continued to demand the naive simplicities of story-telling, and story-telling, and more story-telling.

67

Putting content into a play is like trying to contain water in a sieve. Johnston seems well aware of this fact and counterpoints his static discussion against the tension of a containing action. Tausch and the audience know that the police will arrive at a certain time, and so Tausch attempts to prolong the discussion while making furtive glances at the prominently displayed clock. In other words, Johnston brilliantly has his cake and eats it. Having his cake means developing the case for and against industrialism, practicality and the onward march of civilization; eating his cake means developing the tension of an engrossing action. As in Shaw, though, his argument is about as engrossing as his plot; and that argument, in which he finally opts for impracticality and idealism and the old ways, seems to me the central theme, but not the final point, of the play.

(Curiously, in an introduction to *The Old Lady Says 'No!' and Other Plays*, Johnston remarks that in Dublin, *The Moon* 'has always been suspected of harbouring a superior ascendancy smile at the expense of the noble native, and it has never been popular there on that account.' And yet nothing could be closer to de Valera's ideal of an Arcadian rural Ireland than the backward look of the play's theme. The point is, no doubt, that a conventional patriotic statement must be made in a conventional, traditional way. *The Old Lady* says rather the same thing as *The Moon*, but says it backward, satirically rather than admiringly. If it has been somewhat more popular than *The Moon*, the reasons are undoubtedly Mac Liammóir's playing of Emmet and the Dublin penchant for snickering at any topic whatsoever. In any event, *The Old Lady*'s popularity was relative; it was no *Juno*; it was not even a *Passing Day*.)

Having debated, if not yet quite decided the point, the playwright must conclude the action of the police arriving, and then he must introduce a new action for the third act. Dramaturgically the new action must be introduced to conclude Act II and, even more important, it must top the previous action. Conventional dramaturgy demands a big first act curtain and a bigger second act curtain. Many second act curtains are cliff-hangers and leave the audience wondering what will happen next. Johnston's second act curtain is a cliff-faller and leaves the audience startled, nonplussed and wondering what has just happened. It is a dangerous device because it demands that the audience react unconventionally. In a note, Johnston says:

> Occasionally a curtain falls on the second act without as much
> as a clap of a hand from the audience. And, oddly enough, this
> phenomenon is regarded by those who know the play well, not as
> a disgrace, but as an indication of a really fine performance.[11]

And, one might add, such a reaction is the most experimental of
writing because it demands an untheatrical response.

Part of Johnston's untheatrical daring has to do with when Blake
is killed and how the audience regards him. In conventional
dramaturgy, you can kill the bad guy off at the end of the play, and,
if you can pull off that *tour de force* called tragedy, you can also kill
the good guy off at the end of the play. Hotspur is enormously
appealing, but he has got to go for thematic reasons, and the
audience is satisfied enough about the matter because he is faultier
than the hero. (The ritual killing of Falstaff at the end of *Henry IV,
Part II* is not nearly so successful, because Falstaff's faults have
become much more enchanting than Hal's virtues.) In Johnston's
play, Blake is killed too soon, only two-thirds of the way through,
for conventional dramaturgy; and also the audience has begun to
like him. Only the fact that Johnston has a stageful of other
appealing eccentrics to take up the slack palliates the matter. However, the death of a major sympathetic character at the end of Act II
is indicative of the shocking quality of both dramaturgy and theme.
Johnston never has to make a character lecture to the audience that
'Attention must be paid.'

The third act tidies up, as all third acts do, the loose ends of what
will happen to the characters; then it goes on to the central thematic
debate between Tausch and Dobelle, with Dobelle unconventionally but convincingly winning. What the debate is about has now
become more than practicality versus idealism; it is now the proper
definition of right and wrong. Indeed, in noting how right causes
such pain and opting therefore for wrong, Dobelle sounds very like
Dick Dudgeon, Shaw's Devil's Disciple.

A great difference between Shaw and Johnston is that Shaw's
right and wrong, which are usually quite the opposite of society's,
are defined and clear but Johnston's are not. Tausch stands for
reason, practicality and industrial progress, but he also stands for a
love of art, of family, of humanity and for a kind of idealism.
Dobelle stands for impracticality, for the status ante quo and for
industrial regress, but also for a logic beyond practicality as well as
for selfishness and a lack of human sympathy. The issues, as in life,

are not clear cut; the argument, therefore, is a little more complicated than the usual stage plot-argument. That plot-argument has basically a simple three-part structure: boy meets girl, boy loses girl, boy gets girl; or John Wayne knocks Ward Bond down, Ward Bond knocks John Wayne down, John Wayne knocks Ward Bond out.

In such a simple argument, the plot would be over after the Tausch-Dobelle debate, and all the playwright would then have to do would be to construct a quick and effective curtain. In *The Moon*, however, the statement is not yet completed, and so the plot must have two more convolutions. When that master of structure, Ben Jonson, handled a conventional plot as in *Volpone*, he sat Right and Wrong on opposite ends of a seesaw. One was up and now the other; and, as the play progressed, the seesaw went faster and faster until Wrong was finally knocked off. In *The Moon*, after Idealism has been totally defeated by Blake's death, it unexpectedly and startlingly wins when the powerhouse is blown up by a comic fluke. The comedy is necessary as a dramaturgic antidote to the previous debate, but it also keeps the triumph of idealism from being sentimental and mawkish.

Sentimentality and mawkishness are charges that have been levelled at the very ending of the play. After the destruction of the powerhouse has cleared most of the actors from the stage and completed the major public action, Dobelle's daughter Blanaid wakes up and comes sleepily down the stairs. Dobelle sees with a start that she resembles his dead wife, and for the first time extends his sympathy and kindness. This is a very necessary development for Johnston's theme; Dobelle has intellectually won and presumably converted the audience, but his intellectuality is a cold and selfish one. For his conversion of the audience to be complete, he himself must be partially converted and leavened with the audience's humanity. On the plane of action, this abrupt about-face must be extraordinarily well done, for it has little psychological preparation, and has certainly seemed in poor stagings to be simply the author prostituting himself for an upbeat ending. Thematically, though, the action is utterly integral; and well staged it could work most touchingly.

The very final scene is simply a coda or dying fall which re-emphasizes the statement about human sympathy and the value of the race. Dobelle and Blanaid have dropped off to sleep. The comic servant, Agnes, enters, having successfully delivered the offstage baby, and opens the curtains. The sun comes up. This is all conventional enough, trite even, but a good deal of necessary dramaturgy is trite.

Although ramblingly discussed, this, I believe, is how the basic structure of the play works and what the play generally says. A full discussion of Johnston's dramaturgy would have to go through the play scene by scene, if not speech by speech and word by word, to point out the utility of everything. In a production, such a weighing and evaluation happen during rehearsal. In criticism, except in rare and lengthy instances, there is not the time or the space for such close evaluation.

However, as one symptomatic instance of Johnston's thoroughgoing care for structure, we might contemplate the first short scene of the play to see what it does and why it is there. If we decide that the first scene lasts until Agnes' final exit, there are only about twelve speeches; and yet in them Johnston quickly and firmly establishes the basic comic mode of the play and the strategy of the whole act.

At rise, the girl, Blanaid, is sitting in the window seat reading. She has a couple of actions but no lines. There is also the occasional sound of offstage typing. Agnes is laying the table and has an opening soliloquy which introduces the scene's two jokes. The first is about the suffering of woman, as instanced by a neighbour's imminent childbirth (and the announcement of the birth is the appropriate symbolic content of the play's last scene). The second joke is the dramatization of Agnes' cavalier attitude towards her job. The first joke is summed up by the line, 'God knows it's a terrible thing to be a woman'. The second joke is repeated with variations throughout the scene. First, Agnes ignores the knock by saying 'That was a knock at the door', and then continuing what she is doing. When the knock is repeated, she starts to answer it, but stops to talk some more about Mrs. Mulpeter's birth pains. Then the knock is heard a third time, and Agnes finally answers it with the shout, 'Are you the ignorant bosthoon that's banging and hammering away at my knocker?' This response is so nicely comic that Johnston repeats it by giving Agnes two more short speeches of berating the visitor before exiting with 'Ttt-ttt-ttt! Shocking, shocking!' That line punches her exit and probably works both as comic sympathy for Mrs. Mulpeter and comic irateness against the visitor.

Catching the audience at curtain-rise is difficult in the commercial

71

theatre where for the first five minutes latecomers are pushing through the aisles, locating their seats and treading on people's toes. What is needed dramaturgically is something arresting onstage, something to dissipate the audience's distraction, something big, broad, and catchy enough to be repeated. This Johnston adroitly gives, as at the same time he raises the question of who is knocking. Also he leaves two bridges to the following scenes, the silent Blanaid and the offstage typewriter. Each speech and each line of his opening seems to me defensible as adding either to the comic effect or to the audience's curiosity; and the scene is effectively concluded by Agnes' exit lines which summarize her eccentricity, and emphasized by the bewildered reaction of the visitor. If the visitor's bewilderment is visually broad, the bewildered audience will laugh at his confusion, which is more stupid than theirs, while awaiting interestedly the answers to its own questions.

The Moon is a most tightly written play. If the acts are chopped up into the – in the French sense – scenes, nearly each detail of each scene will be found to have its utility.

The use of Agnes to open the play is sound dramaturgy because she is the most conventional of the comic characters, and interest will be built by the introduction later of successively more engaging and – for lack of a better word – 'original' characters. Some of the characters are, like Agnes, what one might call anti-stereotypes. A stereotyped servant would be efficient, practical, diffident and self-effacing, as well as quite accepting his lower position in the social order and his lesser importance for the audience. As an anti-stereotype, Agnes is funny because she contradicts all of the qualities which the audience expects, and we laugh, therefore, at the incongruity. The anti-stereotype of the servant has been a fixture of comic writing from Greek comedy to Wodehouse; and Johnston's Agnes as an Irish variant is no particularly original creation. Some of his other anti-stereotypes are more original, but the originality stems paradoxically from their being counterpointed to our traditional expectations.

The character of Aunt Columba, however, is somewhat different. Columba is a variation of a stereotype. She is in the play because, like all of the characters, she is a necessity for the development of the theme and plot. She is in the play also for the comic value of her stereotype, which is that of the decayed spinster, of which literature has many examples – Hepzibah Pyncheon, the Hon. Impulsia Gushington, etc., etc. She is crusty and dotty but basically kind. Her comic value stems from the original variations of dottiness that Johnston has invented for her. Much to his credit, she stays just this side of the absurd. The story of her one failed love affair, in its details about the wedding gift of the mowing machine, is just within the bounds of plausibility. Johnston's imaginative details are never quite farcical but always fanciful, but they are details that go with Columba's basic character of the stereotype.

The last woman in the cast, Blanaid, is much more delicately detailed, and is an interesting mixture of both stereotype and anti-stereotype. As the stereotype of the thirteen year old girl, she is quiet, shy, sensitive, and painfully desirous for her father to love her. By themselves, these characteristics would only make her a bland, usual and dull role that could figure in a run-of-the-mill romance. Against these stereotypical characteristics, however, Johnston counterpoints two contradictory anti-stereotypical ones – an over-sophistication and an over-naiveté. Both qualities, in themselves and in juxtaposition, cause not laughter, but gentle and charmed amusement. Consider, for instance, her early speech to Tausch:

> I think that every girl needs an education nowadays in order to prepare her for the battle of life. She wants to be taught deportment and geography and religious knowledge and – oh – mathematics. I adore mathematics, don't you?

The word choice here suggests both sophistication and naivete, and is beautifully, delicately done. As much of the comedy in the play is very broad, this gentle charm is a welcome contrast and also an indication of the range of which Johnston is capable.

Doubtless it would be hyper-obvious to investigate every character, to explain why he is necessary for the plot or theme, and to analyse his comic characteristics. However, one character, Dobelle, should certainly be looked at.

If the play has a lead, it is Dobelle. His was the part that Claude Rains took in the New York run and Esmé Percy in the London run. He is the most intelligent character, the one who wins the debate, and the one who changes and grows. Nevertheless, Dobelle is also a borrowing: he is Hamlet, he is the Misanthrope and, above all, he is the Shavian teacher whom we have seen in Sidney Trefusis, Owen Jack, Jack Tanner, Caesar and even Henry Higgins. The Shavian teacher is right, or for the most part right, but Shaw was clever enough to give that rightness some wrongness, some flaws, eccentricities and engaging warts. Dobelle lacks the inimitably Shavian panache, but perhaps just for that reason he comes a little closer to reality than Shaw's theatrical characters.

Some commentators have thought that Johnston's characterisations were richly, thickly observed renderings of reality. None is; they are all theatrical and with theatrical antecedents. Johnston was not writing case studies or Dreiserian novels, but theatre. His characters, even Dobelle, are larger than life. If they are not as monstrously theatrical as Falstaff or Micawber, they are quite distinctly of that memorable but unreal family. In short, once again Johnston's originality has firm roots in conventionality.

Johnston's fine workmanship is nowhere more apparent than in his language, which too is a consummate use of theatrical convention. To take an obvious example, many of the characters speak in different dialects – Agnes in Moore Street Dublinese, Tausch in Germanic English, George in a breezy Anglo-Irish which is contrasted with the low Cockney of his pal, Captain Potts. Dialect has always been a prime device of the comic writer. The quaint divergences of pronunciation and diction of an Irishman, a Scotsman, a Welshman, or a black man from some norm of civilized speech are a source of critical laughter from the audience, as well as a quick shortcut to characterization.

Most of the other traditional linguistic ways of getting laughs have also their examples in the play; to chart some of them, one might mention the mispronunciation or semi-malapropism, as in George's rendition of Tausch's name as 'Splosch'. This seems stupid on the page, but a lot of passable theatrical humour really is stupid on the page; the answer to the charge of stupidity, of course, is that theatrical humour properly belongs not on the page but in the theatre. The 'Splosch' joke is worked several times, and is, like Agnes and the knock at the door, what might be called a 'running gag'. There are about ten running gags in the play, and the utility of the device is evidenced in its popularity in hundreds of comedies – even in *Charley's Aunt* with its famous line 'I'm from Brazil where the nuts come from.'

If the repetition of 'Splosch' seems low on a sliding scale of humour, it should be noted that the scale in this play runs from such nonsense to wit. One can find examples of half-puns, puns, allusions, inverted clichés, anecdotal jokes, that flip near-wit which might be called banter, and that hallmark of wit which is called the epigram.

To give a handful of examples: there is a half-pun in George's 'This gun is what we call a muzzle-loading, four-inch-slow-firing-Potts-shot. Now explain, Potts.' From the half-pun of 'potshot,' we might turn to a full pun in Act III. Tausch has been trying to phone the Minister to relate what has happened, but is interrupted by the explosion, and Dobelle picks up the phone to ask, 'Did the Minister get that report?' There is a nice bit of nonsense in this exchange between Blanaid and Willie:

BLANAID: What were they talking about?

WILLIE: They didn't say, miss.

There is a good use of the inverted cliché in this exchange between Columba and George:

AUNT: . . . Been drowning your troubles in drink, I suppose, as usual.

GEORGE: No, but we've been giving them a damn good swimming lesson.

Dobelle is fond of paradox, such as 'The Will of the People is a tender delicate bloom to be nurtured by the elect few who know best. The icy blasts of a general election are not for it.' Some of Dobelle's best paradoxes and epigrams are vivified by figurative language. For instance, his 'Here by the waters of Lethe we may believe in fairies, but we trade in pigs.'

As one might expect from the author of *The Old Lady*, the play contains many allusions, most of them ironically used. After Lanigan's defence of his killing Blake, he goes off and Dobelle remarks, 'The Moor has done his work. The Moor may go.' A good deal of the writing is, like this, fairly subtle for the stage. Sometimes instead of allusions, one gets what one might call reminiscences. For instance, Dobelle's line, '. . . take away this cursed gift of laughter and give us tears instead,' is reminiscent of Mrs. Tancred's and Juno's most famous lines. (As a matter of fact, Captain Potts has some points of resemblance to Captain Boyle.) As yet another example of word finagling which is deft but unobtrusive, note the following exchange between Dobelle and Tausch:

DOBELLE: . . . That leaves just you and I.

TAUSCH: I agree. Yes. Just you and me.

Tausch's tacit correction of Dobelle's grammar is a marvellous minor touch to condemn the correct formality of Tausch's own character. Or note how in Act I Blanaid's charming ignorance is quietly suggested by a mistake she makes. After telling Dobelle that she was born in Germany, she mentions that the town was Bratislav.

There is no end of quoting from the many traditional devices that Johnston uses in his deftly, tightly wrought dialogue; but one last device might be mentioned because it is unusual, dangerous and successful. I have in mind the comic anecdote which has nothing whatsoever to do with the plot. There is at least one anecdote in each act – the story about shooting the horse has already been cited – and each anecdote stays just perilously this side of the silly. But it is not merely the nature of the anecdotes, but even the actual telling of them that is dangerous. Telling a joke is really for social conversation and not for theatre, because in a theatre the expectation is that one will not be told jokes but shown them. Johnston's jokey anecdotes, especially the one about the drowning of Mrs. Potts, are so fancifully bizarre, however, that they succeed in enchanting.

I have spent so much time in cataloguing Johnston's most noticeable devices of dialogue, that it must be obvious that I think his dialogue is the most achieved excellence of the play. Nevertheless, he makes excellent traditional use of the audience's eyes as well as ears. He puts what the audience sees to fine melodramatic use in the hypnotic clock of Act II; he puts what the audience sees to fine, simultaneous melodramatic and comic use when Columba hides the last shell from the police by covering it with that incongruous item of domestic utility, a tea cosy. He uses what the audience sees with good farcical effect when Willie drops the explosive shell, catches it, drops it again, and catches it again, as the other characters throw themselves on the floor or freeze in petrified horror. He uses farcical effect when George and Potts tap a shell with a hammer to see why it has not exploded, or when Willie does a semi-pratfall as he pushes the gun offstage.

In sum, even in this unsystematic and probably only too obvious catalogue of dramaturgic devices, I have hardly begun to touch upon the variousness, the soundness and the multiplicity of what Johnston has done. One wants to cite his consummate use of comic reversal (see the melodramatic and farcical scene of the masked gunman, Willie, being berated by his mother, Agnes, and finally being pushed to complain piteously that she should not be so violent).

Denis Johnston's horse laugh

Nevertheless, perhaps enough points have been made to illustrate that *The Moon in the Yellow River* could be used as a textbook of technique. My real point, however, is that it is a textbook of traditional technique, and I mean this totally in admiration rather than in denigration. Despite all of the matter about the necessity for new forms and for experimentation, and despite Johnston's own reputation as an exponent of new forms and experimentation, the theatre is the stronghold of tradition. That is its strength, and that is Johnston's strength, and the best hope for the survival of his plays upon the stage.

Bad playwrights, ordinary playwrights, boulevard playwrights all exploit the theatre's traditions, but they exploit them poorly. Johnston has exploited them brilliantly. If that has kept him off the stage, it may also in years to come put him on it. That is what happens to classics.

NOTES

1   Denis Johnston, 'Humor – Hibernian Style,' *The New York Times* (5 February 1961), Sect. 2, p. 3.

2   One is reminded of the great F.J. McCormick, who played Johnston's Dobelle, coming before the rioting audience of O'Casey's *The Plough and the Stars* to hope the audience would not identify the actors with their roles.

3   Denis Johnston, 'Let There Be Light,' *The Old Lady Says 'No!' and Other Plays* (Boston: Little Brown, 1960).

4   R. Hogan and M.J. O'Neill, eds., *Joseph Holloway's Irish Theatre, Vol. I* (Dixon, California: Proscenium Press, 1968), p. 75.

5   On the same day, the Guild gave in Boston the world premiere of Shaw's *Too True to be Good*, and this review appeared above Johnston's.

6   J.B., 'The Guild Goes Irish,' *The New York Times* (1 March 1932), p. 19.

7   J. Brooks Atkinson, 'With Its Irish Up,' *The New York Times* (13 March 1932), Sect. 8, p. 1.

8   'Westminster Theatre,' *The Times* (25 September 1934), p. 12.

9   'Haymarket Theatre,' *The Times* (24 November 1934), p. 10.

10 Howard Taubman, 'The Theatre: Irish Irony,' *The New York Times* (7 February 1961), p. 40.

11 Denis Johnston, *The Old Lady Says 'No!' and Other Plays*.

JOHNSTON, TOLLER AND EXPRESSIONISM

RICHARD ALLEN CAVE

To peruse Denis Johnston's many comments on Expressionism made between the 1920s and today is to read the record of a fierce enthusiasm on the wane. Micheál MacLiammóir, reminiscing about his first encounters with the dramatist, describes him in this 'his earliest and perhaps most spectacular period' as 'an ardent Expressionist'[1]; but Johnston came rapidly to resent the label as a too convenient pigeon-hole in which to dispose of his talent. Prefacing his *Collected Plays* in 1960 he owned he had 'long since given up the Augean task of denying . . . that I am a disciple of Ernst Toller'[2] and the disclaimer intimates a weary exasperation with the matter. Within the last year in commenting on a suitable method of staging *A Bride for the Unicorn,* a play often categorized as Expressionist, he asserts that the work was never intended as such, 'and is not usually improved by this somewhat dated form of approach'.[3]

To contribute an essay on Expressionism to this celebration of Denis Johnston's genius might appear at best foolhardy and at worst downright rude, but I have no wish to go forcing so rich a talent to conform to limiting definitions. Expressionism was however the dominant new theatrical mode of the formative years of Johnston's theatre practice, though by the time he began to write plays it was already past its prime. One can appreciate Johnston's resentment of the tracing of influences on his work that often accompanies the art of pigeon-holing, for it tends to leave one with the sense that the play under discussion is somehow entirely derivative.[4] Johnston may borrow an idea occasionally (he is always honest about his sources in his Prefaces) but he borrows to transform. Nicholas Hern began a recent article on German Expressionism by writing a pastiche of a typical play in the style 'to emphasize the intense homogeneity of the genre'. His scenario was 'composed of recurrent elements from well over a dozen plays written around the end of the Great War'.[5] No play of Johnston's will fit Hern's pattern, any more than one could devise a pastiche scenario that would apply to each of his many dramas. There is an essential sameness about Toller's major plays – of tone, of vision and purpose, of dramatic method.

To claim Johnston as Toller's disciple is patently absurd. What Johnston took from Expressionism suffered a sea-change under the pressure of his imagination into something decidedly rich, frequently strange and wholly unique.

There is no doubting the ardour of Johnston's engagement with Expressionism in the late 1920s. From 1925 when he returned to Dublin, his involvement as actor and director with the Drama League and other Little Theatre Groups such as The New Players helped in large measure, as Micheál MacLiammóir affirms, to make the Expressionist method available in Ireland.[6] Of his three major productions in 1927-29, two were of plays by Kaiser and Toller and the third, *King Lear* at the Abbey, was staged in settings realised by Dorothy Travers-Smith from Johnston's sketches that were Expressionist in inspiration, as was the lighting and the disposition of the actors for many scenes in still, sculpture-like masses.[7] In preparing for his production Johnston purposefully visited a staging of the tragedy in Munich and that in itself is indicative of his indefatigable enthusiasm in searching out the best that European theatre had currently to offer. He was to visit Toller before mounting *Hoppla!*[8] for the Drama League and regularly at this time attended performances at Peter Godfrey's Gate Theatre Studio in London, often in O'Casey's company. The Gate was the one London house that offered an Expressionist repertoire since being a club theatre it could ignore the ban imposed for political reasons by the Lord Chamberlain on public performances of most German examples of the genre. When the Abbey turned down *The Silver Tassie*, O'Casey was telephoned by Shelah Richards anxious to produce the play with Johnston.[9] Given this factual record it is not surprising that Expressionism came to be identified in many Dublin playgoers' minds with Johnston's name. Joseph Holloway, a staunch traditionalist in his tastes, tended by the 1930s to see any attempt at theatrical innovation as 'impressionism [sic] of the Denis Johnston pattern';[10] O'Casey's *Within the Gates*, for example, he dismissed tersely: 'Only a Denis Johnston . . . could see beauty in such a wilderness of outspoken filth!'[11]

When one looks at the vast range of plays referred to in this fashion by Holloway, one realises that he is confusing what in its strictest application is a term referring to a particular genre of German drama with a method of production. Because of the extreme radical sentiments they expressed most of the German Expressionists had to look for the initial productions of their plays to small, often makeshift theatre groups whose limited resources compelled them to be inventive with coloured lighting and shadows, with make-up and with stylised arrangements of simple stage-units, groups of rostra and dark curtains, to achieve the aesthetic effects demanded by the dramatists. Incapable of realising in precise detail the swiftly changing visual dimensions of these plays, the directors had to effect a compromise and find a form of staging that approximated to the tonal atmosphere of each scene. Noticeably the production which set the seal on this style of direction, Fehling's version designed by Strohbach of Toller's *Masse-Mensch*, ignored the dramatist's stage-directions completely and through changing patterns of massed figures caught in shifting spotlights evoked the essential mood of each scene instead. In retrospect one sees that this production-technique had a more pervasive influence than the actual plays. Indeed in Kenneth MacGowan's influential study, *Continental Stagecraft* (1922), which did much to arouse interest throughout Britain and America in post-war developments in German theatre, only two productions of contemporary Expressionist plays are illustrated by Robert Edmond Jones although over half his sketches are of Expressionist productions. The most impressive illustrations are of Jessner's staging of *Othello* and *Richard III* and these two productions are most memorably evoked in MacGowan's text.[12]

The Expressionist production-style was a god-send to the Little Theatre Movement that grew up in the Twenties in Europe and America for its relative economy and adaptability particularly in its reliance on an inventive use of lighting. It became a standard practice with companies like Terence Gray's at the Festival Theatre, Cambridge (1926-1933), where it was applied to a repertoire ranging from Greek through Renaissance to Modern drama. It was Peter Godfrey's preferred style too, because of his shoe-string budget and the remarkably cramped dimensions of his stage at the Gate Theatre Studio. The same motivation obviously applies to the work of Dublin's New Players as described by Johnston himself: they had pioneered 'Ireland's first expressionist productions in the drawing rooms of private houses with the aid of a complicated set of curtains, wires, cardboard boxes, and sheets of beaver board worthy of Heath Robinson'.[13] Given accounts of the stage provision at the Peacock Theatre, it is not surprising to find in studying the illustrations to Bulmer Hobson's *The Gate Theatre* that it became Edwards and MacLiammóir's house style too, at least until the Gate acquired larger premises. It was therefore inevitably the mode in which they approached *The Old Lady Says 'No!'* and *A Bride for the Unicorn*. But performance-style is not the same thing as the dramatic method of a play.

There is always the danger in the theatre with a successful play that it will become too readily identified in audiences' minds with the artistry of the first performers and director. But as the decades pass, what seemed definitive to one generation may well appear dated to the next; techniques in production which startled initial audiences into new modes of apprehension will through repetition become commonplace; effects which worked well will in all likelihood be used again in the context of other plays because they have proved themselves 'good theatre' and so lose their 'bite', that capacity to administer a psychic shock to an audience. It is sad to find Hilton Edwards in 1958 describing *The Old Lady Says 'No!'* as 'old history' that 'belongs properly to the late Twenties when, youthful and defiant, we first produced it at the Dublin Gate Theatre'.[14] But what had aged in people's awareness was the play as produced by Edwards in the Expressionist style and not the play as written, where the defiance has a perennial youth and vitality. The recent Abbey production celebrating the play's fiftieth anniversary showed it in the wake of several years of renewed violence in Northern Ireland to be no museum-piece. The discomfort Johnston creates in his audience comes from the realisation that the nightmare he is analysing is a continuing condition, that they cannot dismiss history as just a matter of the past. But each generation is going to have to find a new visual language in the theatre to excite that horror for if the production technique is in any sense dated then audiences will rapidly seize on that as an excuse for relaxing into apathy with regard to the play's meaning. *The Old Lady* poses a challenge but one which most audiences would prefer not to face.

It is here that one can begin to draw some distinctions between Johnston and the German Expressionists. *The Old Lady* bears some resemblance to Toller's *Hoppla!* in that both plays show an ardent political rebel confronting the reality of the world for which he has sacrificed himself. But whereas Toller's Karl Thomas finds the process of his awakening such an acute disillusionment that his only response is suicide, Johnston's Emmet refuses to recognise his experience as an awakening at all but stridently insists upon the truth of his private vision. Surrounded by a modern Ireland for which he is in part responsible that has all the appearance of Dante's

Inferno, Emmet extols it absurdly with his rhetoric about an Eden regained. Where Toller's is a play of unrelieved despair that achieves variety of pace by using film sequences and a device of playing several scenes simultaneously on a divided setting, Johnston's preserves a sharp black humour throughout a fantasy structure that constantly defeats one's expectations while elaborating his central theme about the dangerously blinkered condition of the fanatical Emmet. For Toller the despair is all; despite the mechanical complexities of Piscator's first production, *Hoppla!* remains a stark, direct text. *The Old Lady* on the other hand has a rich dialogue brimming over with witty social references and literary parodies. It is with the quality of the text in these plays that we confront a major difference between them in the attitude each takes to history. *Hoppla!* has only the actors' costumes and perhaps details in the filmed sequences to establish it in a particular period; the career of Karl Thomas's former collaborator Kilman who renounces his activist past and rises to power within the Establishment carries no specific reference to the instabilities of the Weimar Republic. The play generalizes and abstracts without making clear its grounds for so doing; the target of its satire is so vaguely defined that its attitude of despair seems mere emotionalism. Toller's ambition is to write a political Morality play but the controlling vision is so private that the play inevitably seems dated to an audience today. (There is more than an element of self-pity in that attitude of despair given the circumstances of the author's imprisonment, and the play's conclusion is tragically prophetic of Toller's own suicide in 1939 after the Nazis had compelled his exile from Germany.) There is no denying that the feeling out of which *Hoppla!* is written was one that audiences in the late 1920s could identify with (the popularity of revivals through Europe attests to that) but it is feeling that has not been objectified into art by observation and insight and so it remains closed to the imaginations of audiences nowadays, of interest only to the theatre-historian through having been a vehicle for Piscator's directorial methods.

By contrast Johnston's very subject is the historical process: the power of the past to condition the shape of the present, especially if that past is wrongly understood and the danger in this of mythologising men like Emmet who had no vision of a future state they were fighting to establish but who saw revolt as the end in itself. Without a proper appraisal of its past such a nation has no future.

The range of witty references, historical, social and literary, intimates the pervasiveness of the delusions that in Johnston's view have paralysed Ireland's soul. Emmet fed Ireland's heart on fantasies and taking his distortions for truths, Ireland has come to share his condition of wild dreamer. The play holds at once a mirror up to Emmet and to the whole nation and Johnston's generalisations unlike Toller's are meticulously based in fact. His success comes from his brilliant and unique dramatic method which contrives to blend precisely observed social satire with the transformational structure of Strindberg's dream plays where characters go through a series of metamorphoses that expose the true nature of their psyches. That Emmet's darling Sarah Curran can turn into an embodiment of Kathleen ni Houlihan who can then show herself a weeping *mater dolorosa* or a foul-tongued, vindictive hag by turns as occasion demands is however an exposure less of her intrinsic self as would be the case in Strindberg than of the spurious emotionalism compounded of adolescent infatuation and self-pity in which Emmet's flaunting of himself as hero takes root. All the transformations amplify like this our knowledge of Emmet; by contrast Strindberg's dreamers – Indra's daughter in *The Dream Play* and the Student in *The Ghost Sonata* – seem somewhat colourless, being the *occasion* rather than the *cause* of the transformations in others. They journey as observers of life and accept their dream-visions; Emmet is an observer too but his journey stimulates an impulse to self-discovery that he struggles ever more forcibly to repress. To accept it would be to deny what he sees is his own worth and he fails the challenge of that true test of the hero.

If Johnston writes out of despair with his nation, it stimulates in him a wealth of satirical invention where detail after detail achieves an apposite weight of symbolic truth: Grattan for all his commonsense being reverenced by the modern age as just another of Dublin's many statues; Ireland's great truth-tellers in the tradition of Swift, Joyce and Yeats reduced to wailing and gesticulating shadows derided by the mob; within the dreamscape every theatrical image sustains an intellectual thrust. Toller invites his audience to share an emotional mood; Johnston provokes his to use their minds to root out the apathy in themselves and cauterize the wounds with laughter. Despair is here seen to mask an exhilarating challenge – and that is the play's major transformation. Myth may offer romantic attractions but reality as Johnston presents it has (along with its clear-eyed, dispassionate control) its imaginative splendours too.

First audiences for *A Bride for the Unicorn* at the Gate might be forgiven for supposing that Johnston was reworking the proven formula that made *The Old Lady Says 'No!'* such a triumph. It is perhaps Johnston's most demanding play from the actor's and director's point of view and it is understandable why Hilton Edwards should have resorted to a production style that reproduced many of the most striking features of his direction of *The Old Lady*: the garishly painted, cartoon-like designs on curtains to effect rapid scene-changes; the projections of gigantic shadows; the isolating of individual faces out of darkness by sharply angled spotlights; the monochrome black-and-white effect aimed at throughout giving, to judge by photographs, an impression of a series of animated Expressionist woodcuts; the intoning of choral passages by a cast frozen in tableaux.[15] And yet *A Bride for the Unicorn* is a very different play from *The Old Lady,* its subject being no longer the quality of man's political consciousness but the nature of his metaphysical imagination. In this it is more truly a Morality play than any of Toller's attempts at the type. *Transfiguration,*[16] for example, examines many similar experiences – the enormity and horror of warfare; the misery of domestic poverty – but Toller's motive is always to show how man's transfiguration could come through his political enlightenment; his rhetoric invites a change in man's soul but that change is towards Toller's idiosyncratic style of socialism and the stress is invariably on man's material condition, even though the virtues of charity and fellow-feeling are called into play. Certain of Toller's scenes, especially those concerning the Great War, have a memorable intensity of vision – the skeletons whitened with quicklime dancing about the craters in No Man's Land or the parade of cripples with grotesque artificial limbs, who are the pride of the hospital professor because they show that science has achieved at last the equal of the Resurrection. But *Transfiguration* is a play in which the parts are damagingly greater than the whole: the intensity referred to is uniformally macabre to a degree that renders the play's theme of a possible way to achieve mankind's regeneration a pathetically frail hope.

The true affinities of *A Bride for the Unicorn* are once again with Strindberg in Johnston's ability to create surreal theatrical images through which an audience can recognise psychological truths. Much more is at work here, however, than mere influence. Compare, for example, the Cook in the last scene of *The Ghost Sonata* with the Nanny who haunts Jay Foss in his night of despair. The Cook is a monstrously bloated creature, a parasite who extracts all the nourishment from the Young Lady's diet for her own satisfaction; she emblematises everything the Young Lady fears about life, which she dreads confronting, but to which she renders herself a prey in the very act of seeking to retreat from it. The Young Lady's room is not a sanctum but a prison and the vindictive Cook is the neurosis that reduces her to a state of vegetative existence. Johnston's Nanny shares this emblematic status but she represents all those childhood pressures to conform to a standard of behaviour that threaten Jay's pursuit of individuality and so must be struggled with and renounced though at a considerable cost given the powerful sentimental circumstances in which such pressures took hold:

> I told you little horror stories of an improving nature and was your closest companion all the most impressionable years of your life. My monogram is stamped on your cranium.[17]

Like Strindberg, Johnston can so meticulously hit on the exact surreal verbal image to match his visual caricature that he compels an audience's complete imaginative engagement with the horror being defined. How rich the pattern of associations that last remark of the Nanny's calls to mind; yet how tersely matter-of-fact (and so 'in character') the expression.

Johnston is here using in the Nanny a traditional comic British stereotype but he converts her into a figure of nightmare or trauma. Though hers is a small role in the action, it is characteristic of the way Johnston ensures that his chosen dramatic method informs every detail of the whole. There is here none of that imbalance between method and theme which mars Toller's play. Johnston's theme in *A Bride for the Unicorn* is the triumph of banality in the modern world through its capacity to rob life of any transcendent value, though ironically in Jay Foss it cannot stifle a hunger for some kind of spiritual permanence. That impulse to go on questing, given the strength of the forces ranged against him, both social and privately psychological, invests Jay with heroic proportions. The trials besetting this modern Jason are not tests of his wit and physical prowess but attempts to suppress his sense of his own individuality by compelling him into the mould of a stereotype – businessman, dutiful husband, soldier, social dignitary.

To illustrate his theme Johnston employs two devices throughout the play: a large chorus; and a technique of burlesquing popular theatre styles and situations. The chorus with their choreographed ensemble-work (the precise stage term for this is significantly 'a routine') either threaten to engulf Jay in their frenetic activity, as in the Stock Exchange Scene where he all but disappears amidst the showers of money and rushing hordes of speculators; or with deliberately calculated myopia lose all sight of him as an individual in the Courtroom Scene, though he should be the focus of attention as the defendant, by following through the process of a trial as just a mechanical ritual, a collage of sounds, movements and legal commonplaces. The tone and the procedure are appropriate but the speech is nonsense; no-one is interested in Jay as a specific case whose nature might offer extenuating circumstances. The element of burlesque is evident even here but the focus gets even sharper in the small-scale scenes which explore Jay's intimate relationships where his anguish is defined by his inability to adjust to the conventions in dialogue of the scene in which he finds himself with his various friends. Each of them has a limited awareness which is exactly defined by the theatrical idiom in which he or she seems trapped: Psyche, the perennial adolescent, infatuated with a Rodgers-and-Hammerstein idyll of love on the farm ('I love my love with a Ess because he's Special');[18] Philly echoing Noël Coward's many poor little rich girls ('Actually Bermuda can be a terrible rut')[19] while living off her alimony and her nerves; and – most significant for our purpose – Barney caught in an Expressionist tangle of barbed wire on some foreign field and pursuing death in battle as the only logical end to his world-weariness ('In sleep we will each have our own world. Here we have only a world in common').[20] Jay refuses to be the dupe of such romantic delusions. What gives him the strength to resist them is the confidence that man can experience states of transcendent awareness. Jay's tutor in this is oddly (but appropriately, given the self-conscious theatricality of the play) a Harlequin figure; the transformation he conjures forth with his music is psychological not spectacular, a mystical apprehension of a mode of being beyond Time, that is represented by the image of a masked, silent girl of seraphic composure dancing 'with great dignity' in the shadows – an emblem out of Yeats's plays for serenity and perfection.

It can be seen at once from this what demands *A Bride for the Unicorn* makes on its performers for they must be versatile in mime, dance, song and capable of playing within a range of recognisable theatrical styles but with sufficient detachment to bring out the subtleties of satire. What is wanted is a performer with the technical virtuosity of the revue artist but with a sensitivity to the play's underlying moral theme which shapes the apparently fragmented structure to some purpose. The problem for actor and director is that that theme – the pressure to find spiritual ardour and the difficulty of sustaining it in a diverse, jazzy age – must be everywhere stressed in performance but it is nowhere actually stated. It is partly Johnston's purpose in the play to show that the modern theatre lacks a language with which to describe spiritual understanding and so the dramatist must resort to other forms of theatrical expression through which to encourage an audience to infer a meaning.[21]

Many Expressionist plays like Toller's *Hinkemann* or Kaiser's *From Morn to Midnight*[22] evoke powerfully the miseries of poverty by showing in the one case the levels of degradation to which an individual will submit to secure the fundamental necessities of living or in the other the lure of crime to get access to a little colour and excitement in life and the overwhelming sense of shame society and religion foster over such a desire to relieve the menial round. But the power here comes from the relentlessness with which such a theme is projected over the span of a whole play. No Expressionist playwright envisaged a technique of dissociated acting which allows an audience to engage with imaginative immediacy in such an abject condition from within as Johnston does with his portrayal of Jay's marriage with Hera. Against a backdrop suggesting cosy domesticity, she works at the family ironing while he reads a newspaper; they mime with naturalistic freedom; when they speak, it is either to utter stage directions describing what they are doing or to voice a deep, hidden self that lies predatory and spiteful, watching the other partner ruthlessly and waiting for the chance word or gesture that will permit the unleashing of a spate of vindictive nagging:

HERA: She hands him the hot iron. Indicating the fireplace.

JAY: Burnt! Ow! How is he trained to such tasks?

HERA: By appealing to his better nature. She has, for instance, given him the best years of her life.

JAY: Which have enriched him largely in responsibilities.

87

HERA: She is a good wife who knows her limitations. She relies on his decisions in almost everything.

JAY: So long as he decides acceptably.

HERA: And yet he does not seem to be satisfied. If only someone would tell her what it is that men really want she would have tried to get it for him – to do it for him. But nobody seems to know, and he knows least of all.

JAY: Beloved enemy of the spirit – seated in the holy of holies – knowing all his futilities, and ventilating them every one at inappropriate moments. As every action springs from many motives, so with unerring fingers she will seek out the meanest, and display it to his eyes as though it were the only one.[23]

The tension in this speaking silence is prevented from gaining release in an open quarrel by the presence of an elderly relative who hogs the fire and the radio, rocks relentlessly on her chair and emits only mindless squawks like a parrot. If one is reminded of The Mummy in Strindberg's *The Ghost Sonata*, it is only to appreciate how completely Johnston has adapted the inspiration to his own ends to depict the extreme selfishness that often accompanies senility and the way that an object of one's charity can rapidly cease to be cherished and become just tolerated out of a sense of duty. The exceptional theatricality of the scene generates a tension that makes one immediately apprehend the pettiness of spirit that poverty has caused Jay and Hera to inspire in each other. The grimness of the experience is the more telling for the incisiveness of its presentation. The method is perfectly judged to embody the theme. Theatricality with this purposefulness (and it is true of all the scenes of the play) bespeaks a wit of the highest order. Indeed it is just that wit that sets the play quite apart from anything produced by the German Expressionist School, whatever may have been suggested to the contrary by the style of Hilton Edwards's first production. It is the organising principle of wit behind its conception that ensures the play's timelessness of appeal. Johnston has, as it were, pushed beyond Expressionism into a surreal form of total theatre in pursuit of a greater complexity of awareness, psychological and moral.[24]

The force of this last point can best be illustrated by a comparison of Toller's *The Blind Goddess* (1932)[25] with Johnston's adaptation

88

of the play, *Blind Man's Buff* (1936),[26] which he undertook at Toller's insistence. A few weeks before the Abbey's production of Johnston's version of the play, Toller wrote in an open letter to the *New Statesman* about the condition of drama in England that plays ought not to be produced simply because they express 'the right convictions. The best convictions have no meaning in the theatre, can indeed only do harm, unless presented and allied with true aesthetic force to give them form and significance.'[27] Johnston had warned Toller that in revising *The Blind Goddess* he would reverse the moral emphases of the play, that Toller's 'heroes' would be 'my villains and vice versa', but Toller had urged him on regardless.[28] What *Blind Man's Buff* seems to question is whether convictions as such are a proper subject for drama, however aesthetically shaped and presented. Throughout the Thirties Johnston took an increasingly critical view of O'Casey's new plays because of their 'passionate insistence on a point of view'.[29] It is the lack of any debate with regard to the issues being explored in *The Blind Goddess* that Johnston seeks to remedy in *Blind Man's Buff*. Toller's play is fundamentally about a trial and trials are public debates about moral issues. Trials also make for very powerful theatre but the theatrical effectiveness of the situation can mask stereotyped or even prejudiced thinking on the part of the dramatist. As Johnston remarks:

> On the Stage, any person on trial is usually the centre of the picture, and is generally required to be innocent. With one or two notable exceptions, trial plays culminate either in a triumphal acquittal or in a wrongful conviction – a practice that has placed judges and prosecuting counsel in the unfair position of being, as a rule, character villains.[30]

A strong curtain can always be got by showing the defendant as the victim of some 'malice, corruption or . . . active ill-will on the part of the State'.[31] For all its power and originality of presentation, *The Blind Goddess* in its ideas and judgements fits this traditional mould.

Franz Färber, a doctor, is arrested for the murder of his wife, largely on the strength of the calumnious accusations of a servant, Marie Hacker, who chooses to interpret his attempts to resuscitate the dying woman as his way of killing her. She reveals that Färber has been committing adultery with his secretary, Anna Gerst, and this is seized on by the Prosecution as the motive for Betty Färber's poisoning. There is evidence to suggest that Betty committed suicide, but a pathologist argues that, as his tests have shown that she died of small doses of poison administered over a protracted period, it is unlikely that she took her own life; suicides generally take a single lethal dose. The jury are seen to be divided in their assessment of the case: some are conscious that merely circumstantial evidence like Marie Hacker's, the importance of which is a matter of personal judgement, can be manipulated by a clever barrister to prove anything; but they are outnumbered by others whose judgement is coloured by moral disapproval of the defendants' adultery and who bring in a verdict of guilty. Anna and Färber are shown in prison; the rigours of the system cannot quench her fierce passion for him but he becomes a prey to despair, attempts suicide and plans to effect an escape by arranging for a fellow prisoner to poison a guard. Some years later, the pathologist admits that his recent research has proved to him that his former interpretation of the facts of Mrs. Färber's death was wrong and that she could have died of a single dose of arsenic which confirms certain cryptic comments in the woman's diary to the effect that she planned to kill herself as a perverse act of revenge. Anna and Färber are released and return to his home to find the townspeople who were formerly accusing and aggressive are staging a welcoming reception. Alone with Färber, Anna admits that she experiences only loneliness and repulsion in his touch; suffering for her love has steadily eroded her capacity to feel for the man:

> Even an emotion can have its day and die, like a word. . . . I have loved you very, very dearly . . . I loved you so much that I really could have killed your wife.[32]

This is an undeniably strong curtain-line coming at the climax of a scene in which Anna and Färber grope through long silences to an awareness of how their passion was kept alive by their need to assert their innocence against the machinations of the State and the pressure of public opinion; once that need is removed, they know no peace, only a sense of bitter waste. The scene is suffused with this negative emotion, which Anna gradually finds the courage to define. If it fails to move one profoundly it is because it is difficult to reconcile this emotionally drained, clear-sighted Anna with the impulsive, passionately determined woman of the prison scenes who is prepared to admit to the crime if it would allow Färber to go free. Undaunted opposer of a cruel system and degraded victim of it – two situations that allow for maximum pathos, but they destroy the psychological credibility of the character. The one connection between the scenes lies in the dramatist's private convictions about the evils of the state legal system and his concern to project his sense of that evil as emotively as possible. Toller's strengths as a dramatist lie either in the presentation of short, varied scenes, 'stations' as he called them, that illustrate a single theme as in *Transfiguration* and *Masse-Mensch* or in the gradual intensifying of a character's perception of the absoluteness of his despair as in *Hinkemann;* the psychological subtleties which Toller is patently aiming for in *The Blind Goddess*, the changes in a character's awareness that complement changes in his circumstances, are of a kind that his dramatic method cannot sustain.

A further weakness in the play is the way the State is represented. For the most part the officers of the State merely perform the functions required of them as barristers, judges, gaolers; all are coldly impersonal, even the pathologist whose revising of his initial opinions of the case is so necessary to bring about the final tragic ironies of the plot. There is, however, one character who of necessity had to be omitted from the summary of the play's action and that is Max Franke. He nowhere directly affects the progress of the narrative but is everywhere used by Toller to provide an ironic commentary on Dr. Färber's fate. Max is a philanderer, a sexual and political opportunist; without ever being instrumental in Färber's shaming, he is invested by Toller in all the deep-dyed colours of the traditional villain. Hypocrisy is his only nature: though he has procured an abortion for his girlfriend, Marie, he voices moral effrontery the loudest amongst the citizens when Färber's adultery is revealed and he offers Marie herself no help when she is convicted for the abortion. Max starts the play in the humble position of Clerk to the local District Council; by the end he is Chief Councillor himself and is organising the reception welcoming Färber on his return; his seductions and chicanery continue undetected. It is difficult to determine his function in the play if it is not that of embodying the corruption of the state bureaucracy in which he is achieving advancing status. He is offered by Toller as an emotive emblem of the blindness of Justice, as he sees it, in the modern world and as such is an all-too-recognisable stage-type calculated to provoke a precise and immediate response. His presence in the play amounts to a sleight-of-hand on Toller's part, a way of side-stepping a detailed investigation of the processes of the law which is his declared theme. The audience is invited to project its detestation of Max as rising bureaucrat on to Bureaucracy at large and the Courts of Justice in particular.

The Blind Goddess has power but it is of a raw kind, for the theatricality disguises a want of intellectual rigour in approaching the subject. A possible explanation for this lies in the fact that the play is more directly autobiographical than any of Toller's other works for the theatre. He had been imprisoned on political grounds by a repressive regime; in the Stadelheim prison he had rejected a plan for escape 'because it could have cost a warder his life'[33] – an experience that taught him how the abject conditions of prison life could compel an intellectual rebel to become a criminal in earnest out of sheer desperation; when Toller was finally released in 1924, it was to find himself a celebrated dramatist in a world where the ideals for which he had suffered were even further from realisation. Many of the ironies of the play had been personally experienced by Toller; the problem is whether that personal experience can carry the weight of generalisation which he is seeking to impose upon it. Toller wrote out of his experience as defendant; Johnston out of that of a barrister and so his view of the courts of law was informed by more than emotional reactions. The critic of *The Times* reviewing Johnston's adaptation, *Blind Man's Buff*, made a significant distinction between the two versions: Toller's original he found 'heavy with propaganda'; Johnston's revision was every bit 'as disturbing *while remaining completely human*'.[34] This was a perceptive response in line with Johnston's own attitude to *The Blind Goddess* as related to Joseph Holloway:

He [Johnston] told me that he practically rewrote the play which was full of propaganda with scenes showing life in prisons etc., and all the characters were puppet types and not real people.[35]

Behind the two plays lie two quite fundamentally opposed attitudes both to the law and to the theatre. 'The Expressionists', Toller wrote, 'were not satisfied simply to photograph. . . . Expressionism wanted to influence environment, to change it.'[36] Johnston prefers to make an appeal for understanding: the shortcomings of the law are not in the process itself but in the essential humanity of its officers. Toller's dramaturgy invites his audience's emotional assent; Johnston's stimulates their powers of discrimination and discrimination is a prerequisite of true justice.

In *Blind Man's Buff,* Johnston retains the basic shape and situations of *The Blind Goddess*: Dr. Frank Chavasse's wife dies by poisoning; he is arrested on a charge of murder largely because of the vindictive gossip of his servant, Mary Quirke. There is a trial in which Chavasse's adultery with a Dr. Anice Hollingshead is offered as the motive for the murder even though Chavasse and Anice assert that their relationship terminated too long ago to have any bearing on the case. The fact of the adultery and the State Pathologist's claim that Mrs. Chavasse was slowly poisoned over a period of time are used by the Prosecution to secure a verdict of guilty. The death-sentence is commuted to life imprisonment because of the dubiousness of most of the evidence. Much hangs on the apparent loss of the poison-bottle which the Prosecution believe Chavasse destroyed as incriminating evidence; its discovery throws doubt on the Pathologist's report and Chavasse is released. He is now not a broken man like Färber but soured, corrosive and mean-spirited.

What such a summary cannot take into account is the true focus of the action in *Blind Man's Buff* which is on the interplay of character as *creating* the events of the plot; character is not as in Toller defined as the product of events. In *Blind Man's Buff* the officers at the trial are all named as individuals: Theobald Thin (Defence); Henry Harrican (Prosecution); Liam Poer (State Solicitor) and Mr. Justice Drooley. They are not the anonymous agents of doom they appear in Toller, relentlessly accusing and without charity. Here each respects the others for their established reputations; knows the precise intellectual gift on which those reputations are based; and so views the trial as a matter of tactics, the matching of mind against mind, where each can predict from his intimate knowledge of the personalities of the others how severally they will choose to interpret the evidence. The only unknown quantity in the trial is Dr. Chavasse. He has been advised by Thin to pursue a particular pattern of behaviour that will substantiate the Defence's line of argument but Chavasse chooses in court to be himself and so becomes the architect of his own downfall. His accusing Poer subsequently of recklessly persecuting an innocent man shows that Chavasse is the blind one in this game not the figures of Justice and what he is blind to is his own unprepossessing nature.

It is here that we touch on Johnston's radical departures from Toller's script. The melodramatically conceived Max is excised completely by Johnston as serving no valid function in the plot but much of his malice is retained in the servant Mary Quirke so that her role is substantially elaborated. As Johnston develops her, she becomes more certainly Chavasse's evil genius and counterpart than Max was in relation to Färber. Mary illustrates the biblical dictum: judge not that ye be not judged. Finding evidence of Chavasse's adultery with Anice and that Anice was pregnant but lost her baby (by a natural miscarriage in fact), she puts the basest interpretation on their two characters, never stopping to ponder on extenuating circumstances or motives. Clearly her evil gossip did much to goad the now dead wife to despair. Johnston makes the outcome of the trial hang on the admissibility of her evidence. Defence, Prosecution and Judge alike can read Mary's true character behind the moral rectitude she so violently asserts. No evidence exists to show that the adultery was continuing at the time of Mrs. Chavasse's death; but both Thin and Harrican know from their experience of juries that if the subject of sex is once introduced into the trial the jury will seize on it as the motive whatever the evidence to the contrary. They appreciate that Mary Quirke's deposition against Chavasse could only be revealed to the jury if the Defence called her character into question as a witness when the Prosecution would have every right to expose Chavasse's character to scrutiny. Both Thin and Harrican view this as shady dealing, but the attraction they feel to demonstrating their expertise with tactics urges them on to play with the possibility of allowing this turn of events to happen. Neither expects that it will but Harrican delights in setting up hurdles which if faltered at might lead to such a development, knowing full well that Thin can effortlessly cross them and will take equal pleasure in showing his proficiency at doing so. So proud are they in their ability to control events that neither suspects that their tactics will unnerve Chavasse who is on trial for his life and cannot see that their gentlemanly sparring is an admission that there is essentially no case against him; in his view it looks like a wanton conspiracy to misrepresent Mary Quirke's character and he makes the wrong assumption that the Court will correspondingly travesty his innocence. Out of sheer desperation he turns a harmless question during his cross-examination into a way of making a bid for freedom by imputing the whole course of events to Mary Quirke's ill-will. The unexpected now becomes the inevitable and a verdict of guilty is assured.

The court scene has considerable tension and excitement but

every development in the situation, however surprising, is psychologically convincing and substantiates Johnston's moral thesis. The trial is a miscarriage of justice that illustrates no romantic tenets about the law but a shrewd awareness of the difficulty of administering justice when it is a general habit of mind in man to debase another human being as the readiest mode of affirming his own rectitude or superiority. This is a temptation that Mary Quirke flagrantly succumbs to and everyone openly despises her for it; but more subtly and insidiously it is the temptation ultimately held out to the jury; moreover it is a judgement against Thin and Harrican that they let their pride in their technical skill outweigh their sensitivity to the defendant's nature and so are directly responsible for laying the temptation before him too. What makes Chavasse's outburst such an astonishing and memorable *coup de théâtre* is that Johnston during the trial has so sharpened the audience's discrimination that they can at once feel for Chavasse in understanding the occasion for his virulence against Mary yet also be profoundly shocked at what is palpably a moral failure in him. This complexity of response in the audience is activated as a consequence of Johnston's major innovation in adapting *The Blind Goddess* and that is his wholly original conception of the doctor's supposed accomplice, Anice Hollingshead. By choosing to make her the moral centre of his play he achieves a psychological impetus for his last act which is quite lacking in Toller's.

In *Blind Man's Buff* Anice is not arrested along with Chavasse as Anna is with Färber. Their affair is definitely over. This allows Johnston the opportunity to devise a new scene in which to introduce Thin, Harrican and the State Solicitor as private individuals away from the formalities of the Courts and to sketch out for his audience's information the reasons behind the tactics to be pursued at the trial. Thin questions Anice rigorously about her relationship with Chavasse; convinced by the pain the discussion causes her of the truth of her replies about her miscarriage and the ending of the affair, he explains why it is essential that the relationship is not so much as intimated in court and why on no account must the veracity of Mary Quirke be called into question. Anice herself will be required as a witness simply as the local Dispensary doctor who was summoned by Chavasse to help attend his wife and register her death. Out of her sense of moral disgust Mary Quirke had refrained from carrying the Doctor's message to Anice who had come to Chavasse's aid two hours later when he had himself frantically telephoned her. Mary had brazenly lied about the situation and insisted that it was Anice's decision not to come to the house. As the initial crisis of the play it did much to establish both Mary's character as a vengeful fury of dubious moral status and the peculiar tensions in Chavasse's household which the rest of the play will explain. It is characteristic of Johnston's economy and his sense of organic structure, his capacity to turn a spotlight on the apparently incidental to invest it with an unsuspected relevance to his purpose, that he should use this episode as the focus of his moral argument during the trial.

In court, the discrepancy in time between Chavasse's summoning Anice and her actual arrival emerges almost by accident but Harrican seizes on it as a means of setting up another hurdle for Thin. Aware from Thin's admonitions of the danger of imputing any ill conduct to Mary, Anice under Harrican's questioning takes on herself responsibility for the delay. All too conscious of the point of Harrican's tactics, she perjures herself to avoid accusing Mary of perjury, even when it draws down on her the Judge's shocked disapproval of what he believes to be her criminal negligence in respect of the dying woman:

> Whatever may be the outcome of this case there are certain aspects which reflect no credit on the parties concerned. I can only hope that they have not escaped the attention of the Press.[37]

With selfless courage and out of respect for Chavasse's innocence, Anice acquiesces in the defamation of her own character and the jeopardising of her career. The Judge's generalised wording is a masterstroke in deflecting the audience's attention away from Anice at whom he specifically directs it and on to the procedure of the trial itself. The moral culpability at this moment rests with Harrican and Thin. If Anice excites the audience's admiration as a victim of the legal process, it is on far subtler and more convincingly defined grounds than obtain with Toller's Anna. Here is true charity and the stature with which Anice is endowed in the audience's awareness is what renders Chavasse's outburst morally reprehensible in its meanness of spirit.

Interestingly this shaping of the scene to its moral climax appears to have been a late development in Johnston's revision of Toller. Amongst the Abbey papers in the National Library in Dublin is a typescript of the play as rehearsed at the theatre with sketches of the sets required and handwritten notes about moves and effects of character.[38] The synopsis of scenes given on the page of contents suggests that at one time Johnston followed Toller's sequence of scenes more closely than in his published play. Act II is here recorded as having two scenes; the first is the trial in 'The Central Criminal Court, Green Street, Dublin' which is all that occupies the second act of the published text; the second is described as 'The Jury Room. The next night' which clearly was to be an exact parallel for Toller's episode, but when Johnston's trial takes the turn that it does, the verdict is such a foregone conclusion that it renders a scene for the jury redundant. On the contents page the provision for this second scene is crossed through and the text for the scene itself is missing from the typescript. What is more remarkable is that in the trial scene as it stands in this document Anice is not called to the witness box by Thin at the start of the case for the defence; instead he summons Chavasse immediately. Without the episode with Anice the play in its implications remains very much confined within the limits of its plot; but with it, *Blind Man's Buff* begins to stimulate a metaphysical debate about the nature of guilt and responsibility and about the dangers of relying on legal procedures rather than a sensitively attuned moral imagination in the pursuit of justice. The trial scene in the typescript expects its audience to be detached if excited spectators; in the trial as printed a greater degree of imaginative participation is urged on them. Harrican and Thin's delight in their skill is infectious (verbal sparring invariably makes good theatre) but it all turns very sour for the audience with the hounding of Anice when Harrican's continuing pleasure appears rank smugness and Thin's failure to come to her protection is just as distasteful. The final miscarriage of justice is profoundly disturbing because the audience is all too aware of how much that has a bearing on the case has been deliberately kept out of the trial, yet has accepted the reasonableness of this calculated move on the grounds that to admit it is to risk inviting a sordidly sensational interpretation of events, which is an even greater travesty of the truth. The audience is placed in the position of at once seeing the necessity of judging and yet of appreciating the difficulty of doing so in a way that takes into account a properly compassionate awareness of human fallibility. If Toller activates outrage in his audience, Johnston exacts humility from his before the experience we call Justice.

It is Anice who dominates the last act. Admiration for her

courage and assurance compels the State Solicitor, Liam Poer, to reopen his investigations into the manner of Mrs. Chavasse's death, though he is unsure how to explain Anice's character to himself. She appears 'either a very foolish woman or a very daring one' – two possibilities that share the basic assumption that Anice is still nonetheless guilty.[39] Anice quickly points out that there is a third way of judging her conduct – that she is urged on by outraged honesty – but that would require Poer totally to revise his moral opinion of her. The act explores how he comes to do just that as admiration is changed steadily to respect. Poer is no impersonal, undeviating figure of fate but a man whom circumstances compel to recognise his fallibility and admit it in gaining Chavasse his freedom. There is courage in his generosity and it excites respect for him in Anice too. Beside the magnanimity of these two, Chavasse remains selfish, petty and shrill. Appreciating the current of imaginative sympathy in Poer that led him to work against the drift of his personal convictions about the case, Anice cannot withhold her shock and distress when Chavasse threatens Poer with litigation: 'I and my good friends will get you yet'.[40] The shock kindles a final insight in Anice: it releases a flow of imaginative sympathy for the dead wife. Chavasse's conduct in the trial and again now substantiates fears she had felt intuitively years before at the too-demonstrative relief he showed when her miscarriage saved them from the need to make choices about their future together which would challenge public opinion. The pain she felt when questioned by Thin about the past is now seen to be generated not by the act of remembering itself but by recalling the ease with which she could face the ending of their relationship. Her shame is that the relationship should be deemed of more value than it proved. Chavasse's reception of Poer shows her how little he will understand of what she has done. Just as Poer has unwittingly shown her the truth about Chavasse so, she realises, her adultery with him even if known about only after the event through Mary's discovery of the correspondence (and how true that detail is that such an essentially selfish man as Chavasse should make the sentimental romantic gesture of preserving Anice's letters!) had brought the dead woman to a similarly exact awareness of her husband's nature. Through the long silences of the last scene, Anice comes to a full understanding of the tragedy that separates her from Chavasse: that his innate banality puts him beyond the reach even of her pity; no-one can *touch* him. Her final words virtually echo Anna Gerst's but they are charged with a greater intensity of significance: 'I wonder if we really did kill Elizabeth? I wonder if we aren't guilty after all?'[41] Identifying now imaginatively with the dead wife's misery, she can accept her particular responsibility for the fatal outcome: unwittingly Anice brought Elizabeth to a knowledge of how complete was the waste of her own best self; that knowledge Anice now shares and after such knowledge, what forgiveness can there be? Beside the imprisoning labyrinths that guilt can create in the sensitive mind, the processes of the law can seem little more than a game of Blind Man's Buff.

Working within Toller's plot-structure for his first and final scenes, sometimes astonishingly making only the slightest shifts of emphasis in his dialogue, Johnston has transformed *The Blind Goddess* into a profoundly tragic exploration of man's moral sensibility. It is a matter for regret that difficulties with Toller's estate have made it impossible to reprint the play in either of the collected editions of Johnston's works. Of course before even embarking on his adaptation Johnston had recognised a similarity between Toller's storyline and the events of a nineteenth-century murder trial which he had made the subject of an unperformed radio play earlier in 1936. In the mid-1950s Johnston resurrected this play about William Burke Kirwan and rewrote it using most of the original material (especially the central trial scene and the developing relationship between the defendant's mistress and one of the senior representatives of the law, though in this version it is the Chief Superintendent of the Police not the State Solicitor) which he had devised for his Toller adaptation. '*Strange Occurrence on Ireland's Eye*' carries the same argument as *Blind Man's Buff* and follows the same pattern of revelations and dramatic climaxes but it has an air of contrivance about it lacking in the earlier play. The situations are now rather too obviously created to point the themes. Here it is the Chief Superintendent who races to conclusions about the defendant's character, presses charges and hastens the trial; when he reopens his investigations in the final act a wealth of evidence emerges proving Kirwan's innocence which in his zeal he had overlooked or not bothered to pursue as in any way crucial. But there are rather too many such discoveries in the space of a couple of scenes and the theme does not so much emerge from the action as seem forced on one by the author's manipulations. The device whereby the audience for '*Strange Occurrence*' are to suppose themselves the jury in the trial scene and are addressed directly by the Judge who urges them to mark certain stages in the proceedings as relevant has a similar elbow-nudging quality to it. The audience for *Blind Man's Buff* is brought to engage with the action by far subtler means. Further, by keeping the freed Kirwan out of the action of the final scene Johnston loses the beautifully sustained tragic ironies of the earlier play in its conclusion; his heroine now is merely a disinterested pursuer of justice and not like Anice confounded by a deepening sense of responsibility. *'Blind Man's Buff'* is an infinitely richer play than *Strange Occurrence* and deserves to be better known; it is too so very different from Toller's *The Blind Goddess* that it really merits being ascribed only to Johnston.

Blind Man's Buff marks the end of Johnston's involvement with both Toller and Expressionism; but a glance at Johnston's subsequent career as a dramatist will show how fertile an inspiration his work on revising *The Blind Goddess* proved to be. The use of a trial as a means to defining the essence of personality occurs as a central situation in *The Golden Cuckoo*; in *The Dreaming Dust* and the operatic version of *Nine Rivers From Jordan* the trial is a pervasive image that acquires spiritual and metaphysical weight where the wisdom of the biblical proverb about the dangers of taking on oneself the right of judgement over others affords an organic thematic principle that allows Johnston to keep a firm control over spectacularly wide-ranging material. *The Dreaming Dust* particularly has affinities with *Blind Man's Buff* in the way scenes reveal the distorting subjectivity of individuals' perceptions as an explanation of their incapacity to feel compassion. Whereas *Blind Man's Buff* is in the realistic mode, *The Dreaming Dust* returns to the surreal theatricality of Johnston's earliest works. The dramatic structures of *The Old Lady Says 'No!'* and *A Bride for the Unicorn*, as we have seen, stand as images of the psyches of the central characters, for Emmet tortured by his fanaticism or Jay questing for metaphysical assurance; the structure of *The Dreaming Dust* is as fragmented but it works somewhat differently in portraying the mind of Jonathan Swift. A group of Dublin intellectuals, Friends of St. Patrick's, have come together to perform in the cathedral a masque to raise funds, and get involved in a debate about the celebrated Dean. Each has his own explanation to offer about the mysteries surrounding Swift's relations with Stella and Vanessa and to substantiate his theory pinpoints a moment in the Dean's life as of emblematic importance. But these symbolic scenes when acted out quickly reveal themselves for what they are – travesties of the truth that expose the want of a proper imaginative insight in the perpetrators. But having let their imaginations run loose on the subject they find it asserting an autonomy that takes corporate possession of them: Swift the man emerges, despite their private fantasies about him, as both infinitely greater and infinitely pettier than their minds could conceive. The pity of it is that what is so superhumanly courageous about him and what compelled him to exact a superhuman courage from Stella derives from his absurd though wholly credible struggles to keep secret the facts of his birth. The actors flee in terror or repulsion from the truth, but the audience is invited to contemplate the wonder that so much creativity came from such despair despite the self-disgust Swift knew at the emotional cost of it all to Stella and Vanessa, which only rendered the despair even more acute. The brilliance of the play lies in the manner in which Johnston confronts the problem of exposition, always a difficult matter with a historical subject: the device of travesty-scenes at once fulfils that need while illustrating the theme that perception and vision are so subjective that though they constitute one's individuality they immediately render the individual vulnerable to the criticism of humanity at large, and that is the source of Swift's despair which compels him to curse the day of his birth. His quoting from Exodus 'I am that I am' which reverberates throughout the play is a challenge to posterity, a plea for compassion and the cry of a man in the full knowledge of his loneliness willing himself without success into a state of acceptance. The fragmented structure of the play might appear like the stations of an Expressionist drama (the critic of *The Times* reviewing Hilton Edwards's production for the Dublin Theatre Festival in 1959[42] actually described Johnston's technique as 'Expressionist'), but the comparison is not a just one: no Expressionist play can match this for the density and incisiveness of its psychological insights, for the assurance and fullness with which it establishes the grounds for its generalizations, for the rich complexity of response it invites from its audience in exciting the imagination into new realms of awareness and, above all else, for the sheer exuberance of invention, the ability to illuminate a given theme in ways that are convincing for their very unexpectedness. Toller had the courage of his convictions which proves a strength and a limitation; Johnston is more flamboyant and more disciplined as a thinker and as a dramatist. To label Denis Johnston as Expressionist is to misprize his genius and originality.

Denis Johnston: a retrospective

NOTES

1   Micheál MacLiammóir: *Theatre in Ireland*. Dublin, 1964. pp. 44–5.
2   Denis Johnston: Preface to *The Collected Plays* of 1960). Reprinted *The Dramatic Works of Denis Johnston*, Volume Two. Gerrards Cross, 1979. p.6.
3   Ibid. p. 15.
4   Johnston writes with acerbic wit on the subject of pigeon-holing in his 'Letter to a Young Dramatist', *The Listener* LVI. 30 August 1956. pp. 305–6.
5   Nicolas Hern: 'Expressionism' in *The German Theatre*, edited by Ronald Hayman. London, 1975. p. 108.
6   See Micheál MacLiammóir: 'Problem Plays' in *The Irish Theatre*, edited by Lennox Robinson. London, 1939. p. 218.
7   I am indebted here to the fine account of the production given by Christopher Murray in 'Early Shakespearean Productions by the Abbey Theatre', *Theatre Notebook* XXXIII. No. 2. 1979. pp. 69–74.
8   Joseph Holloway records this fact in his diary on 6th March, 1929. See *Joseph Holloway's Irish Theatre*, Volume One: 1926-1931, edited by R. Hogan and M.J. O'Neill. California, 1968. p. 46.
9   See *The Letters of Sean O'Casey*, Volume One: 1910-1941, edited by D. Krause. London, 1975. p. 258.
10 The remark is made about Lord Longford's play *Yahoo* on 19th September, 1933. See *Joseph Holloway's Irish Theatre*, Volume Two: 1932–1937, edited by R. Hogan and M.J. O'Neill. California, 1969. p. 26.
11 Ibid. p. 29.
12 See Kenneth MacGowan: *Continental Stagecraft*. London, 1923. pp. 130-143. Fehling's production of *Masse-Mensch* is described on pp. 144–156; it was mounted at the Berlin Volksbühne in 1921.
13 Denis Johnston: 'The Making of the Theatre' in *The Gate Theatre*, edited by Bulmer Hobson. Dublin, 1934. pp. 12–13. The very cramped conditions on stage at the Abbey in part dictated the choice of the Expressionist style for Johnston's production of *King Lear* to judge from Christopher Murray's account cited above.
14 Hilton Edwards: *The Mantle of Harlequin*. Dublin, 1958. p. 40.
15 Photographs of the production are included in Bulmer Hobson's *The Gate Theatre* pp. 94–95. Illustrations of the Gate's productions of *The Old Lady Says 'No!'* feature on pp. 73 and 127–129. The same volume also contains accounts of his method of directing both plays by Hilton Edwards, pp. 29 and 36. Micheál MacLiammóir describes both productions in *All For Hecuba* (London, 194) pp. 82–87 and 173-4.
16 *Transfiguration* (*Die Wandlung*) was first performed in 1919 in Berlin. It has never received a performance in England. A translation of the play by Edward Crankshaw is included in *Ernst Toller: Seven Plays*. London, 1935. pp. 55–106.
17 Denis Johnston: 'A Bride for the Unicorn', *The Dramatic Works* Volume Two. p. 54. I have chosen this rather than an earlier version as Johnston's currently preferred text.
18 Ibid. p. 34.
19 Ibid. p. 48.
20 Ibid. p. 66.
21 It is interesting to compare the play on this point with Eugene O'Neill's *The*

Fountain which Johnston had directed for The Dublin Drama League in May, 1928. O'Neill's hero, Juan Ponce de Leon, is like Jay Foss in quest of some mystical apprehension of the nature of being and believes it will be found if he can discover a fountain that he has been told of by an old American Indian. He spends a lifetime searching for it in the New World and meets his death in an ambush while still pursuing this elusive goal. As he dies the brackish spring near where he falls is transformed into a vast fountain in which ghostly figures appear singing of the nature of time and eternity and of life's powers of renewal. For all its scenic spectacle, O'Neill's play remains essentially a play of statement; its theme is not as in *A Bride for the Unicorn* to be imaginatively worked for by the audience and steadily apprehended. Moreover O'Neill's rhetoric in his moments of illumination so strives after intensity of significance that it comes dangerously close to bathos. Clearly the dramatist has failed to find a language adequate to express spiritual understanding. One can but suppose that difficulties with directing these scenes in the O'Neill play taught Johnston how necessary it was for the modern dramatist to find more indirect modes for defining such experience.

22 *Hinkemann* was first performed in Leipzig in 1923 and was directed by Peter Godfrey at the Gate Theatre Studio, London, in 1926. *Von Morgens Bis Mitternachts* was written in 1912; Denis Johnston's production of the play for The New Players was the opening performance in the Peacock Theatre on Sunday 13th November, 1927.

23 'A Bride for the Unicorn', *Dramatic Works,* Volume Two. pp. 45–46.

24 In this Johnston much resembles his contemporaries, Auden and Isherwood, and O'Casey was to do likewise in his later works. Details in *A Bride for the Unicorn* call to mind *The Dance of Death* (1933) with its central figure of a silent dancer who controls each change of scene and compels the chorus of actors to imitate his rhythms and style; or again the satirical use of pantomime and musical comedy in *A Dog Beneath the Skin* (1935) and the ironic placing of polite ritual in contexts like the Ostnian public executions which renders such decorum of behaviour obscene. One is reminded too of the various surreal images involving dance, music, mime and song through which O'Casey celebrates the return of Dionysiac energies to the modern world. But with these three dramatists the surrealism and satire have a stronger political motivation than is ever the case with Johnston's works.

25 *Die Blinde Göttin* was written and first performed in 1932 in a production by Fehling at the Raimund-Theater, Vienna. Its first performance in England was by the Welwyn Folk Players at the Barn Theatre, Welwyn Garden City, in 1934.

26 *Blind Man's Buff* opened at the Abbey in a production by Hugh Hunt on Boxing Day, 1936, and for some time held the record as the theatre's longest running success. Chavasse was played by Arthur Shields; Anice Hollingshead by Eileen Crowe; Mary Quirke by May Craig; Thin by M.J. Dolan and Liam Poer by Fred Johnson. A production at the Arts Theatre, London, opened on 26th September, 1938, in which Chavasse was played by Bernard Lee; Anice by Antoinette Cellier; Thin by Richard Goolden and Poer by E. Martin Browne.

27 *The New Statesman and Nation.* New Series, XII, 290. (12 September 1936). p. 351. Cited in Nicholas Hern's article, 'The Theatre of Ernst Toller' in *Theatre Quarterly.* II, No. 5. (Jan.–Mar., 1972). pp. 72–92. I am deeply indebted to Hern's essay for much of the information about Toller contained in this study.

28 Denis Johnston: 'The Scales of Solomon', *Dramatic Works,* Volume One.

Gerrards Cross, 1977. p. 319.

29 Denis Johnston: 'Sean O'Casey: A Biography and an Appraisal', *Modern Drama*. December, 1961. p. 327.
30 'The Scales of Solomon'. p. 317.
31 Ibid. p. 318.
32 Ernst Toller: *The Blind Goddess*. Translated by Edward Crankshaw. London, 1934. pp. 103–104.
33 'The Theatre of Ernst Toller'. p. 76.
34 *The Times*. 30th December, 1936. (My italics.)
35 *Joseph Holloway's Irish Theatre*, Volume Two. p. 64. The diary entry is for 4 January 1937.
36 Ernst Toller: 'Post-war German Drama', *The Nation*. CXXVII. 1928. p. 488. Cited in 'The Theatre of Ernst Toller'. p. 86.
37 Ernst Toller and Denis Johnston: *Blind Man's Buff*. London, 1938. p. 84.
38 MS. 21, 486. p. 62.
39 *Blind Man's Buff*. p. 97.
40 Ibid. p. 119.
41 Ibid. p. 124.
42 *The Times*. 25 September 1959.

*The author wishes to express his gratitude to the trustees of the Ellis-Fermor Memorial Research Fund of Bedford College in the University of London for their generous gift of an award which enabled him to travel to Dublin to undertake some necessary research towards the completion of this article.

THE GOLDEN CUCKOO: 'A VERY REMARKABLE BIRD

CHRISTOPHER MURRAY

The cuckoo, as all the world knows, is a rather mysterious bird. The poet Wordsworth[1] offered the notion that it was in fact 'No bird, but an invisible thing', which may seem somewhat extreme; but we could perhaps agree that it seems 'but a wandering Voice', disembodied and somehow impish and even magical. It is a bird that has it both ways, for it is earthy and remote at the same time, realistic and mystical. To Shakespeare, its song 'mocks married men';[2] but to Wordsworth, 'Thou bringest unto me a tale/Of visionary hours.' Indeed, we are to believe, the cuckoo's voice can evoke 'That golden time again' of youthful happiness, hope and love. Wordsworth's lines serve well enough to introduce Denis Johnston's own symbol of the mysterious and the miraculous in nature, *The Golden Cuckoo*.

The play, if I might refresh readers' memories, concerns an eccentric old man, Dotheright, who writes an obituary notice, on request, for a local newspaper and is then refused payment on the grounds that his subject is still very much alive. (It emerges later that the editor deliberately created the story of a man's death, for his own gain.) Dotheright protests, fails to be paid, and then takes action. The action is symbolic, though ludicrous. He assaults a post office and declares a one-man republic, in obvious imitation of Patrick Pearse in 1916. He is, of course, seized and charged with malicious damage to property, and only escapes a prison sentence when his friends testify to his mental instability. Dotheright regards himself as betrayed by God and man. He gets a chance to be released from the mental institution, however, and he has a final interview with a young couple, his friends, whose marriage was in process of dissolution all through the play. They have in some strange way been affected by the old man's personality, have become reconciled to each other, and do not want to see Dotheright locked up. But he is now resolute that his home is in the mental institution, and he chooses (freely) to return there. Before he goes, he leaves his gospel, as it were, with this couple: 'let us all be happy in the facts, whatever they may be', and in signal that facts can be super-rational he performs a miracle: the 'cock' in the loft which was Dotheright's dwelling lays an egg which drops on the head of Paddy, the young man, his disciple, so to speak. The 'miracle' certifies a world of experience beyond reason, and Paddy must now bring into unison a sense of pity for life's sufferers and a sense of 'happiness' in the facts (i.e., reality).

The play, even from the above inadequate summary account (omitting all of the minor characters), attempts to comment seriously on such matters as the nature of justice and the nature of freedom, and it seeks to provide by way of symbolic action a comment on modern values, ethics and culture. It is a philosophical play in the form of a farce; a criticism of life using the materials of conventional romantic plot. It presents us with a modern Don Quixote, whose foolishness transcends comedy, finally, and faces us with the possibility of pure love and pure holiness in what Shakespeare calls 'a naughty world'.[3]

But before discussing at any length the themes of *The Golden Cuckoo*, and before offering some sort of considered interpretation, it is necessary here to say something about the text itself. Johnston is a notorious reviser of his work. He will be dabbling, let the critics say what they will. Various versions of many of his plays exist, and the latest volumes, *The Dramatic Works of Denis Johnston*, carry on his practice of altering and amending texts already published and staged. There is something obsessive about this habit, perhaps; it seems, certainly, to be characteristic, as if Johnston believed life itself to be a palimpsest, a text constantly revising itself and super-imposing one scene on another. Indeed, some of the experiences in the plays themselves seem to enact this very idea, e.g., the double use of time in *The Old Lady Says 'No!'*, that moment at the end of *The Moon in the Yellow River* when Dobelle suddenly sees his daughter as his dead wife come again, and the whole plot of '*Strange Occurrence on Ireland's Eye*', which is a reconstruction of a crime, of the 'facts', in search of the elusive detail that may make the truth take new shape. There may, then, be something fundamentally expressive about Johnston's revisions of his plays; they may be part of his statement.

Be that as it may, *The Golden Cuckoo*, first staged at the Gate Theatre in April 1939, was first published in 1954.[4] It was not included in the two volumes of *Collected Plays* (London: Jonathan Cape, 1960), but appeared as number six in the Irish Play Series published in 1971.[5] It was recently included in the second volume of

The Dramatic Works, published by Colin Smythe (1979). There are, then, three editions of the play to be considered. I propose to look at Johnston's alterations as evidence of his continuing concern to master time, to keep his play relevant to and in communication with the present.

One may distinguish minor from major alterations here. The minor alterations comprise changes in phrasing, cuts and additions. A detailed comparison between the 1979 and the 1971 texts indicated to me that every single page has undergone such revision as only a Variorum could properly illustrate. I would offer by way of example the following brief example, from the first page of dialogue:

1979 edition	1971 edition
whom	who
the car	a car
wondering	saying
Didn't you say you didn't see	I thought you said you didn't see
too bloody fair	a little too fair
with a handsome smile	*With a smile*
Well. One can hardly	One can hardly
One adores. Now, can one?	One loves. Can one?
reluctantly smiling back	*smiling back*
Maybe not. I like the way	I love the way
and mean	and silly
anyhow it's	Well, it's

Generally speaking, the simple changes include idiom, tone and vocabulary. They would appear to be directed towards a greater degree of verisimilitude or modernisation. For example, the monetary value of Dotheright's debt is revised from the old currency to the new decimal currency (15 February 1971 was the so-called Decimal Day, when Ireland and England changed over to the new form), and also reflects contemporary inflation, by jumping from £1-6s.-8d. to £3.50 plus tax. Mrs. Vanderbilt's *'capacious bag'* (1971) or *'large and capacious bag'* (1954) becomes *'a metal Supermarket trolley'* for the opening of Scene Three. Johnston likewise makes room for the modern habit of freer speech on stage: 'swine' becomes 'shit' (1979 edition, p. 244). Revisions of this minor kind are prevalent all through the 1979 edition.

The larger changes comprise cuts, additions and change of location. Approximately two hundred lines are cut from the 1971 text; some of these are replaced but many of the cuts remain as excisions, the purpose of which seems to be to modify slightly the characterization. Paddy and Letty Golightly, estranged when the play opens, are more plausibly reconciled than heretofore. Paddy's faults, especially his cynicism, are toned down while his rival Chaplain's faults, especially his self-interest, are played up. Lowd, the editor and also the father of Letty, is rather less of a cynic and more of a crook. The rather preachy manner he formerly had, in speaking to Letty and Paddy about marriage and divorce ('You can get out, when the fancy moves you, and by God you do—at the first creak of the bedsprings', p. 20, 1971 edition), is no longer tolerated, nor is he allowed to say things like, 'Well, this is the twentieth century and you know your own business best,' as if he belonged to another century himself. The alterations to Mrs Tyler I shall leave aside for the moment. Dotheright himself is now rendered less of a King Lear, if that phrase can be accepted, and rather more of a Holy Fool. In the 1954 text he is more angry and more vocal than ever he is in later versions; Johnston gradually quiets him down. In Act III of the 1954 version, for example, Dotheright enters rehearsing a speech to be delivered to the Judge, and this is cut from the later versions:

> So when I obey my voices in this High Court of Injustice, here is what I shall say: 'You charge me with rebellion—you who condemn the thief by night and aid the thief by day. I am a rascal if I pick a well-lined pocket. But I may pillage the starving by free contract, and drive them out of doors to raise a rent or satisfy a usurer. And in all this you will aid me, righteous Judge—God's ape upon the high bench. . . . I must be hanged if in the heat of blood I slay a single foe. But to unleash a million souls upon each other is no crime if one is great enough. Then take me away and lock me in the jail, for such is the apt reward of honest men, when craft and villainy alone are honoured, and to be strong makes sin an ornament (pp. 111–12).

Besides this speech, there disappears from the 1979 version the strong note of pathos found still in the 1971 version in such lines as: 'Forgive me, gentlemen, if I do not rise, for to tell you the truth I am a little tired, and lately I have not been sleeping very well. But

The Golden Cuckoo

before long I shall sleep better and this derisive world that calls me mad will trouble me the less – will trouble me the less' (p. 52). A tougher, less self-pitying Dotheright emerges in the later version.

The additions in the 1979 text include use of a cuckoo clock, a boy and a goat. The first scene begins and ends with the clock shouting 'Cuckoo', whereas formerly this scene ended with the cock crowing; similarly, the clock sounds again at the end of the play. This is a simple effect, no doubt, but it serves to establish and retain tone, rather in the manner of the 'buckineeno' in O'Casey's *The Bishop's Bonfire*. The Boy, a new creation, appears at the opening of the play and four times thereafter, each time very briefly. He seems to have two functions. One is to mediate between play and audience, thus breaking the dramatic illusion. The rising of the curtain, according to Johnston's stage direction, discovers *'a small boy who appears to be supervising its ascent. . . . He takes a look at the Audience to see that they are all seated and he is at liberty to make some helpful remarks if they are not. . . . When all are comfortably seated the boy begins'* (p. 207). His opening speech is in the nature of a prologue, reminiscent, somewhat, of Yeats's prologue for *The Death of Cuchulain*, and in like manner we soon have the sense that this is the playwright's *persona*. The boy informs the audience of the location, and calls for a sound cue, a knock at the door, to signal the arrival of Letty Golightly and Chaplain. A goat whinnies off stage just as the boy says, 'I shall go and let in the . . . Leading Lady,' a nice ironic touch; he then tells the audience to ignore the goat. The opening dialogue between Letty and Chaplain is interspersed with brief comments from the boy, who then remarks: 'Well now that you've started so well, I'll leave you to go on with the Scene' (p. 208) and he leaves *'with a friendly salute at the Audience'*. He re-enters shortly afterwards *'pulling a reluctant goat which he attempts to lead to the Horse Box'* (p. 213). Interrupting the scene just beginning between Letty, Chaplain, Hooley and Penniwise, the boy apologises archly: 'I'm sorry but it's not supposed to be in this Act at all.' Johnston calls here for *'some extemporary business and ad-libbing while the animal is pushed and prodded into the horse box'* and then the scene continues, the boy interrupting with brief remarks until Penniwise shows irritation and says pointedly: 'Nobody wants you here.' The boy agrees to leave, adding: 'But nobody out there will understand a word if I do.' In accordance with the conventions of naturalism, the other characters are not aware of the audience, so Penniwise, looking where the boy is pointing, asks, 'Out where?' (p. 214). The

109

boy then takes his leave with the assurance to the audience that 'Mr. Dotheright will be on shortly, and he's the only character that matters. However, call me if there's any more trouble.' He does in fact return unsolicited before the end of this scene, when Hooley is telling Dotheright about his exploits in 1916 and the medal received 'for services rendered to the rights of Man' (p.222) ('to the old cause', p.18, in the 1971 edition). The boy calls through the window: 'Wear it, Hooley. You're supposed to be wearing it,' and eleven new lines are added here, resulting in Hooley's pinning his medal on to his outer coat.

The boy next appears in the company of Dotheright, Hooley and Penniwise at the newspaper office (Scene Two), where thirty-nine new lines are added. In this passage, the boy carries a large notebook in which he makes notes, on behalf of 'All these other people' (p. 231). As before, the other characters then stare out at the audience *'and see nothing'* (p. 232), at which the boy asks 'Why don't you go on with the Play?' He has only two further appearances, which are very brief and will be discussed below. Throughout the play, the boy variously gives his name as Alexander, Peter and George and yet when he is called a liar he insists: 'I'm the only person in this mess who means exactly what he says' (p. 231). His function is ironic; he is a messenger not from Godot but from the playwright himself, and so as breaker of illusion he is necessarily the voice of truth. The goat is, of course, another matter. I take it that unicorns are in short supply. A joke at Johnston's own expense, perhaps, as well as the kind of signature only the supremely confident artist will supply.

The second function of the boy is to incite and make imaginative the revolutionary gospel at the heart of the play. He gives Hooley the inspiration to wear his military medal, in the scene referred to above; and, early on also, he somehow appears to Dotheright as an ally. In the newspaper office Dotheright remembers meeting the boy before, mystery figure though he is, 'And I found him quite inspiring in some ways' (p. 231). Before that scene ends Dotheright identifies the boy with a revolutionary attitude. Whereas in the 1971 text Dotheright said, 'We will now pass on to the Second Phase' (p. 28), having failed to get justice through peaceful and reasonable means, he now says in the 1979 version: 'We will now follow in the footsteps of our young [George]' (p. 235), and the boy leads him off the stage. In the scene of 'rebellion' itself, the boy enters with his goat and delivers only two lines: 'He's right, you

110

know. You have to occupy the Post Office,' at which point he is described rather pointedly by Paddy as 'Saint George Washington with his Dragon' (p. 244). The boy thus plays a role in expressing the major theme, as Johnston consistently gives this in his 1954 and his 1979 Introductions: 'the moral duty of the put-upon to break the law from time to time' (p. 11, p. 198 respectively). In one sense, Dotheright crosses over from one realm to another at this point; from illusion to reality, if one accepts that the boy's 'world' is (as was suggested in preceding paragraphs) disjunctive from the 'illusionary' world of the other characters. I am reminded of certain events which took place in Dublin in 1972, immediately after Bloody Sunday, when thirteen people were shot down by British paratroopers in Derry. At a mass meeting in Merrion Square, a speaker ran through all the wrongs done to Ireland and to Irishmen by English governments over centuries past; each episode was greeted with enthusiasm by his listeners, as an orator is always applauded in Ireland, but after a time the speaker suddenly pointed to the nearby British Embassy and declared, so a friend informed me, 'and now we are going to burn their embassy down!' The cheers subsided, as heads turned to observe a man climbing on to the embassy building and affixing explosives. 'My God, he means it!' my friend recalls saying, and suddenly the occasion altered from a histrionic to a real and violent one. The embassy was burned to the ground. What Johnston records, it seems to me, is just this crossing of a threshold. In the midst of a rather festive occasion, dedicated to recalling bygone rebels, Dotheright seizes the microphone and announces: 'We must be angry men, unashamed of our anger' (p. 247) and after further rhetorical flourishes he suddenly leads an attack on the post office, breaking the windows, occupying the building, and crying 'To arms! To arms!' (p. 248). He finds, to his dismay, that he is alone, the others having scattered as soon as Dotheright took real action.

Then there is the change in location. The 1954 text is apparently set in England. The stage direction for the opening of Act II refers to a *'red letter-box'* outside the small shop-cum-post-office (p. 71); in Ireland the letter-boxes are green. Also, when Dotheright takes down the striped awning and waves it as a flag, he comments on the scarlet in connection with 'that pretentious and hypocritical whore who stands above the Old Bailey' (p. 84). Again, the public speaker with whom he engages, and whom he thought he won over to real revolution, is an American descendant of Wat Tyler, come to do honour at his birthplace. When Paddy interviews her she says: 'You must remember [him] from your history books. . . . This is his birthplace, you know. And somebody thought, as a part of this radio programme, it would be nice to get a section from the very spot, spoken by somebody like me' (p. 73). An historical context, the Peasants' Revolt of 1381 (which was led by Wat Tyler), was thus supplied for the 1954 text. A certain ambiance was also supplied by Paddy Golightly's cynical attitude towards Mrs Tyler and her entourage: 'a lot of damned hypocrites – honouring Rebels, my bloody eye!' (p. 82). In this context, Dotheright stepped forward and made his gesture of rebellion, declaring itself 'tired of the self-righteous cynicism of this young man who believes in nothing himself and considers himself entitled to lecture us on that account. So I propose to hold a Rebellion' (p. 82). In the 1979 text, Johnston, as we have seen, makes the young his *direct* inspiration. More to the point here, the context and ambience of this scene are vastly altered in the 1971 text. The play is now clearly set in Ireland, though purportedly still just 'somewhere in the British Isles' (p. 5, as in 1954, p. 21). The red pillar-box disappears, as do the lines on the flag, Mrs. Tyler turns into Mrs Graves, wife of a Minister in Dáil Éireann (p. 37), come to distribute medals among Old Comrades. This character suffers quite a sea-change. Her speech to the meeting has nothing whatever to do with Wat Tyler and bears instead on Irish history and the struggle for Irish freedom: 'Where are the men of '41, of '89, of '98, of '48 – the men of 1916?' she wants to know (p. 33). The subsequent attack by Dotheright on the little post office then appears a hilarious parody of the 1916 rebellion. But in the 1979 version Johnston abandons the Irish setting and goes back to Mrs Tyler, wife of an American senator, come 'to unveil this Memorial on the wall of the humble birthplace of his distinguished ancestor—the great English Rebel and Reformer of the 14th century, Watt Tyler' (p. 243). She then speaks of the American Revolution, and provides quite a different context for Dotheright's gesture.

I do not think that what we have here is a simple case of a return to square one. With Johnston it is always a return to square one *a*, or square one squared, if I can use that phrase to suggest the addition of a new dimension. These alterations of setting and milieu indicate Johnston's various attempts to make his central action – the revolt of Dotheright against socially enforced injustice – suitably metaphoric. Though he drew his story from an actual happening in

Ireland in 1926, Johnston seems to have felt the continuing need to make it immediate, and for this purpose he needs the currency of universal symbol or myth. History can provide this currency, as, for example, Shaw had shown in *Saint Joan* or Arthur Miller in *The Crucible*. But since it is the moral action itself, the gesture of revolt, which is significant in Johnston's story, and not historical process, he is willing to alter location or context in accordance with contemporary concerns. Topicality is what Johnston is striving for, perhaps because he views history not as any kind of absolute or deposit of facts but only as relative to the present plight and moral state of man. I recall a stage direction in *Storm Song*, for Act III: '*We are back in the living-room at Tigh na Beith, except that on this occasion we view the room from another angle.*'[6] This seems to me the rationale behind Johnston's revisions, in the larger sense: he wants to look at the same material, the same scene, from another angle. (The exceptional thing about *The Scythe and the Sunset*, in this regard, is that the 'original' was not by Johnston but by O'Casey.) And the purpose behind the second (or third) look is to keep drama plastic, to deny it the permanence of irretrievable statement. If this sounds like a formula for ephemeralism, I can only say that it is not incompatible with comic theory, with its idea of the second chance (or resurrection) as presented by Northrop Frye in *Anatomy of Criticism* and, especially, in *A Natural Perspective*.

To return, with apologies for the digression, to the particular case of *The Golden Cuckoo*. In Act III of the 1954 version, Mrs Tyler is in dread of the American reaction to her involvement in a 'rebellion'. The probability of her being 'investigated' (p. 89) conjures up immediately the days of the Committee on Un-American Activities. This context did not obtain in 1971, but it may be said that an I.R.A. context certainly did. 1966, the jubilee of the 1916 rebellion, saw a resurgence of nationalism in Ireland, and the momentum carried through into 1969, when the Civil Rights Movement in Northern Ireland flared up into guerilla warfare and rapidly led to a fresh chapter in the I.R.A.'s engagement with the British army. In the south, a government crisis arose in 1970 when two Ministers were dismissed and later charged in the courts with conspiring to use government funds for arms for the I.R.A. The trial, and all its implications for the security of the government, was one of the most bitter in recent times.[7] Fear and uncertainty shook the party in power, Fianna Fáil, the traditional, republican party. A line like Mrs Graves's in *The Golden Cuckoo* thus carries

113

contemporary value: 'There will be questions asked in the Dail about this. I had nothing to do with this nonsense at all. You all know that' (p. 37). When Hooley, who has just received a 1916 commemorative medal from Mrs Graves, backs her up she replies: 'I can see that you are a very sensible man. I will remember this, Mr Hooley, if you stick to that truth. My husband, the Minister will remember it too.' Whether or not Johnston was entirely aware of the Arms Trial, as it was known, his Irish setting gave this section particular point in 1971. Why, then, it may well be asked, has he abandoned the particularity of an Irish context for the 1979 version? The Arms Trial is past history now, and would mean little or nothing to a wide audience. Moreover, as said already, it is characteristic of Johnston to return to an earlier version and view it anew.[8] In restoring Mrs Tyler he now alters the ambience from 1950s American to 1970s American, with its emphasis on youthful revolution. Mrs Tyler now has none of the paranoid quality of her 1954 attitude in Scene Four (Act III): 'I was asked to take part in a broadcast. That was all. Is that an offence in this country? If so my husband, the Senator, will have something to say about it' (1979 version, p. 250). She is no longer the image of failure of nerve in the face of totalitarian observation; Johnston merges her with the other participants in the 'revolution', whose self-protective reflexes soon swamp their concern for Dotheright.

In *Nine Rivers from Jordan* Johnston said: 'I am one of the chaps who starts things – that is all I am: so it is not incumbent on me to do more than provide the Myth.'[9] In *The Golden Cuckoo* he provides Dotheright with mythic status. The theme of search for justice in society combines with the necessity for the individual to offer resistance; but if the play does not end with this fusion. It ends on a heroic note, if one understands by heroism some action which has positive social results, as, for example, Oedipus' sufferings do finally purge Thebes, or Thomas Becket's death regenerates the women of Canterbury. Such references may be out of key here; perhaps Ibsen's Dr Stockmann comes nearer the mark. Like Stockmann, Dotheright is a comic figure, a scapegoat; but like Stockmann his betrayal energizes his vision of society and his buoyancy inspires new hope. In terms of plot, Dotheright's failure results in the flourishing of love between Penniwise and Miss Peering, and the renewal of love and faith for Letty and Paddy Golightly. It is worth noting that this latter renewal begins in violence, as Paddy floors Chaplain during the scene where Dotheright starts his 'revolution.'

114

The quality of the 'myth' is entirely characteristic of Johnston. He does not write like Ibsen, though he shares Ibsen's concept of revolution, as Ibsen expressed this in a letter to Georg Brandes in 1870: 'What matters is the revolution of the spirit, and you must be one of those who march in the van.'[10] But Ibsen's myth points towards man's self-destruction, as the stories of Brand or Mrs Alving or Hedda Gabler signify. Johnston's is a comic Muse, and he may be closer to Shaw than to Ibsen. But Shaw was a Fabian, whose politics underpinned his parables of human action. His socialist analysis implied a Utopian teleology. Social change is always just around the corner in Shaw (even if it is a long corner, as in *Saint Joan*). Johnston has no such vision. His is a mystical, or at any rate a highly spiritual, subjective experience. Blake, rather than Marx, is his mentor.

It may be felt that Johnston makes a great deal of fuss over nearly nothing, in Dotheright's case. Nobody dies, after all, nobody suffers apart from Dotheright himself, and his sufferings are hardly on a par with the great sufferers, Prometheus, Job or Lear; all is conducted on the level of farce. Johnston has set himself the task of extracting significance from farce, because only if he keeps the stakes small will the paradox emerge clearly, 'the less the more'. He has, of course, to make a transition, to move the play at a certain point on to a level of meaning above the trivial. The point is akin to the moment in Shaw's *Major Barbara* when Barbara sees herself as betrayed by God (in that scene in the West Ham shelter when the Salvation Army accepts her father's cheque in spite of its origins[11]). Dotheright, having learned that he is regarded judicially as insane, cries out: 'I am betrayed. Oh Heaven – betrayed! . . . But my voices – my voices? Do they not want my – my services? (*He grows very calm as he gazes upwards.*) Is there nobody up there?' (1979 version, p. 263). Whereas in Shaw this is the point of a new departure for Barbara, who comes eventually to a new concept of salvation by social revolution, according to the 'gospel' of Undershaft, in Johnston this is the moment of tragic awareness. The technique might be termed 'absurdist', if by that loose term I can invoke the names of Dürenmatt and Ionesco and can imply their strange use of comedy for tragic purposes. Johnston uses the word 'absurd' himself in the text, even in the 1954 edition. In Act III, Letty insists that if Dotheright took the money owed him at this point, 'the whole thing becomes meaningless and absurd' (1954 version, p. 94). This conviction must be felt by the audience also.

115

It seems to me, finally, that *The Golden Cuckoo* is something of a personal statement by Johnston. In *Nine Rivers from Jordan* he tells of his anger at the charge of fraternization, simply because as a war correspondent he accepted apple cakes from the defeated Germans. He resolved to fight this attitude: 'If that is the law, I am going to break the law. I am going to break it as often and as openly and as ingeniously as I can; which to my Irish mind is the acid test for legitimate law-breaking' (p. 347). Dotheright takes a very similar line. And in *The Brazen Horn*, which is subtitled *A Non-Book for those who, in revolt today, could be in command tomorrow*, Johnston speaks of the knowledge of evil as lethal, which is Dotheright's insight also; but then Johnston offers a way out, through what he calls 'Grace': 'Grace is not a prize for Piety or for Agenbite of Inwit. It can be better described as a graduation certificate for those who prefer danger to boredom, and who in making this choice can also manage to be right, or accept the consequences if they are not.'[12] Grace is, surely, what Dotheright manifests, above all, at the end of *The Golden Cuckoo*, and the 'miracle' is its outward sign. In his latest version, Johnston makes the miracle happen through the agency of the boy, the playwright's representative, his Ariel. The ending marks, it seems to me, the culmination of a religious response to the ineluctability of a moral stance in an indifferent or amoral world, 'this great stage of fools.'[13]

Man and boy, Johnston has for fifty years been presenting his metaphors of nightmare or self-deception or human fallibility, always with a satirical eye to man's tendency to worship false gods. Through all of his work the duality of shadow and substance persists, and ultimately he opts (in any given play) for neither one nor the other, but insists on both. It is as if he were asserting that the realm we inhabit is richer and more complex by far than we commonly realize, as we elect materialism or spiritualism to be our guides. Life merges the two, superimposing realms of experience. As Eliot put it, 'the rose and the fire are one,'[14] but as Johnston put it: 'Here and Now is the focus of a saltire, or perhaps more accurately, of a double cone, as has been depicted by Yeats in his book, *A Vision*, and which opens out from the Observer in both directions – towards Past and towards Future.'[15] Being 'happy in the facts', which is Dotheright's final state, implies acceptance of this multivalence, and opening oneself to other possibilities than conventional 'realism' or logical positivism supplies. Being happy in the facts, the facts of later twentieth-century life being what they are, and yet retaining 'pity', which Dotheright also insists upon, is the 'cuckoo' duality which this play, in all its versions, offers. It is 'golden' because, as Johnston says elsewhere, gospel is golden.[16] It is not so much Wordsworth's bird we encounter, then, in the end, as it is an *eikon*, and we may recall the words of Blake: 'The hours of folly are measured by the clock, but of wisdom: no clock can measure,'[17] and adapt them accordingly, 'no clock but the cuckoo clock.' This is, perhaps, a point of view verging towards what in the 'sixties was termed 'Hippy'. Not bad for an eighty-year old. Truly, a remarkable playwright!

NOTES

1 'To the Cuckoo', in *Wordsworth: Poetry & Prose*, with an Introduction by David Nichol Smith (Oxford: Clarendon Press, 1948), pp. 95–6. The following quotations are from the same text of 'To the Cuckoo.'

2 'The Song: Spring,' *Love's Labour's Lost*, V.ii.909. The edition used, here and for footnotes 3 and 13, is *The Complete Works of Shakespeare*, ed. Hardin Craig (Chicago: Scott, Foresman and Co., 1961).

3 'How far that little candle throws his beams!/So shines a good deed in a naughty world,' *The Merchant of Venice*, V.i.90–91.

4 Denis Johnston, *The Golden Cuckoo and Other Plays* (London: Jonathan Cape, 1954). In his Introduction, Johnston concedes that the texts differ from those staged.

5 *The Golden Cuckoo (Revised Edition): A Play in Three Acts* (Newark: Proscenium Press, 1971).

6 *The Dramatic Works of Denis Johnston,* Volume 1 (Gerrards Cross: Colin Smythe, 1977), p. 217.

7 See Conor Cruise O'Brien, *States of Ireland* (London: Hutchinson, 1972), pp. 247–58. See also the Prime Minister Jack Lynch's recent comment in 'Jack Lynch: An Interview,' *Etudes Irlandaises*, No. 4 (Decembre 1979), pp. 229–30.

8 'My plays seem to resemble those racing cars that appear at one event in a certain condition, at the next with a different engine, and at a third with quite a new body.' Denis Johnston, Introduction, *The Golden Cuckoo and Other Plays* (1954), p. 5.

9 Denis Johnston, *Nine Rivers from Jordan: The Chronicle of a Journey and a Search* (London: Derek Verschoyle, 1953), p. 326.

10 Michael Meyer, *Ibsen: A Biography* (Harmondsworth: Penguin Books, 1974), p. 346.

11 Bernard Shaw, *Complete Plays with Prefaces* (6 vols., New York: Dodd, Mead & Co., 1963), I, 403. *Saint Joan* is, of course, an obvious parallel for *The Golden Cuckoo*, but it is worth noting that Joan recovers her faith in her 'voices' and chooses death rather than imprisonment (Ibid., II, 407-8); i.e., Joan is a martyr, where Dotheright is a casualty. Inasmuch as he discovers 'heartbreak,' Dotheright also bears some resemblance to Captain Shotover.

12 Denis Johnston, *The Brazen Horn: Lenaea 5* (Alderney, Channel Islands, 1968), p. 172. See also the later edition (Dublin: Dolmen Press, 1976), p. 169.

13 'When we are born, we cry that we are come/To this great stage of fools,' *King Lear*, IV.vi.186–7.
14 T.S. Eliot, 'Little Gidding,' *Four Quartets,* in *The Complete Poems and Plays 1909–1950* (New York: Harcourt, Brace & World, 1962), p. 145.
15 Johnston, *The Brazen Horn*, (1968), p. 152. Dolmen edition, p. 147.
16 Introduction to *The Brazen Horn*, p. [v]: 'Gospel is golden, and is very properly dispensed from the right horn of the altar.'
17 'Proverbs of Hell,' *The Marriage of Heaven and Hell*, in *William Blake: The Complete Poems*, ed. Alicia Ostriker (Harmondsworth: Penguin Books, 1977), p. 183. Johnston has said of Blake: 'His Proverbs are as prophetic as the Book of Isaiah, and we should be glad at any time to act as Ushers at his Marriage of Heaven and Hell.' *The Brazen Horn* (1968), p. 216; Dolmen edition (1976), p. 219.

'HE IS ALWAYS JUST ROUND THE NEXT CORNER.' DENIS JOHNSTON'S *IN SEARCH OF SWIFT*

MAURICE ELLIOTT

I

Let Professor Quintana deliver the verdict of the lower court: 'Denis Johnston's *In Search of Swift* (Dublin, London, and New York, 1959) makes highly exciting reading, but it can only be said that the startling theories it advances concerning Swift's parentage and his relationship with Stella have won no support from the leading Swift authorities of our time.'[1]

An admirer of Mr. Johnston who feels uneasy at civil strife between the man of letters (dramatist) and the professional scholar (authority), and who detects echoes of A. S. P. Woodhouse's friendly grumble 'ingenious' (meaning 'unsound'), may pass on to the next essay. As Professor Quintana would seem to have the critical scales heavily weighted in his favour, and recalling that there are still to be found 'Men of much Haste and little Ceremony' who prefer to enter the palace of learning by the back door,[2] young men in a hurry may perhaps be forgiven for preferring to ignore the unflattering sights and smells of exhumation. I am not very interested in disinterring from 'that deep Grave, a Book,'[3] the dry bones of the victims of academic warfare, but I did enjoy *In Search of Swift*. I should like to think that I read the book, not simply as part of the lively and elegant output I have seen and heard from Mr. Johnston in other contexts, but in Swift's own spirit: 'When I am reading a Book, whether wise or silly, it seemeth to me to be alive and talking to me.'[4] In order to appeal the critical verdict and to try to set out why the book should be remembered as more than a mere curiosity of Swiftiana, it is necessary to rehearse part of the drama.

II

Mr. Johnston's personal and public search for Swift has been very

119

intense. Inspired by Lord Longford's play *Yahoo* (1932) and W.B. Yeats's *Words Upon the Window-Pane* (1930-34), it spans more than twenty years. It begins with the radio broadcast in 1938 of *Weep for Polyphemus*, and the dramatic result, *The Dreaming Dust* (1940), extensively revised for both stage and television before its final appearance in *Collected Plays* (1960), and cost him 'more time and trouble than anything else I have ever written'.[5]

In Search of Swift is the culmination of Mr. Johnston's passionate encounter with the enigma of a fellow-Dubliner and the delayed response to the 'catastrophic'[6] reactions to his first theoretic approach to Swift's origins presented at a meeting of the Dublin Historical Society in 1941.[7] It seems to have been irritation at the neglect and the derisive civil leer of 'leading Swift authorities' which provoked Mr. Johnston to enlarge his examination of the biographical accounts of Swift, and to attempt to set his theory of Swift's relationship to Hester Johnson ('Stella') and Esther Vanhomrigh ('Vanessa') in a lucid and sturdy framework, 'a tome studded with footnotes and terminating with a bibliography.'[8] The result is by no means the dull reading which Mr. Johnston promised as the recognisable hallmark of such works.

Mr. Johnston contends that Stella was indeed the illegitimate child of Sir William Temple, as some contemporaries suspected. He claims that Swift, who seems to have deliberately obfuscated his origins, far from being married to Stella, as was sometimes believed, was actually her uncle. He argues that Swift was the illegitimate son, not of Sir William Temple (also rumoured), but of his father, Sir John Temple, Master of the Rolls in Ireland. This claim is based upon Mr. Johnston's examination of the 'Black Book' of the Kings Inn, a minute and account book used at one time by Jonathan Swift the elder, putative father of the Dean, whose unlikely Stewardship of the Kings Inn was signed for by Sir John Temple. This Jonathan, says Mr. Johnston, died ten months before the birth of Swift. He is 'the invisible scrivener' and his early death is 'at the back of all the dissimulation and contradictions that infest everything that we are told about [Swift's] birth and background.'[9] The secret consanguinity of Stella and Swift obviously prevented their marriage, but the intense relationship which had developed between them since she was a child ('of my own rearing and instructing')[10] precluded marriage to any one else; hence the tragic difficulties of the unwanted if not entirely unrequited passion of Esther Vanhomrigh.

When Mr. Johnston was considering the problem for dramatic

representation, he says that he soon found himself dealing with what seemed a set of very eccentric characters. Perhaps I may be forgiven for summary which is never an entirely fair reflection of an argument and comes close to distorting a lucid and perspicuous presentation.

III

Mr. Johnston complained that his theory did not receive much attention when first broadcast, but the sympathies of the reviewer in the *Times Literary Supplement* in September 1941 brought some rather unhelpful interest best described as 'twartin' and tormentin'.' Sir Harold Williams in the role of sergeant-at-arms hauled the offending outsider before the bar of scholarly authority without much ceremony. He accused Mr. Johnston of fixing his sights on theory and reaching for questionable assumptions to support it; of unfair and wholesale dismissal of previous biographers; of conjectural dramatizations; of accepting false authority; and of asking us to suspend our disbelief for too long.[11] He did not accuse Mr. Johnston of purchasing 'Knowledge at the Expense/Of common Breeding, common Sense'[12] – but that was to come.

Swift's *Ode to Sir William Temple* provides some convenient descriptive terms for a variety of attacks on *In Search of Swift*, and presented very briefly they do offer a kind of negative instruction for dealing with embarrassing theories. I. *The Lumber of the Schools*: a closing up the wall with our English dead. This is where the defence of previous scholars against an outsider is not easily distinguished from professional protectionism and is employed in the belief that young men who read undocumented papers to small learned societies are necessarily ignorant. The most cursory reading of *In Search of Swift* demonstrates that this approach will not protect the authorities and Mr. Johnston's polite criticism of Swift's early biographers remains unanswered. II. *The Roguery of Alchemy*: this is to suggest that Mr. Johnston's own scholarship is faulty, that 'he does not practise his gospel of accuracy as fervently as he preaches it.'[13] These critics are described in *The Tale of a Tub* as belonging to the 'Race of Men, who delighted to nibble at the Superfluities, and Excrescencies of Books.'[14] As with any argument based on the assumption that truth can be made by standing lies on their heads, this approach is difficult to sustain and simply demonstrates equivocation.

121

A third method is more honest, and properly applied could be positive and constructive. III. *The Hope of Golden Rules*: this is to find fault with the theory on the basis of established fact either ignored or unknown by Mr. Johnston and subsequently uncovered. For example, Abigail Erick, Swift's mother, seems to have been born in Ireland and is ten years younger than Mr. Johnston claims. She now appears to be much closer in age to Jonathan Swift the elder, and although by no means impossible, it does seem less plausible that she is a returned mistress of a much older Sir John Temple.[15] Fair dealing would demand that the book be responded to in detail by such sifting of the evidence, but this was not the case with *In Search of Swift*.

I am not a scholar with any specialized interest in Swift, and I was not able to respond with either the outrage of party or the amused tolerance sometimes shown to the 'amateur'. To a certain extent, like all true amateurs, I am dependent on the 'leading Swift authorities', but I am not at all sure that Mr. Johnston's diffident claim that his enterprise 'ought to have been undertaken by somebody else' will stand (*DD*, 4). I can see weaknesses in Mr. Johnston's case, but I can also see that he has not been answered fairly or confidently. If I am unable to declare in Gogarty's brazen tones: 'His findings have been accepted by me,'[16] I may at least feel uneasy at the way the reception is going. Other books come to mind where the violent reaction may well be the symptoms of a critical malaise which needs periodic disinfectant. It is for these reasons that I have always valued the first edition of F.W. Bateson's *Wordsworth: A Re-Interpretation* (1956), in spite of his characteristically courteous recantation in the preface to the second edition. Likewise, is seems foolish to reject out of hand Professor Norman Fruman's *Coleridge: A Damaged Archangel* (1972), although I find myself in disagreement with almost everything he says. But I cannot feign deafness. At least I am made aware of my own weakness for the pieties of admiration and am sharply confronted with the need for rediscovery and regeneration of response. A preliminary conclusion to all this might be that the laws of the critical courts are not entirely just, and their verdicts must be contestable.

Mr. Johnston insists that he is not forcing answers or proving any particular thesis. He does indeed provide a series of warning posts for others (*S*, x), like Goethe and Coleridge wishing to spare the young from circuitous paths. He knows that no positive proof can ever be forthcoming about matters of historical paternity; and he understands that it is purely a matter of opinion whether Vanessa was Swift's mistress (*S*, 147, 109). If Mr. Johnston has been led up mock alleys in the very Swiftian pursuit of conclusions to their unwelcome ends, there is no reason why I should follow him blindly. Rather I should be encouraged and refreshed by his bold questioning of the authority of the printed page and by his willingness to make judgements.

Ultimately, I think it is possible to preserve disinterest in the speculative part of *In Search of Swift*, because the major contention concerning the 'scandalous unreliability of the existing record' (*S*, 222) is of permanent interest to the biographer. The exposure of the contradictory and conflicting evidence in Mr. Johnston's account of the 'library of eminence' (*S*, 24), which Sir Harold Williams seems to have found so impertinent, raises questions which are still unanswered. It is regrettable that members of Mr. Johnston's cast of eccentrics have faded in this world of specialists and are properly discussable only over those long dinners and circling port of ages long past. To whom may one talk about Letitia Pilkington, 'proud *Hibernia* had the Happiness of producing this brilliant Wit'(*S*, 59)? Why is she so casually dismissed as a gossip? Why is 'CMP' of the *Gentleman's Magazine* of November 1757 so despised and of 'dubious credit'? Surely it is not simply because he or she printed the account of Stella almost twelve years after Swift's death? And what of Tom Sheridan, to whom Swift was the 'best of Deans'? If I seem a kind of prehistoric belle-lettrist beyond help of the deconstructionists and unable to discriminate my Swiftianisms, let me cool the blood by recalling Ezra Pound's bleak question as he memorializes Gaudier-Brzeska: 'What do we, any of us, know of our friends and acquaintances save that on such and such a day we saw them, and that they did or said this, that or the other, to which words and acts we give witness?'[17]

IV

Leigh Hunt, complaining of the contradictions of historians and of their airs and graces, makes an observation which casts a fierce light on the verdict with which I began: 'I felt, though I did not know, till Fielding told me so, that there was more truth in the verisimilitudes of fiction than in the assumptions of history.'[18] The antithesis parallels Professor Quintana's, but gives it an Aristotelian kick. The reception of *In Search of Swift* also forms up into two ranks – here dressed for convenience. On the one side there are the responses to the wit and ingenuity of the work which find it highly readable, entertaining, energetic, and even astonishing! If readers were not all moved to tears, like Harold Nicolson, they could appreciate a 'satisfyingly' offered solution.[19] On the other side, some thought that the method was dull, or that the book was turgid, cross, and hard-going; that exposure makes tedious reading. Few could claim with such devastating certainty that 'the truth is far otherwise.' Of Mr. Johnston's major opponents, only Professor Herbert Davies has the generosity to say that he has conducted a 'brilliant defence' of his case.[20]

It is clear that the book appeals to those who like the chase of the hunt, who like riddles and puzzle-solving, and who support Mr. Johnston's own contention that the case has 'all the fascination of a good detective story' (*S*, 8). There are some obvious dangers here. For all the invigorating brio of the presentation, particularly the opening chapter ('The Dean's Ride'), a serious argument is in danger of being treated frivolously as fiction or brusquely dismissed:

> Sir our Accounts are different quite
> And your Conjectures are not right.

Moreover, detective stories are not to every one's taste. It may be a weakness for example, to keep a reader in two hundred pages of suspense before producing the villain; in this case, Sir John Temple. It may well be felt, when we finally know whodunit, that Sir John's damning signature in the Black Book is an unacceptable example of a favourite Swift aphorism: *maximus e minima suspendens*.

When Mr. Johnston says that he will 'dwell at length on some of the clues and cross-examine fully the more suspect of the witnesses'(*S*, xi), he really uncovers his strengths. These are not so much the dogged determination and patient temperament of the sleuth. They are expressed in the management of briefs; in asides and instruction; in intelligent reconstruction; in short, in the creative handling of court-room drama. The successful deployment of such talents frequently produces an intangible but quite distinct atmosphere of suspense at a trial. There is a continual threat of exposure as motives are uncovered by cross-examination, and the air of conspiratorial uneasiness begins to trouble the most innocent. In the case of Johnston v. Swift all the participants become involved in 'an accumulation of lies, exaggerations and plain nonsense,' in the 'fog' which Mr. Johnston says is partly of Swift's own making (*S* 68,9). For the defence, Professor Ehrenpreis concludes that his client simply misled his biographers.[21]

'The question may, without much regret, be left in the obscurity in which he delighted to involve it.' Dr. Johnson's lofty dismissal is echoed in Professor Ehrenpreis's admirably detailed and imposing biography: 'I have been less concerned to add than to eliminate fables, and those readers who look for my views on a long train of legendary Swiftiana will search in vain.'[22] Yet I can see that Professor Ehrenpreis occasionally rests an argument on speculations which, for all the suave unconcern of his introduction, are equally based on 'fables',[23] and a phrase like 'we can speculate', uttered with confidence and repeated frequently enough, begins to make everything seem – in the words of another American – 'perfectly clear.'

If a biographical heretic cannot be ignored, or burnt, perhaps he may be laughed out of court and hustled into that 'astonishing world of legend and hearsay'[24] which *In Search of Swift* so patiently tries to expose. Enquiries which contain mysteries connected with the Temples or Stella which belong, in one view, to the 'back kitchen of history', are attacked as bad manners. W.H. Auden expresses this at its most extreme: 'Biographies of writers, whether written by others or themselves are always superfluous and usually in bad taste. A writer is a maker not a man of action.'[25] This is the most insinuating form of what Mr. Johnston aptly calls 'literary terrorism'. It is to insist that biographical reflections are 'rather a bore', or 'rather tiresome', because 'it is usually hard to see how settling such issues . . . would enhance our understanding of Swift's work.'[26]

If *In Search of Swift* is to be of value to readers of Swift as well as to readers of Mr. Johnston, it will be by means of the directions provided for an understanding of Swift in his works. In the volatile 'No Go' area between biography and criticism an author's work must be caught in the light of the details of the life if those details are to be more than the mere 'Tattle' which 'by the help of Discretion will wear off' (*C*,II,150).

V

The driving force of Mr. Johnston's search for Swift is not a love of gossip, a fascination with detection, or even his view of life as performance. It is his compassionate view of Swift as a tragic figure, Archbishop King's 'most unhappy man on earth' (*S*, 4). It would have been easy, he says, 'to draw a stage portrait of the Dean of St. Patrick's as a scatological problem-child with a hatred of the sex-act and an obsession with lavatories, or as a tormentor of women who drove two of them into the grave, or simply as an unusually angry old man' (*DD*, 3). The people who knew him, however, and were his friends, insist that he was no monster, and Mr. Johnston derides the suburban gentility that prefers cads to bastards.

It is clear that Mr. Johnston feels a kinship with his fellow-Dubliner, and his view that 'we are all inclined to visualise public characters in terms of ourselves' is underscored by his dramatic work.[27] In the final version of *The Dreaming Dust*, his masque characters, 'those mysterious gifts of the spirit', each accuses Swift of his own fault: 'money must have been at the back of it'; 'Swift loved women more than money'; 'He was always criticising and offending his superiors'(*DD*).

It is possible to draw parallels between *In Search of Swift* and another 'chronicle of a journey and a search,' Mr. Johnston's memoir of the Second World War, *Nine Rivers From Jordan* (1953). Both works explore the way in which controversial history comes to be written and both seek understanding by imaginative reconstruction. One of the most moving parts of *Nine Rivers From Jordan* is the sensitive recreation of the relationship between two young lovers which is drawn from his discovery of the letters of a German girl to a serving soldier in the Afrika Corps. This story of Georg and Anneliese counterpoints Mr. Johnston's account of the tragedy of domestic suffering and loss and the catastrophe of world war. It is no 'hard-mouthed imagination running away with reason', but a tender exploration of an episode which haunts Mr. Johnston's personal odyssey of self-discovery and search for a meaning to the tragedy of life.

Caught in the web of his origins, Swift cannot escape the consequences of two of the most complex of emotions, love and pity. The commandment 'that ye love one another – love one another' (*DD*, 65), can be desolating, and pity can be seen as a plague to man.[28] Mr. Johnston's view of Swift as sexually normal, 'only a man – just like other men', is strengthened by the loyalties and hatreds, greatness and sins, the contradictions and paradoxes which mark his genius; and the compassionate observation of Swift's suffering, validated as part of the fabric of life, is of a piece with the acolyte's prayer at the end of *Nine Rivers From Jordan* that tribulation be the 'measure of my joy in being alive.'[29] When *In Search of Swift* is seen in the context of Mr. Johnston's personal quests, I think it can be viewed as a kind of 'sacred biography' which Dr. Johnson claimed 'kept mankind from *despair*.'[30] Whereas I felt that the laws of the critical court were not entirely just, I should now suggest that they are not enforceable, like Non-Fraternization Orders.

The searcher must be led to Swift's writings after all, for (and it is a pity there is no way of indicating a Dublin accent in print) 'if you ask me there's no man knows a man better than his own man' (*DD*, 72).

VI

It is not difficult to find paradigms for the enigmatic secrecy and elusiveness in the formal qualities of Swift's works: the irony and raillery, the plural forms. Here comes everybody in various guises: Bickerstaff, the Hack, the Drapier, the Proposer, Gulliver, all are masks for that exposure of weakness or 'unmasking' which Swift felt had never been given fair usage, 'either in the *World* or in the *Playhouse*.'[31] Such creations could be seen as part of what Flann O'Brien calls 'aestho-autogamy' for it is no great leap from Shem the Penman to Sham the Punman. The narrator of *The Third Policeman* expertly glosses Swift's autobiographical fragment: 'I considered it desirable that he should know nothing about me, but it was even better if he knew several things which were quite wrong.'[32] Both Swift and his successor O'Brien/O'Nolan/na gCopaleen/the Brother/etc., are 'ontological polymorphs'[33] gaining much of their shrewd perspective by preserving their distance as outsiders, by conserving a bleak isolation. I should add, of course, Muldoon/'N' or 'M'/Yourman or E.W. Tocher (author of *The Impact of the Unreadable*) who points out 'It does not require more than a superficial examination of these schemata to expose this polymanual authorship, and the fact that the 'Writer' is not a person at all, but a Quest-Hero on whose personality there is not even substantial agreement.'[34]

It is no surprise to find that Swift claimed raillery as 'the finest part of conversation' for it is a kind of Prestolinguistics he made his own: 'something that at first appeared a Reproach or Reflection: but by some Turn of Wit unexpected and surprising, ended always in a Compliment, and to the Advantage of the Person it was addressed to.'[35] Of such an expert it is said with complete justification that 'we do not know how to take him', although to recognize the essentially social and compassionate nature of such a gift is to be sharply aware of the tragic contrast of the cruel senile decay of Swift's last years.

Swift's final work, *Polite Conversation*, exploring a neglected but useful and innocent pleasure,[36] the most agreeable pleasure perhaps, finds an informal equivalent in his correspondence; and I have found it rewarding to read Swift's letters (and those to him) holding in mind Mr. Johnston's sympathetic view.

Swift's description of Stella as the 'happy conjunction of civility, freedom, easiness and sincerity,'[37] might well be a definition of the art of conversing together agreeably, and when she died in 1726 it could seem that friendship itself ceased to have meaning: 'I think there is not a greater folly than that of entering into too strict and particular a friendship, with the loss of which a man must be absolutely miserable; but especially at an age when it is too late to engage in a new friendship. Besides, this was a person . . . who excelled in every good quality that can possibly accomplish a human creature . . . Dear Jim, pardon me, I know not what I am saying; but believe me that violent friendship is much more lasting, and as much engaging, as violent love' (*C*,III,145). This is an intensity, as Mr. Johnston puts it in *The Dreaming Dust,* 'above the cheap embellishments of kisses', and yet friendships continue: 'He seems to gain by his Distress/His Friends are more, his Honours less.'[38] Never did a correspondence show a man more beloved by his friends. Even allowing for the convention of compliment, it is instructive to glance at the openings of letters from Addison in 1710, through Lord Peterborough, John Barber, John Gay, Alexander Pope, Mrs. Pendarves, Lord Orrery, to Michael Clancy in 1737.[39] Mrs. Pendarves can speak for them all: 'I find your correspondence is like the singing of the nightingale; no bird sings so sweetly, but the pleasure is quickly past; a month or two of harmony, and then we lose it till next spring' (*C*, IV,251). Swift said that his solitary way of life was 'apt to make me talkative upon paper' (*C*,IV,29).

Certain familiar aspects of Swift as a correspondent have possibly had a distorting effect when used to support the more familiar pre-1959 views of Swift, and indeed any letters can be dangerous weapons unprotected by gesture and context: for example, his sharp views on Ireland in the 1730s expressed to Dean Brandreth and Francis Grant, or his vigorous, blunt approach to Thomas Sheridan: 'You believe, every one will acquit you of any Regard to temporal

Interest, and how came you to claim an Exception from all Mankind? I believe you value your temporal Interest as much as any body, but you have not the Arts of pursuing it' (*C*, III,94). Turning to the letters from *In Search of Swift* I found two things which do not seem to have been noticed very often, and which I should have ignored but for the search. Swift's strong sense of responsibility and duty are well known from his pressing successfully for the rights of the Clergy, but this quality is overwhelmingly clear in those letters which are written at the close of his life before the channels of his energies were blocked by disease and pain. A second quality is the way in which Swift's pity and compassion are enhanced by his austere restraint, his dignified and unsentimental acceptance of the tragedy of life. Vanessa once said to Swift, 'a charming compassion shines through your countynance'(*C*,II,364), and given that wonderful glimpse I should like to conclude with an illustration from a letter of condolence to Alexander Pope on the death of John Gay (*C*, IV,103-5).

At first it seems that Gay's death is a local event which can be generalized and which serves only to provide Swift with material for epigram and with the opportunity to reflect on his own isolation:

> I received yours with a few lines from the Doctor, and the account of our losing Mr Gay, upon which event I shall say nothing. I am only concerned that long living hath not hardened me: for even in this kingdom, and in a few days past, two persons of great merit whom I loved very well, have dyed in the prime of their years, but a little above thirty. I would endeavour to comfort myself upon the loss of friends, as I do upon the loss of money; by turning to my account-book, and seeing whether I have enough left for my support? but in the former case I find I have not, any more than in the other; and I know not any man who is in a greater likelyhood than my self, to die poor and friendless.

As the letter continues, the discriminations become sharper. Swift's reflections gradually narrow the careful distance conveyed in the opening gesture. The abolition of the promise of a future is balanced by the fruitful past validated by memory:

> You are much greater loser than me by his death, as being a more intimate friend, and often his companion; which latter I could never hope to be except perhaps once more in my life for a piece

129

of a summer. I hope he hath left you the care of any writings he may have left, and I wish, that with those already extant, they could all be published in a fair edition under your inspection.

Swift now takes up the subject of Pope's *Use of Riches* which he has just seen, and continues with remarks on mutual friends, Dr. Delany and Lord Orrery. The idea of friendship draws him back to Gay and closer to Pope:

> If you are acquainted with the Duchess of Queensbury, I desire you will present my most humble service: I think she is a greater loser by the death of a friend than either of us. She seems a Lady of excellent sense and spirit. I had often Postcripts from her in our friends letters to me, and her part was sometimes longer than his, and they made up a great part of the little happiness I could have here. This was the more generous, because I never saw her since she was a girl of five years old, nor did I envy poor Mr. Gay for any thing so much as being a domestick friend to such a Lady.

From such a delicate glance at the past and the happy tenderness of domesticity – and Mr. Johnston's Swift says 'There has been little enough of tenderness in my life' – he moves to comfort his friend by recognizing the sorrow of human attachments and the consolation of accepting human limitation. This is friendship in its greatest height:

> I desire you will never fail to send me a particular account of your health. I dare hardly enquire about Mrs. Pope, whom I am told is but just among the living, and consequently a continual grief to you: she is sensible of your tenderness, which robs her of the only happiness she is capable of enjoying. And yet I pity you more than her; you cannot lengthen her days, and I beg she may not shorten yours.

The changing perspectives of this letter narrow and qualify the opening distance as the two friends finally share and face the miseries of survival with the affirming of human bonds. It is no wonder that Pope later said that he could never write to Swift 'without drawing many of those short sighs of which we have formerly talked' (*C*, IV,217).

VII

Mr. Johnston suggests that each man searches for his own Swift, yet as Yeats observed, he remains elusive: just around the next corner. *In Search of Swift* and *The Dreaming Dust* both invite new explorations of Swift's work and help to narrow the gap between Swift and ourselves by creative sympathy. It was once said of Coleridge, that however unfinished his work, it put one in the way of better reading. I think this would be a suitable appeal court ruling on Mr. Johnston's work, for appeals to aesthetic exploration are heard when 'Authorities' are overbearing; it is a writing which offers gratitude for pleasure and instruction, and suspends final judgements.

NOTES

1 Ricardo Quintana, in *Fair Liberty Was All His Cry. A Tercentenary Tribute to Jonathan Swift, 1667–1745*, edited by A. Norman Jeffares (London: Macmillan, 1967), 345.

2 Jonathan Swift, *A Tale of a Tub*, edited by A.C. Guthkelch and D. Nicol Smith (Oxford: Clarendon Press, 1920), 145.

3 'Ode to Sir William Temple,' *The Poems of Jonathan Swift,* edited by Harold Williams (Oxford: Clarendon Press, 1958), I, 27.

4 'Thoughts on Various Subjects,' in *A Proposal for Correcting the English Tongue, Polite Conversation, Etc.,* edited by Herbert Davis and Louis Landa (London: Basil Blackwell, 1957), 253.

5 Denis Johnston, *Collected Plays* (London: Jonathan Cape, 1960), Preface to *The Dreaming Dust*, 4. Hereafter cited in the text as *DD*.

6 Denis Johnston, *The Golden Cuckoo and Other Plays* (London: Jonathan Cape, 1954), 16.

7 'The Mysterious Origin of Dean Swift,' *Dublin Historical Review*, III, no. 4 (June–August, 1941).

8 *Golden Cuckoo*, 16.

9 Denis Johnston, *In Search of Swift* (Dublin: Hodges Figgis, 1959), 46, 72. Hereafter cited in the text as *S*.

10 *The Correspondence of Jonathan Swift*, edited by Sir Harold Williams (Oxford: Clarendon Press, 1965), III, 145. Hereafter cited in the text as *C*.

11 *Times Literary Supplement*, September 13, and November 29, 1941.

12 'Ode to Sir William Temple,' *Poems*, I, 27.

13 John P. White, 'Jonathan Temple Satirist,' *Tablet* (November, 1959).

14 *A Tale of a Tub*, 98.

15 Irvin Ehrenpreis, *Swift. The Man, His Works, and the Age,* Volume One, *Mr. Swift and His Contemporaries* (London: Methuen, 1962), Appendix C, 270–274.

16 Oliver St. John Gogarty, *Intimations* (New York: Abelard, 1950), 81.

17 Quoted in Donald Hall, *Remembering Poets* (New York: Harper and Row, 1978), xiii.

18 *The Autobiography of Leigh Hunt,* edited by J.E. Morpurgo (London: Cresset Press, 1949), 142.
19 Comments by James Sutherland, C.H. Peake and Lilian Haddakin, Sir Herbert Davis, Vivian Mercier, Harold Nicolson, and Donald Davie.
20 Comments by Frank Kermode, Howard Spring, Matthew Hodgart, Sir Harold Williams and Sir Herbert Davis.
21 Ehrenpreis, 3–4.
22 Ibid., ix.
23 See particularly Ibid., 32–33.
24 Nigel Dennis, *Jonathan Swift. A Short Character* (London: Weidenfeld and Nicolson, 1965), 112.
25 W.H. Auden, Foreword to *A Certain World.*
26 John Hayward, quoted in *Search,* 223; Pat Rogers, 'Swift and the Idea of Authority,' in *The World of Jonathan Swift,* edited by Brian Vickers (Oxford: Basil Blackwell, 1968), 25.
27 Denis Johnston, *Nine Rivers from Jordan. The Chronicle of a Journey and a Search* (London: Derek Verschoyle, 1953), 59.
28 Ibid., 448
29 Ibid., 451.
30 *Boswell's Life of Johnson,* edited by G.B. Hill, revised by L.F. Powell, Volume IV (Oxford: Clarendon Press, 1934), 53.
31 *A Tale of a Tub,* 173.
32 Flann O'Brien, *The Third Policeman* (New York: Lancer Books, 1967), 67.
33 *Irish Times,* 21 February, 1944.
34 *Nine Rivers From Jordan,* 294.
35 *A Proposal for Correcting the English Tongue,* 91.
36 Ibid., 88.
37 Jonathan Swift, *Miscellaneous and Autobiographical Pieces, Fragments and Marginalia,* edited by Herbert Davis (Oxford: Basil Blackwell, 1962), 228-229.
38 *Poems,* III, 1041 (Thomas Sheridan).
39 *Correspondence,* I, 163, 235; II, 167; III, 414; IV, 217, 270, 370; V, 83.

A HUMANE AND WELL-INTENTIONED PIECE OF GALLANTRY: DENIS JOHNSTON'S *THE SCYTHE AND THE SUNSET*

JOSEPH RONSLEY

Denis Johnston's play, *The Scythe and the Sunset,* was written over forty years after the event it dramatizes, the Easter Rising of 1916, and over thirty years after O'Casey's play on the same subject, the title of which Johnston parodies in his own. In a way it is surprising that it took Johnston so long to get around to writing a play about Easter Week, considering that he has generally written his plays on historical subjects, that his personal experience of that occasion had given it a special significance for him in addition to its effect on the nation, and that O'Casey, for better or for worse, has always been a playwright of special interest for him.

O'Casey wrote and had produced those first three great plays of his while Johnston was spending his theatrically formative years directing and sometimes acting with the Dublin Drama League; since that time Johnston has written nearly a dozen essays and reviews on O'Casey. While the relative merits of O'Casey's plays is now a controversial subject, most of us, including Johnston, still consider *The Plough and the Stars* to be among his two or three greatest dramatic achievements. Johnston has said that *The Scythe and the Sunset* follows *The Plough and the Stars* like the 'smell following the motor car', and has written more officially in 1960 that his own play 'shows every sign of turning out to be one of those elusive phenomena – a play without a public.' He goes on, however, to explain that he likes the play very much himself, but that being 'an antimelodrama on what has now become a sacred subject', it is 'distasteful to the sea-divided Gael, and is concerned with a matter that the Sassenach has chosen to forget.'[1] I suppose it is at least true in a qualified way to say that the play is without a public – certainly it has nowhere near the popular success of *The Plough and the Stars.* That its treatment of its subject is distasteful to Irishmen or embarrassing to Englishmen today is I think rather doubtful; besides, the same could be said of O'Casey's play, if this were the case. And in

133

fact, *The Scythe and the Sunset* is not without melodrama. But it does not contain the sticky kind of melodrama that nearly spoils *The Plough and the Stars.* In comparison, the melodrama in *The Scythe and the Sunset* might be considered cerebral – if there is such a thing as cerebral melodrama.

The richness and ebullience of many of the characters ultimately give O'Casey's plays more popular appeal than Johnston's, and this may be said of *Juno and the Paycock* as well as of *The Plough and the Stars.* Speaking of *Juno,* Johnston has said that O'Casey sees his characters 'in the round, and not as cardboard figures spouting abstract ideas. And even when they are didactic,' he says, 'and expressing political viewpoints dear to the author's heart, he does not cease to regard them objectively and to laugh at them when need be . . . [*Juno and the Paycock*] is the work of an honest heart and not of a fallible head,' Johnston concludes. 'It does not deign to argue, and its poetry is entirely natural. It preaches no sermon and it points no moral, except whatever sermon or moral you choose to draw from it yourself.'[2] I am not sure this last statement is true either of *Juno and the Paycock* or *The Plough and the Stars,* and probably it cannot be said of *The Scythe and the Sunset* either. But if Johnston is didactic, he most likely annoys his audience by not being didactic enough, or at least his didacticism is of a finely spun intellectual sort that does not allow the audience readily to see where it is supposed to stand, a sort just the opposite of O'Casey's.

The play has, in fact, been admired in some quarters from the beginning. A review in the *Irish Independent* for 20 May 1958 called it 'all in all . . . the most vital play by an Irish author which Dublin has seen in many years.' The play received generally mixed reviews in Dublin, many reviewers comparing it disadvantageously with O'Casey's. Robert Hogan is I think more astute when he says that '*The Scythe* is a companion to and not a rival of *The Plough.*'[3] The two plays, in fact, approach the Easter Rising from very different perspectives.

That Johnston admires *The Plough and the Stars* is made clear in his preface to *The Scythe and the Sunset.* He also makes clear that the parody of O'Casey's title implicit in his own is intended not to mock *The Plough and the Stars,* and even less so 'to debunk 1916', but to present his own view of the affair, which is pointedly different from O'Casey's. Primarily, Johnston cites the fact that *The Plough* is essentially a pacifist play, implying that if only man had 'a tither o' sense', these outbreaks of destruction and bloodshed would never occur, whereas he himself, 'as a quiet man, who nevertheless, is not a pacifist,' could not 'accept the fact that, theatrically, Easter Week should remain indefinitely with only an anti-war comment, however fine.'[4] 'Cynics and pacifists,' Johnston has asserted in the preface to another play, 'sometimes argue . . . that wars never settle anything, but this is absurd. Of course they settle things. They settled American Independence, and they settled Slavery. They settled Tsarism, and they settled the Boers. That is to say, a hard-earned military defeat decided that the Boers should eventually have the whole of South Africa, instead of a couple of minor republics.'[5] Certainly it is arguable that military defeat in the Easter Rising settled something for the Irish, though undoubtedly not as much as it did for the Boers. Making his own comparison of the two plays, Harold Ferrar says that 'O'Casey's Easter Week . . . is death-dealing. He relentlessly denies the Rising any value. Johnston, in contrast, refuses just as relentlessly to equate violence with evil.' Furthermore, he continues, 'in the sphere of personal experience it afforded many Irishmen their first sense of intense aliveness and purposefulness.'[6] This side-effect of war is a subject with which Johnston deals at length in *Nine Rivers from Jordan*. It is not that he likes war, but he finds it inevitable, a manifestation of the evil side of man's nature, which is also inevitable, and which, if we are to affirm life and humanity, must be embraced along with the good even as we work against it. Both the mode and the emphasis are different, but the ultimate viewpoint is very close to Blake's, and to Yeats's. As to the Rising, Johnston says that 'Whether or not we hold that the actual fighting was widespread or of first-rate quality, we must agree that the affair, on the whole, was a humane and well-intentioned piece of gallantry. And the more one sees of how these uprisings have since been conducted elsewhere, the more reason everybody has to be pleased with Easter Week.'[7]

Despite their differences in perspective, Johnston and O'Casey have similar outlooks on certain important aspects of the 1916 historic event. In 1946, writing an article entitled 'It's So Good There'll be Trouble' as a kind of introduction to a broadcast version of *The Plough and the Stars*, Johnston points to the fact that,

> During the Easter Week Rebellion of 1916 an incident took place that has not been included in the lore of those Homeric times. A very brave and romantic young man, by name Joseph Plunkett, stepped out of the rebel stronghold in the General Post Office

135

and began to read the proclamation of the Irish Republic to the assembled citizens at the base of the Nelson Pillar. He had not gone very far with the news when there was a crash of broken glass from nearby, and the cry went up 'They're looting Noblett's Toffee Shop.' With a whoop of delight that far exceeded their enthusiasm for the Republic, the sovereign people departed, leaving young Plunkett to finish his proclamation to the empty air.[8]

Johnston's dramatic method differs from O'Casey's, among other ways, in that he makes more use of specific historic events, and he puts the looting of Noblett's Toffee Shop into his play. While O'Casey does not do this (though he does include the reading of the proclamation, and there is certainly a good deal of looting in general), there can be no doubt that he too would or must have been somewhat grimly amused by the event. Both playwrights approved removing the glamour from violent revolution. But as Johnston continues his essay, his view diverges from O'Casey's:

Since that time the Post Office has become a Pantheon – an elastic Pantheon, if one is to judge by the number of people who allege that they were occupying it – and it is not always considered good form to recall such an event as the above. Yet, oddly enough, it really adds a dignity and a deeper poignancy to what Plunkett was trying to do, and it is a very mealy-mouthed view that holds that the courage of the few is in any way diminished by the rascality of the many.[9]

Both Johnston and O'Casey affirm that the real human issue lies in the behaviour of individuals, but whereas O'Casey will readily grant the capacity for heroic action to Bessie Burgess or Fluther Good, he will undermine Jack Clitheroe's courage, making it empty and futile. Johnston, on the other hand, is ready to endow both types with capacities for bravery and an heroic spirit.

Finally, Johnston makes a statement about O'Casey's ultimate effect in *The Plough and the Stars* which, while not untrue, is more to the point in reference to Johnston's own views that to O'Casey's:

To those of us who remember the Rebellion with eyes undimmed by politics, it was a tormented and rather confused affair – a pastiche of heroism and of poltroonery, of individual gallantry and mild ineffectiveness, of outbursts of bad temper and of astonishing kindliness. In short, it was very like life, and in so painting it, O'Casey is not in any sense throwing dirt or contempt on his own people. On the contrary, by etching humanity in its true contours he is investing it with a dignity far beyond that of any pompous melodrama.[10]

A profound human dignity is indeed invested in *The Plough and the Stars*, but I do not think it is very certain that O'Casey did not intend to throw dirt or contempt on at least some of his own people. Johnston's own treatment of the subject is closer to the ideals of Yeats and Lady Gregory during the times of both Synge and O'Casey, and of the political events concerned, ideals that render partisan didacticism irrelevant in the observation and expression of the human spirit. Moreover, his statements are consistent with his own firmly held view that life itself is the most noble of phenomena, and that the rendering of it accurately and convincingly, in all its impulses, is the greatest achievement of art. This outlook pervades *Nine Rivers from Jordan* as well as plays like *The Old Lady Says 'No!'* and *The Moon in the Yellow River*. In fact, it may be the most basic theme running through all of Johnston's work.

This capacity for a broadly human outlook is exemplified in a 1947 BBC radio broadcast entitled 'Middle East Re-Visited,' in which Johnston tells the following story. An old friend, who was a physician, mentioned that he had been a prisoner of Rommel for four or five days during the desert campaign in North Africa. Asked how he had managed to escape, the friend replied:

'Well, I didn't actually escape . . . It was during that very fluid period when there was really no front at all, and everybody was running around, chasing each other. I had a Field Hospital out in the blue, and I had a good deal of operating to do. In fact, the orderlies were bringing in cases all the time. Then, as I worked, I noticed rather to my surpirse that the orderlies that were passing in and out were Germans, and that the casualties were Germans too. I asked about this, and somebody said that our fellows had gone right back, and we were now inside German lines. However I was very busy, so I just went on working, and whenever I wanted supplies or more help I just asked for it, and the Germans provided it. I found before long that most of my assistants were German doctors. They evidently considered that I was the best

man for the job, and they seemed quite happy to work under me
and to take my orders. This went on for four days, and on one of
them Rommel himself came in and took a look around. After the
fourth day somebody came in and said that they were going back,
and that all the wounded would have to be got out at once. I
protested about this and said quite a number of the casualties
weren't in a fit state to be moved, and would probably die if it was
attempted. All right, they said, you show us which of them are fit
to go and which are not. So I went around the tents and pointed
out that this one could go and that one couldn't.'

'And they took your word for it?' I asked.

'Why not,' he said. 'I was telling them the truth. They loaded up
all the least dangerous cases into ambulances, and I went back to
my operating. Presently I noticed that the orderlies coming in and
out were British once again. And so were the casualties. From
which I gathered that I wasn't a prisoner any longer.'

Johnston repeats the story in *Nine Rivers from Jordan*.[11] Certainly
something of this doctor has gone into the making of Dr. Myles
Mac-Carthy in *The Scythe and the Sunset*. More at issue, however, is
that Johnston's conviction that individual human impulses and relationships are more real and more important than abstract
principles is largely responsible for the difficulty of his audiences in
deciding just which side of the dramatic conflict they are supposed
to be on. The idea is commomplace enough, but Johnston's
dramatic exploration of it is particularly interesting. A *TLS* (Oct.
1960) reviewer of the Jonathan Cape edition of the *Collected Plays*
has put the matter clearly:

> Mr. Denis Johnston . . . is a dialectician: he delights in
> metaphysical contradictions. He is not, however, a dramatist of
> ideas in the accepted sense, for the dramatist of ideas presumably
> envisages the triumph of one idea and at a certain point the play
> turns into an exposition. The dialectic arguments that Mr.
> Johnston delights in sustain themselves on the stage because the
> notion that one point of view is any better than another is entirely
> abandoned. Conceived through character, any one of the con-
> tradictory and irreconcilable attitudes expressed may be more
> logical, or more dignified, or more delightful than any other but
> ther is never a hint that it can hold, in any final sense, more 'truth,'
> for truth would rob Mr. Johnston's dialectics of their tragi-comic
> confusions . . .

The point may be exaggerated somewhat, but the issue is central in *The Scythe and the Sunset*, where Johnston does not clearly take sides either between those who find violence worthwhile and those who do not, or between the belligerents in the conflict.

His even-handedness is underscored in the play's preface, when he tells of his family's imprisonment in its own house by the rebels, an imprisonment which bears certain similarities to that of his physician friend in North Africa. The 'captors were soft-spoken and apologetic young men who did the least damage they could,' he says, 'compatible with their orders to turn the house into a fort and to prevent us from leaving.' He remembers principally 'their charm, their civility, their doubts, and their fantastic misinformation about everything that was going on.' And of the British soldiers his memories are equally tender: his abiding 'impression of many cups of tea, of conversations about everything except the business at hand, and of a military incompetence of surprising proportions, even to [his] schoolboy's eye.'[12] Obviously these remarks are intended partially to serve as stage directions for the play, or perhaps we should say character directions. More important is the fact that already when he was fourteen years old Johnston received his first practical lesson leading to a Tolstoyan anti-heroic view of warfare, a view in evidence in his earliest plays, but which was to be made profound in the more advanced lessons provided by World War II.

The occupancy of his house taught him that very few of the real personae were either heroes or villains.[13] Johnston's Tetley, Harold Ferrar has remarked, is unlike Yeats's Pearse who is 'Cuchulain's protégé, a modern reincarnation of the heroic temper. Nor is he the pawn of an "antiheroic" vision like O'Casey's offstage Pearse, eager to kill people to win for himself a place in the pantheon of martyred patriots.'[14] The theatre, Johnston has said, is an easy thing to use as a sounding board for politics, but he does not approve of this use, nor of the oversimplification that goes into it.

In his art Johnston is an iconoclast in the best tradition of Irish writing. To supplement the intimate personal recollection, he notes in his preface, and includes in his play, a goodly amount of more objective historical fact, for instance: the lack of command in the British garrison during the early hours of the upheaval, and the very late arrival of Sir John Maxwell, the British officer renowned for placing the defences of the Suez Canal on the wrong bank, and then in the Easter Rising for presiding 'over the least intelligent part of

139

the proceedings – the executions'; the heroic defence by a few rebels of a bridge over the Grand Canal and the consequent infliction of many British casualities simply because of the breakdown of the most rudimentary communications; the cavalry charge on the General Post Office; the rebels' leaving the 'telephone system of the city in full working order under the impression that the exchange was heavily guarded – this,' 'Johnston remarks with astonishment, 'on the day of Fairyhouse Races!'; the occupation of strongholds with little tactical value; the interference with the Fire Brigade, fire eventually contributing considerably to the rebels' own demise; and the widespread contempt felt by the general public toward the 'Sinn Fein Volunteers.' All of this, especially where it involves weaknesses and blunders, is of course subject for humour and even ridicule. But the ridicule is of a man laughing at the foibles of his own humanity. It is in a sense human frailty that in the end paradoxically helps to save humanity by undermining the abstractions that threaten to subdue it.

Johnston is quite as even-handed as he is in his preface in endowing his dramatic characters with humanity – the rebels, the British officer, and those members of the contemptuous general Irish public who find themselves trapped in the course of events. These last at least begin with greater audience sympathy than do the others, simply because they are distant enough from both the abstractions and the action to be able to see the ironies in the behaviour of others more caught up, and we all enjoy participating in the mockery of pretence and bungling. But it is not Dr. MacCarthy's satire or Roisin's scorn that is the most interesting part of the play's characterization; indeed, their satire and scorn lessen as events of the play progress. Furthermore, the audience's own detachment and contempt decline as its interest increases in the humanity that emerges out of the officiousness of the combatants themselves. 'Brave men,' Johnston says, 'are always exciting to write about, particularly when they are afflicted with doubts, and deficient in technical training.'[15] Here again, Johnston keeps his art as close to life as he can. His 'lack of personal knowledge of any of the leaders [of the actual Rising] is [his] principal reason for not presuming to depict any of them by name, or even,' he says, 'by implication, on the stage.'[16] But what Johnston calls 'a certain similarity' is quite strong between his character Tetley and the rebel leader Pearse, between Williams and James Connolly, O'Callaghan and Plunkett, and between Emer and Constance Markievicz. There is also a marked similarity between the wit of Dr. Myles MacCarthy and that of Dr. Oliver St. John Gogarty, who died in September 1957, when Johnston was writing the play. The other real life character is one celebrated by Gogarty in the opening pages of *As I Was Going Down Sackville Street*, as well as by Joyce. This character, who keeps his real-life name in the play, or at least the name he took after his accident (Joyce gives him a different one in *Ulysses*, but still one that he himself on occasion had assumed) is Endymion, the sagacious fool.[17]

Actually, despite all this historicity, Johnston is an idealist, but his ideals are based on historical fact as well as he can determine it, rather than on false contrivances designed to make the ideals work. He would be the last to lay claim to an objective or absolute truth, his war experience having taught him the futility of such a pursuit, as he tells us in *Nine Rivers from Jordan*. But he constantly strives to strip away lies and illusions in order to get at some kind of con-ceptual truth, whether of Robert Emmet or of Dean Swift, of Irish history and politics or of World War II. A reverence for life over the abstract principle, and especially the patriotic or nationalist prin-ciple that usually leads to death in the name of life, is his own ideal, as it was O'Casey's. The influence of Ernst Toller might be felt here, although the principles involved really need no specific influence, and in fact a congeniality of spirit and opinion may have been responsible for bringing Johnston and Toller together in the first place. Johnston knew Toller first through Toller's early plays during the days of the Dublin Drama League in the twenties, and then personally when they both lived in London in the thirties. He says he liked Toller personally, and found him the best of the German expressionist playwrights, but in their dramatic collaboration *Blind Man's Buff* Toller's contributions stick out like sore thumbs because the two playwrights disagreed on nearly everything.[18] Yet on the humanistic basics they certainly did agree, and Johnston, at what-ever level of consciousness, must have come away from Toller with much the same impressions as did Toller's translator:

> . . . Ernst Toller was a poet with two passions – a passion for truth and a devotion to men and women . . . Toller is a poet, he must know that no man can hold any party doctrine fruitfully, bene-ficially, unless he realizes that there is good in men of other parties. Not in their systems; there is no need to hold that, but in the men and women. It is only the liar who claims to possess the

whole truth. Directly you begin to apply political, economic, social or religious principles, you find yourself compelled to work with and on men and women . . . Have your political system, hold to your own political creed, live, if you wish, in your party house – but take heed that the house has large windows, through which you can see others not of your household, and if you can see them looking at their faces in their mirrors, you will turn back to your own looking-glass and gaze at yourself with a more critical countenance.[19]

Yeats reports similar views of John O'Leary. Johnston makes the issue central in most of his work. In *The Scythe and the Sunset* the two characters he uses most fully to express it are of course Tetley, the Irish rebel leader, and Palliser, an Anglo-Irishman serving as a British cavalry officer.

Palliser is knocked unconscious when his horse is shot from under him during the cavalry assault he is leading against the General Post Office, an exaggerated version of which event is referred to also by The Covey in *The Plough and the Stars* – 'a volley from the Post Office that stretched half o' them . . .' As a result of his fall, Palliser also suffers a dislocated knee and is taken prisoner by the rebels. Since he is not wounded very seriously, Palliser is a potential object of considerable ridicule. His proclaiming his Irishness while serving in the British garrison, his leading an absurd military tactic, his military officiousness when hearing that his troop has 'turned tail and fled' and is now hiding behind the Parnell Monument – 'I shall stop somebody's leave for this' –, and the rather ignominious nature of his wound all make him vulnerable. Johnston's own background, not too distant from Palliser's Greystones one, would not be enough to protect Palliser; in fact it could well make him even more vulnerable. But any look of foolishness on Palliser's part is neutralized by the pretentiousness and bungling of the other side, accentuated from the first by the wit of Dr. MacCarthy and the vitality of Roisin in their mockery, but exemplified in Tetley's forgetting to arrange for the reading of the Proclamation of the Irish Republic, Emer's fanaticism, and O'Callaghan's naivety in asking for Palliser's 'parole' not to try to escape. In addition, the gentle and sensitive O'Callaghan, who later in his confrontation with the other British officer, Clattering, demonstrates that he is really not enough a soldier to shoot anybody, is indignant at the telephone not having been disconnected; he tears out the wires only to have them replaced almost immediately by Dr. MacCarthy. Then there is the captured machine gun that nobody knows how to operate, and Maginnis's sulking at having been left out of the Rising. All this to the accompaniment of romantic music from the piano next door. Still, before the end of the first act, both Palliser, by indications of his relative professionalism, and Tetley, by the expression of lofty enough ideals tempered by an attitude of fairness and a hint of honest doubt, foreshadow admirable, even heroic qualities that will emerge in both men as the play progresses.

In the expression of personal desires, motivations, ideals and doubts, the two antagonists in the second act change from somewhat satiric political objects to human subjects. Tetley does not appear on stage for the first half of the act, leaving Palliser to dominate through his interplay with the other characters.

Palliser functions now not only as a soldier, but also as one person sharing a space with others. To MacCarthy's surprise, he has a taste for William Blake – and for Johnston anyone having this taste cannot be all bad. His intellectual credentials are bolstered further by his responsiveness to Endymion's cryptic wisdom and by his capacity generally to hold his own against MacCarthy's satiric wit. On the other hand, he is gentle and sympathetic with Roisin, in contrast to MacCarthy's satire. Relevant to the larger conflict at hand, he does sulk when chided about his cavalry assault on the G.P.O., and he is further insulted when MacCarthy likens him to a tramways official. But then he comes off well against Williams' amateurishness – his childish whining about the British playing fair (the same complaint about the British use of artillery appears in *The Plough and the Stars*) – and he certainly looks good against Clattering's fatuousness. Both these minor characters serve as foils for the development of Palliser as the character of real interest. Finally, Palliser has a relatively enlightened view of the situation. He opposes the blustering mentality of the artilleryman, being professional enough to wish to avoid the destruction and bloodshed that firing the big guns will cause, and he recognizes the psychological implications of the circumstances, that his purposes can best be served by making the rebels look foolish rather than by turning them into patriots going down heroically to a military defeat. He would thus exploit the already existing hostile attitude of the majority of the Irish public. Most important, he is genuinely anxious to end the fighting, and is shrewd enough to make use of whatever opportunities come to hand.

In the first half of the second act, then, Palliser opposes primarily Williams and O'Callaghan, who are not only inept, but pretentious as well. He treats them with contempt and generally wins the audience's approval. His interplay with Roisin, MacCarthy and Clattering varies from one case to the other, but generally contributes to the emergence of a character that has weaknesses, that can be even foolish at times, but that is on the whole likeable, and competent enough. The appearance of Tetley on stage introduces an element of uncertainty, however, because along with a realistic outlook, devotion to the truth, and honest questioning of his own motives, he brings with him a point of view in direct conflict with Palliser's, and if the audience has been inclined either to mock the Rising with Palliser or to abuse the playwright for giving the mockers so strong a hand, it is now brought back to centre. Tetley most fully represents those 'brave men' that Johnston says 'are always exciting to write about, particularly when they are afflicted with doubt, and deficient in technical training.'

For the most part, though not entirely, Tetley's naivety of the first act is now gone. He is realistic in his attitude toward the enemy's threatened use of artillery, accepting the gamble and the responsibility taken by his own side, and, in contrast with Williams' propaganda, he insists on telling the truth as regards the progress of the battle. In the process he wins the approval and admiration of Maginnis who represents the rank-and-file patriot. There can be little doubt that he has the approval of the playwright as well when he responds to Williams' question 'What kind of a way is this to talk?':

> It's a very good way. I'm not blaming the men. They have all shown great courage in being with us at all, and what we've failed to do is simply a matter of ignorance. Dammit, we're only taking on the British Empire in open warfare for the first time in three generations. It takes us a little time to learn. But we'll never learn by pretending that we've done things that we haven't.

Most likely, too, he begins with this declaration to win a begrudging respect even from Palliser.

Once Williams and O'Callaghan are off stage, Tetley begins truly to dominate the scene, and in so doing further wins the audience's sympathy by his expression of anguish over doubts that have arisen in his mind. Revolutionaries usually, by their very nature it appears, are convinced they have a monopoly on the truth, on the knowledge of what is good or not good for the people. Dobelle makes this observation to Tausch in *The Moon in the Yellow River*, when Tausch is surprised that the Irish 'political idealist' 'does not recognize the machinery of democracy.' To which Dobelle replies cynically: 'He would say that you don't understand democracy. The Will of the People is a delicate bloom to be nurtured by the elect few who know best. The icy blasts of a general election are not for it. There's some sense in it – when you know that you know best.'[20] And the Speaker playing Robert Emmet in *The Old Lady Says 'No!'* proclaims: 'I will take this earth in both my hands and batter it into the semblance of my heart's desire!'[21] – a kind of definitive expression of the revolutionary spirit. Johnston has a certain very real admiration both for Darrell Blake and for Robert Emmet, but it is an especially strong mark of personal endorsement when he has Tetley behave in a different manner. 'I'd fight to the last building and the last man,' Tetley says, 'if I was sure of only one thing – that I was fighting for my country and for my people, and not just for my own satisfaction.' In response to Roisin's hostility he continues:

> You see. She's the people. It's their hostility that's really shaken me – not any question of whether we're going to win or lose. I was watching their faces during the reading of the proclamation, and there was nothing but derision in those eyes – derision, and that murderous Irish laughter. It was as if we were putting on a rather poor entertainment for them, and they wanted their money back.

Emer, on the other hand, takes the more familiar revolutionary line, that the people oppose the revolution because they don't know any better: 'They'll change,' she says. 'We'll show them.' But Tetley pursues his doubts, a pursuit which takes courage given the circumstances of the moment:

> Show them what? That they're downtrodden? You can't show people that if they don't feel it. There we were – in our hands, the first declaration of our independence for the past seven hundred years. But there was no sign of understanding in those eyes. And then . . . at the words 'Ireland through us summons her children to the flag and strikes for her freedom'. . . that crash of glass, and that terrible shout of 'Noblett's toffee shop'. . . Oh, these moments of doubt and self examination! I can stand anything but

145

them. Do I have to pretend to myself that I'm another Jesus Christ – that everyone's wrong except me? Endymion thinks like that. But I'm a sane man – amn't I?

Whereas the 'Noblett's toffee shop' incident as reported by Dr. MacCarthy in the first act generated only derisive laughter, the continuation of that laughter is dependent on an enduring pompous self assurance on the part of the rebels. Paradoxically, Tetley's loss of self-assurance forces the onlookers to take the ideals expressed in the Rising seriously and even sympathetically, no matter where they themselves actually stand on the issues. This is the first step from the wearing of 'motley' to a 'terrible beauty'.

Roisin and Maginnis now go into the kitchen, and Emer moves upstage toward the window to sit near the machine-gun, thus leaving the stage essentially to Palliser and Tetley alone. Tetley immediately unlocks Palliser's handcuffs and offers to let him go, because, as he says satirically but with an element of self-awareness that suggests further enlightenment, he (himself) is 'just a damned amateur'. But in his so doing, the two men are able to meet on equal terms as men, and are now free to abuse each other sincerely on grounds of conduct and motivation. Each expresses his convictions and uncertainties, the interchange becoming a dramatic vehicle for the playwright's attempt at an even-handed exploration of the opposing issues and the human impulses behind them. Palliser, though offered his escape, does not leave. Character integrity is maintained because he too is now intrigued by Tetley, as he could not have been by the Tetley of the first act.

Tetley prefers to fight out the battle rather than to ask for terms from the British; he appears determined to die for Ireland either the easy way, fighting, or facing the much more severe test of his own behaviour if it comes to being hanged. In order not to allow his personal interest to intrude, however, he decides not to participate in the vote on this issue among the rebel leaders. Historically, according to Johnston, while Connolly was satisfied at having successfully made his protest, Pearse was determined from the start to die for Ireland, one way or another. By not voting to continue the fight, however, Tetley avoids voting to satisfy his personal needs possibly at the cost of the Irish people, and is thus presented as a more attractive figure than his historic original. Pearse's only anxiety, according to Johnston, was that he might survive. He suffered from an obsessive romantic egoism, a malaise only too common and destructive throughout Irish history. His Tetley is much more severe in holding himself accountable for his actions. 'Whether we lose or win is a matter that only God can decide,' he says. 'How we behave is something that depends upon ourselves.' The first person plural in this declaration refers both to the Irish people in their struggle and to a rule of collective humanity applied to himself. Tetley wishes to embody in himself his ideal for the nation, and is thus preparing himself for the move he will make at the end of the play towards his own martyrdom.

His last few speeches before he follows Roisin and Maginnis into the kitchen to eat his beans leave Palliser at a moral disadvantage, and in a way challenged to come up with something to reassert his own position. Just why Palliser decides to rig the machine-gun for Emer, so she can fire it and thereby destroy the possibility of ending the hostilities, has evidently puzzled audiences from the play's first productions. So much so, in fact, that Johnston addresses himself to the question at the end of his preface to the play:

> The conflict of the man with the idea against the man of action is as old as the battle of Pope and Emperor, and what each has to say for himself is as important now as it has been since the trial of Jesus. And whether in Cairo, Delhi, or in Jerusalem . . . I can still visualize some local Palliser rigging that machine-gun in a fury. And I would still be asked afterwards why he did so – this in a world where we not only rig machine-guns for our foes but supply them in bulk to the other side with unfailing regularity.
>
> The fact is, that, outside the theatre, men do not act from logical motives as often as they act under the promptings of the urge [of] this thing that the Orientals call 'face'. If it is not permissible to depict this well-known phenomenon on the stage without elaborating the reasons for it, that is the theatre's lookout. Not mine.[22]

Palliser's moral self-assurance has taken a beating at the hands of Tetley. After a brief musical interlude with Miss Garrity, the next-door piano player, in which Palliser tries to cover his embarrassment, Emer takes over to finish the job.

Emer, too, in her own way, displays at least an apparently selfless dedication, though Palliser recognizes that she is also in love with Tetley. (He may not recognize, however, that Tetley's failure to return this love is associated with implications of homosexuality,

147

after Pearse's model. Emer says at one point, 'It isn't with any woman that he's in love.') At any rate, Emer might be viewed as the ultimate romantic. 'You mean, you want to make sure that he's hanged?' Palliser asks her when she makes it clear that she doesn't want him to save Tetley. Emer in response makes no denial, but simply says, 'That's a cruel way of putting it', and goes on to explain that she does not primarily want him hanged, but simply wants 'his life to have its meaning – the meaning that he puts on it himself.' In objecting to the pacifist role O'Casey gives to his women, Johnston points out with satisfaction that 'both [his own] women are killers.' Roisin has certainly goaded Maginnis into battle, and if Palliser was surprised at the extent of Tetley's dedication, he is astonished at the extent of Emer's fanaticism: 'You want a holocaust, do you,' he asks, 'so that your lover can win the only crown he's fit for?' And while his own moral outrage would be sufficient to protect him thus far, despite the vulnerable state in which he has been left by Tetley, he is not really able to withstand Emer's next blow: 'You *are* afraid of him – afraid most of all to see him die. . . . Because you know, for all your talk, that you couldn't face it the way he could.' And with the final twist of the knife, that being a Protestant he could not really understand death or martyrdom, and by implication, courage, the way a Catholic could, she goads him into sacrificing his professionalism to his vanity. Certainly Palliser is not the first to make the trade-off. It is a matter, as Johnston says in the preface, of 'saving face', and Palliser has just been so out-manœuvred by Tetley and Emer in a battle of character, that he cannot be content simply with a defence, but must go on the counter-offensive by offering Emer a counter-challenge. So he rigs the gun for her. 'Well,' he says, 'let's see who's best fitted to look Azrael in the face – the saint or the unbeliever.' But Emer gets the best of him again by taking up the challenge and firing the gun. 'My God!' he cries, 'She fired it!' and then goes a step even beyond rigging the gun, behaving in the irrational manner which has confounded audiences which themselves, Johnston insists, have irrational notions of the way people behave. There can be no doubt that Johnston intends Palliser to fire the gun himself. After his mock reprimand of Emer, 'You really are a very careless girl,' the stage directions read: *'He touches the gun again, and it bursts into action once more. Both he and Emer appear to struggle with it.'* It seems to me, in fact, that whatever the emotional impetus behind Palliser's actually taking up the gun and firing it, whether it be a matter of 'face', of the impulse

148

1. Denis Johnston. A photograph taken in Montreal in 1977. 2. Micheál MacLiammóir and Meriel Moore in the first production of *The Old Lady Says 'No!'* in 1929. 3 and 4. Two scenes from the third (1934) production of the play, with MacLiammóir and Ria Mooney.

5. The 1939 production of *The Golden Cuckoo* at the Dublin Gate Theatre (Longford Productions. L. to R. Mr. Haybottle (Ronald Ibbs), Mr. Pennywise (Michael Ripper), Mr. Golightly (Peter Copley), Mrs. Golightly (Vivien Dillon), Mr. Dotheright (Noel Iliff), Miss Peering (Nancy Beckh) and Mr. Green (Hamlyn Benson). 6. The 1950 production of *The Golden Cuckoo* at the Provincetown Playhouse. The cast was Mrs. Golightly, V. Thoms; Mr. Pennywise, L. Wells; Mr. Hooley, J. Gaudreau; Mr. Pull, P.D. Lukather; Mrs. Vanderbilt, L. Fern; Mr. Dotheright, R. Yasgur; Mr. Lowd, C. Moore; Mr. Golightly, W. Roberts; Gerard Bullock, F. Coreth; Miss Peering, M. Coreth; the Attendant, R.W. Nason.

7. The 1956 production of *The Golden Cuckoo* at the Gaiety Theatre, Dublin. L. to R., Miss Peering (Ann Clery), Mr. Hooley (Seamus Kavanagh), Mrs. De Watt Tyler (Ginnette Waddell), Mr. Pennywise (Joseph Tomelty), Mrs. Golightly (Maureen Cusack), Mr. Golightly (Michael Murray). 8. The 1947 BBC production of *Weep for the Cyclops*, a version of *The Dreaming Dust*. Its cast was the Dean, Fred O'Donovan; Stella, Joyce Heron; Vanessa, Muriel Pavlow; Rev. Mr. Tisdall, Stuart Latham; Rebecca Dingley, Jean Anderson; Charles Ford, Godfrey Kenton; Dr. Berkeley, Ivan Samson; Brennan, Harry Fine. The play was directed by Denis Johnston.

9, 10, 11, 12. The 1936 Longford Production of *A Bride for the Unicorn* at the Westminster Theatre, with Godfrey Kenton as John; Art O Murnaghan, Lionel Dymoke, Harry Fine, Roy Irving, Ronald Richie, Edward Lexy and Cecil Monson as the Seven Companions; Michael Cole as a Drunk Bust; Joan Collier, Shelah Richards, Mary Leahy and Eileen Ashe as the Girls, with the Mask, the Ring, with Ambitions and with the Box. Settings were designed by Joan Hayhurst, except for the front-cloths and Scene VIII which were by Norah McGuinness. 13. Denis Johnston with some of the Longford Productions staff. Peter Powell is on the extreme right.

The first production of *The Moon in the Yellow River* (Abbey Theatre, 1931). 14. Eileen Crowe as Aunt Columba. 15. Maureen Delany as Agnes. 16. Udolphus Wright as Willie. 17. Shelah Richards as Blanaid. 18 (next page). Arthur Shields as George.

19. Cyril Cusack as Mr. Dotheright in the 1956 Gaiety Theatre production of *The Golden Cuckoo*.

21. The 1958 Abbey Theatre production of *The Scythe and the Sunset*, with Michael O hAonghusa as Williams and Denis Brennan as Dr. Myle MacCarthy.

20. Denis Johnston interviewing The Rt. Hon. Winston Churchill at El Alamein in 1943.

22. The 1948 BBC production of *The Unthinking Lobster*, a version of *A Fourth for Bridge*. The cast was: the Air Force Type, Humphrey Lestocq; The Yank, Dermot Palmer; The Pilot, Morris Sweden; The Hussar, Frank Harvey Jr.; The Afrika Korps Type, Channel Mifelow, The Folgore Division Type (The Italian), Martin Benson; The Pole (The Partisan), Liselotte Kristian. The Play was directed by Denis Johnston. 23. A dress rehearsal of *The Tain* produced for An Tostal in 1956.

that gives joy to the solider to be shooting, of an outlet for sexual drive, a subconscious desire, like Emer's, to give Tetley his chance, or whatever, the psychological basis for the action is viable, as is each of these possibilities. Making a precise choice as to which is operative in Palliser's case, however, is beyond my competence.

In terms of the action, the incident does give Tetley his chance, and not only Tetley, but Maginnis as well, who goes back to his men on the Canal for the first time with 'the kind of an order the lads will unnerstan'.' Exactly where it leaves Palliser at the end of the second act in the minds of the audience, relative to Tetley, is less certain, though there can be no doubt that the urbane and humane superiority with which he started is now gone. Our respect for Palliser is not irredeemable – Johnston in fact does not abandon him – but Tetley, the course of events having been determined for him, can now go over to the Post Office to pursue his own destiny as he sees it with a clear conscience. And he enters the last act unquestionably as one of those brave but somewhat incompetent men who 'are always exciting to write about'. Palliser has, wittingly or not, given him his chance.

The moral disadvantage with which Palliser was left at the end of Act II lingers well into Act III; throughout the first half he more or less remains in the background, occasionally covering his loss of stature with remarks of bravado or sarcasm, the openings being provided by Dr. MacCarthy. About half way through the act Tetley reappears, and Palliser resumes his role as foil, now to a Tetley still further matured, ready, for instance, 'to disregard the rules in an intelligent way'. Military tactics of the rebels also indicate increasing competence.

Most profoundly, however, Tetley has now given up his original plan to go down in the flames of the G.P.O., and is determined on a more effective martyrdom as the way ultimately to win Ireland's freedom. His own doubts have been resolved, his dedication is complete, and his means have been provided by the introduction of the new British commanding officer who is strong in the severity of his discipline, if not in his intelligence.

If Tetley's part in the history of his country is clarified, however, Palliser's is made more difficult, because the scenario provides that he play the part of informer, and Palliser, after all, for all his British officering, is Irish too. For Palliser, according to his own lights – which can shine as brightly as anyone else's – has been serving his country – Ireland – as well as has Tetley and his comrades. 'I like my country too,' he has said. Tetley's reply, 'Captain Palliser, I hope we all like our country, however differently we may express it,' while said with satiric intent, can be accepted more at face value both by playwright and audience. Similarly, Dobelle, in *The Moon in the Yellow River*, says to Tausch, in reference to the killing of the rebel Darrell Blake by Lanigan, 'Maybe you are thinking that there are more ways than one in which a man may die for his country?'[23] Palliser had been highly offended in the first act at being called British, and he has from the beginning only shared the sentiments of the majority of the Irish people (who could hardly be called traitors to their country) toward the Rising. Now with this most recent challenge, his Irish identity asserts itself more plainly than ever; recalling a remark of Tetley's in Act II, he says he has no intention of 'playing Judas to [Tetley's] Jesus.' 'It's not my casting, Captain,' says Tetley. 'It's Heaven that provides us with our roles in this fantastic pantomime.' And Palliser responds (with the playwright's sympathy I am convinced), 'Well Heaven can't ballyrag me. I pick my own parts.' His personality, and perhaps his social heritage, make defeat at the hands of these particular antagonists especially humiliating for him, and his recurring displays of arrogance to hide his feeling are psychologically consistent with his characterization. But he comes to respect, and perhaps envy, Tetley's sense of purpose along with his courage and intellectual capacities.

Furthermore, for all his arrogance, there is reason to believe that Palliser may at least at some subliminal level have been converted to the rebels' cause along with Roisin. Roisin, at the death of O'Callaghan, changes abruptly from mocker to partisan, though Maginnis's return from the front, not only as a hero but as a man, has prepared the ground for her conversion. At any rate, Roisin's change of heart demonstrates the effectiveness of Tetley's new tactic: ultimate victory by means of military defeat. Palliser has revealed a certain refined set of sensibilities throughout the play, and the increasing human stature of the rebels that accompanies their decreasing military fortunes does not escape him. It is the story of Yeats's 'Easter 1916'. The behaviour of his own party in the affair, on the other hand, represented by Clattering and the newly appointed British commander, contribute further to the doubts rising in Palliser's mind about the nobility of the cause for which he is fighting. Moreover, the question of why Palliser rigged that machine-gun in Act II preoccupies the major characters in Act III just as it always has the play's audiences. Roisin has turned with a fury on him because rigging the gun led to O'Callaghan's death, but now Tetley accuses Palliser of having rigged it because he 'didn't want to see [his] countrymen climb down without putting up a good fight.' Palliser denies the charge with vehemence, but Johnston has pointedly taken cognizance of the fact 'that speech is as often used to conceal thought as to express it.'[24] It is indeed unlikely that Palliser has acted with any such conscious motive as that with which he is accused, but the accusation certainly increases the doubts rising in his mind concerning his own actions, and the self doubt has the effect of ennobling Palliser now as it had Tetley earlier in the play. His course of action is determined once again, however, by Emer, now in her parting challenge. 'I think *we've* managed to look Azrael in the face,' she says. 'What about you? . . . Now's *your* chance to turn wind into wonderment.' Johnston's women can indeed be killers! Consequently Palliser determines on a martyrdom to match Tetley's own, though unlike Tetley's, it will not alter the course of historic events other than to eliminate his own role in them, which is reason enough for him.

Palliser, nevertheless, never becomes the noble but romantic idealist that Tetley is, or that Robert Emmet is in *The Old Lady Says 'No!'* or Darrell Blake in *The Moon in the Yellow River*. Nor is Johnston himself such an idealist, though he may admire those that are. It is true there is an element of romance in Palliser's sadness at the passing of the British Empire, of which he recognizes the Irish Rising as a beginning. He was enraged when Endymion, with the prophetic wisdom of his madness, had indicated as much early in the act:

The April wind blows cold on royalty,
Swift, Grattan, Sheridan, Wellington and Wilde,
Levees on Cork Hill,
The tramp of crimson sentries in the colonnade.
No more of Suvla Bay or Spion Kop.
The bunting under which we spilled our colours on the globe
Shall hang in gaunt cathedrals
Where no one goes.

Throughout the play Endymion has more or less a choral role, narrating in sometimes cryptic sometimes lucid verse the course of events taking place outside the Pillar Cafe. These events may be immediate, as in the moving of artillery onto the quays, or, as in the present instance, they may be larger and more profound events only implied or foreshadowed by the action of the moment. For Palliser, and the class to which he belongs, and for Denis Johnston as well, the passing of the British Empire, despite its shortcomings, is a setback in the course of civilization. For all the modifications that have taken place in his attitude, Palliser does hold to this esteem. And in this esteem he finds no contradiction to his love for Ireland. As he says to Tetley when they are left alone together:

> When we built an Empire . . . we didn't have much in the way of big battalions. But we had life and an interest in ourselves. Now we're tired of being what we are, and we play the other fellow's game because we're sick of winning. I see it all as if it had happened already. Ireland's only the start. We're going to go on winning every war, but piece by piece we're going to give it all away – not because we're licked, but because we're bloody well bored. So don't be too proud of yourselves. It won't be the first time that people like you have loosened the foundations of a civilization – and at Easter too, by gad. You'll have it in chains again, as you had it before.

There is a good deal of post World War II observation in Palliser's prophecy (when Johnston wrote the passage, of course, it had all 'happened already'), but in replying to Tetley's indignant response, 'In chains? We, who are fighting for liberty?' Palliser echoes words attributed to Parnell by Yeats, and anticipating historic circumstances with which Johnston had already dealt in both *The Old Lady Says 'No!'* and *The Moon in the Yellow River*. 'You don't give a damn about liberty,' Palliser says. 'All you care about is a cause. And causes always let you down. Your admirers will find that out before they've finished.' Perhaps this is what Denis Johnston meant when he told me that *The Scythe and the Sunset* is a play about that statue of Cuchulain in his death throes, with a bird on his shoulder whispering something into his ear. The bird, he said, may be saying, 'I told you so.'[25]

Mutual respect has by now developed between the two antagonists, though their rivalry does not end. 'Perhaps it's just as well you won't be around,' Tetley says. 'I think I shall defeat your general, but I must admit that in some ways you defeat me.' The pride, or arrogance, of Palliser's class will not permit him to respond as graciously, and Tetley follows his compliment with a parting, unreturned, salute. 'If he were the Devil himself,' Johnston has said, 'I would salute my Enemy – dead. It is the best tangible expression that I can think of to illustrate the principle embodied in the dictum – I have cast forth the knowledge of Good and Evil.'[26] Palliser's, and Johnston's, William Blake is in evidence here, but Johnston's World War II experience has also contributed significantly to the attitudes expressed in *The Scythe and the Sunset*. Even during that war, he has pointed out, 'a most peculiar friendliness' was evoked on many occasions 'between men who were engaged in killing each other, and a feeling of warmth – as between the more professional enemies at least – that was totally out of keeping with what was portentously called the "War Effort".'[27] It is apparent that Tetley now is as much a professional as Palliser. And as for Palliser, he returns the salute when he thinks, mistakenly, that he is alone.

During the course of rehearsals for a production of the play directed by the author in Toronto in 1976, Johnston changed the ending. Rather than have Palliser remain in the building as it collapses around him, he had him leave at the last moment, with a wink at the audience, after having won his points against Tetley. This is what Palliser, if he is true to character, would do, Johnston said at the time of making the revision. He will probably quit the army and go to Greystones to play golf or sell insurance. Palliser, Johnston felt, was beginning to act too much like his opponent. Besides, he didn't want two suicides, and felt that the audience found the conclusion unnecessarily grim.[28] Perhaps, too, Johnston remembered a review of the play by Elliot Norton in a Boston newspaper of 15 March 1958, which said that 'Although it is not really convincing, *The Scythe and the Sunset* is a stimulating play and in another era it might conceivably be a blazing success. If these were heroic times perhaps we could respond with full enthusiasm to the final heroism of its principal characters. In our day they seem a little too grand to be convincing; the fault is ours.'

Since the Toronto production, however, Johnston has revised the play back again to its original form, for the change had undercut its dramatic seriousness, almost mocking the author's intentions. Moreover, he came to recognize that the change would have reflected not the natural behaviour of his character, but his own, and he has pointed out that while much of the best Irish drama contains politics, it is the politics of the characters, and not of the play. Palliser, then, continues to try to out-act Tetley to the very end, as he has been doing throughout the play. Besides, he has to 'downface that bitch' who is a killer.[29] Finally, Palliser has undergone a very real dramatic development wherein, without obviously compromising his belligerence, he has caught some of the fire of the revolutionary spirit – not enough actually to support the Rising, but enough to keep him from entering the pages of his country's history as the villain of the piece. He would still prefer to live for Ireland rather than to die for it like Tetley, and his final action is not quite the deliberate suicide that Tetley's is, but if Tetley has taken on his professionalism, Palliser has assumed a sense of purpose to his life nearly equal to Tetley's, along with an historical perspective that goes beyond Tetley's.

So he remains in the building, and as it begins to collapse on top of him he is surprised to hear again Miss Garrity's piano next door. Her piano has been heard from time to time from the beginning of the play, and occasionally Palliser has accompanied her on the piano in the restaurant. The two of them now provide music for the apocalypse: 'Winter gives back the roses to the frost-filled earth', is Palliser's final line as he moves to his own piano to join *'in his part of the duet.'*

One scene in a play Johnston wrote more than twenty years earlier, *A Bride for the Unicorn*, was also entitled 'The Scythe and the Sunset'. In that scene Egbert the Eccentric (in some ways a counterpart of Endymion, and probably of Johnston as well) says to John, the play's hero, 'When we are born we sign a bond with Time that some day we must honour.' And as the piano begins to play, he continues:

> When the singer has sung, are his notes dead? Whatever has been, will be, while Time remains. You would not wish to sprawl through endless space. Why then be bothered that we terminate in Time? Should I be distressed because above my head is none of me except – perhaps a pleasant smell of brilliantine?

John says, 'I hear music. What is it?' And Egbert replies: 'Music? Maybe our lives are nothing but a tune played by somebody upon a piano.' 'Then,' says John, 'we would certainly be immortal.'[30]

Johnston uses an on-stage piano in four of his ten plays, and in each case it is played in association with death. While the last scene of *The Scythe and the Sunset* uses the piano in making operative the title's symbolic implications, death itself has been viewed with the ultimate optimism both in *A Bride for the Unicorn* and again most recently, at length and with extreme complexity, in *The Brazen Horn*. The implications, relevant to Ireland, charge the conclusion of *The Scythe and the Sunset* with this same optimism. And while Tetley plays an obvious and appreciated part in the outcome, it is Palliser, in his more unexpected role, and with certain distinct autobiographical correspondences for the author, who completes the action.

NOTES

1 Preface to *The Scythe and the Sunset*, entitled 'Up the Rebels!' *The Dramatic Works* of Denis Johnston, Vol. I (Gerrards Cross, Colin Smythe, 1977), p. 86. All quotations from *The Scythe and the Sunset* are taken from this edition.
2 ' "Juno" and O'Casey,' *Radio Times*, 21 June 1946.
3 *After the Irish Renaissance* (London, Macmillan, 1968), p. 145.
4 'Up the Rebels!' p. 86.
5 'Arma Virumque,' preface to *A Fourth for Bridge, Dramatic Works*, Vol. 2 (Gerrards Cross, Colin Smythe, 1979), p. 166.
6 *Denis Johnston's Irish Theatre* (Dublin, Dolmen Press, 1973), p. 125.
7 'Up the Rebels!' p. 91.
8 *Radio Times*, 13 Sept. 1945.
9 Ibid., 13 Sept. 1946.
10 Ibid.
11 Home Service London, 27 July 1947. *Nine Rivers from Jordan* (London, Derek Verschoyle, 1953), p. 50. Mark Culme-Seymour tells the same story summarily in this volume.
12 'Up the Rebels!' p. 87. Johnston's mother, he says, brought tea to the rebels who were wrecking the upstairs of the house. In conversation, March 1976.
13 In conversation, March 1976.
14 *Denis Johnston's Irish Theatre*, p. 119.
15 'Up the Rebels!' p. 92.
16 Ibid., p. 90.
17 Endymion lost his sanity when he knocked his head diving into a vat at Guinness's Brewery to save the life of another man. Therefore, he became a hero and a fool at the same time (perhaps not an unusual combination). Joyce gives him the name Cashel Boyle O'Connor Fitzmaurice Tisdall Farrell in *Ulysses*, a name Endymion himself used when registering in the National Library. See Oliver St. John Gogarty, *As I Was Going Down Sackville Street* (New York, Reynal and Hitchcock, 1937), pp. 1–9.
18 In conversation, 29 November 1976.
19 R. Ellis Roberts, 'Translator's Preface,' Ernst Toller, *Look Through the Bars* (New York, Toronto, Farrar and Rinehart, 1937), pp. v, vi.
20 *Collected Plays*, Vol. II (Jonathan Cape), p. 28.
21 *Dramatic Works*, Vol. I, p. 73.
22 'Up the Rebels!' p. 92.
23 *Collected Plays*, Vol. II, p. 80.
24 *The Golden Cuckoo and Other Plays* (London, Jonathan Cape, 1954), p. 7.

25 In conversation, March 1976.
26 Denis Johnston, himself, while a BBC correspondent, saluted the captured Nazi, Hermann Goering, just before Goering was escorted out by his captors from an interview session with the Press at the end of World War II. See Veronica O'Reilly, 'The Realism of Denis Johnston' in *Myth and Reality in Irish Literature*, ed. Joseph Ronsley (Waterloo, Ontario, Wilfrid Laurier University Press, 1977), pp. 281–282.
27 'Arma Virumque,' p. 165.
28 In conversation, March 1976.
29 In conversation, 29 November 1976.
30 *Storm Song and A Bride for the Unicorn* (London, Jonathan Cape, 1955), p. 278.

THE ENDLESS SEARCH

JOHN BOYD

Denis Johnston's marriage to the theatre has been lifelong, more or less faithful, seldom idyllic. The kind of marriage it has been is told in the illuminating prefaces he has written to his plays; and in this essay on his dramatic technique I shall make use of these prefaces and in one instance express disagreement with what is said; I refer to Johnston's view of his own work given in the introduction to *The Golden Cuckoo and Other Plays* (1954). Here it is:

> So in advancing the theory that I am, in fact, a writer who is trying to deal with matters of considerable importance, and who spoils his efforts with a tendency to facetiousness and an inadequate grasp of technique, I am running counter to the prevailing notion that my tricks on the whole are good, but that what I have to say is puerile.[1]

It is a perilous undertaking to contradict a dramatist's judgement of his own work, especially a dramatist such as Johnston who possesses a lawyer's ability to judge most things with a degree of dispassionateness denied to others. But when he advances this extraordinary theory that his technique is inadequate all that I can do is to register a note of disaccord and hazard a guess that the marriage must have been undergoing a considerable strain, possibly as a result of constant irritation from bar-flies writing in Dublin journals. My own opinion (which is of course not confined to myself) is becoming more and more widely accepted: that is, that plays ranging from *The Old Lady Says 'No!'* and *The Moon in the Yellow River* to *The Dreaming Dust* and *The Scythe and the Sunset* reveal Johnston as a dramatist with something important to say and equipped with the most flexible means of saying it. In play after play his technique, what he calls his 'tricks', has been superb. It is his searching vision of life that has occasionally become blurred; his sense of character – notably the protagonist in *A Bride for the Unicorn* – that has occasionally failed him. Saying all this does not place me, I hope, as one of the 'Aristotles in the Big League' from which all of us in the theatre have had to suffer. For as Johnston

157

rightly says '. . . in no other creative field – if you will pardon the expression – are there so many pimps, crooks, exhibitionists and frauds, living off other people's earnings, putting their names to other people's work, and talking and writing nonsense under the guise of technical know-how, as there are cluttering up the stage doors.'[2]

That astringent remark has all the ring of personal experience, Johnston being very much a man of the theatre, and someone who finds theatre people the best possible company. He has acted, directed and written for the theatre; he has been wooed away into radio and television theatre; he has, in short, eagerly embraced the dramatic media that have come his way; and it would be surprising if such a practitioner should not have an almost obsessive interest in technique. Indeed he has admitted this: 'In the endless search for the best way of saying what he has to say, the dramatist has nobody to guide him except himself, and what he overhears in the vestibule.'[3] It is well to note that phrase: 'the endless search'. Johnston holds strongly that all plays require re-writing after their first presentation: only then can their weaknesses be detected; for plays begin their true existence when they are heard and seen and experienced by audiences. A play must be seen to work, and every verbal change, every transposition of text, every scenic addition or subtraction, every move, every gesture, every modification of setting, lighting, costume, all are made with one end in view – to give to the play all of its potential life. Until a play has proved itself before different audiences, until dead tissue has been removed and living tissue substituted, only then can it be given its best chance for survival – survival year after year. And it is partly because Johnston respects his plays technically that their survival value has increased. Other Irish dramatists have achieved greater popularity, flared up quickly and just as quickly fizzled out; Johnston's plays burn with a steadier flame, and revivals have shown how strong and enduring that flame is.

Though Johnston in his self-deflating way calls his technique 'tricks', that term (with its suggestion of trickery and gimmickry) is far from being just. Admittedly his first play *The Old Lady Says 'No!'* is a display of theatrical pyrotechnics. It is an innovator's play; a director's play (almost a director's plaything); a play composed by a young dramatist tired of the notion of a conventional three-act play written in the realistic mode and 'expressing the social sentiments of the stage in the "twenties".'[4] Johnston had other

158

ambitions and his technical influences derived not from traditional Irish models but from abroad – from America and Europe. In 'Opus One', his introduction to *The Old Lady Says 'No!'*, he disclaims the influence of Georg Kaiser (whose *From Morn to Midnight* he had produced for the New Players in 1927) or of Eugene O'Neill (whose *The Fountain* he had produced for The Drama League in 1928), or of Nikolai Evreinov (in whose *The Chief Thing* he had played the part of the Student); instead he claims to owe something to Kaufman and Connelly's *Beggar on Horseback* and to Joseph Capek's *The Land of Many Names*. Like Shaw, Johnston doesn't in the least object to playing the 'influences' game – no original dramatist does – but it would be a mistake to take the game at all seriously. The technical weapons he chose were the sharpest daggers he could find to penetrate the tough hide of the Dublin audiences at the Gate Theatre Studio from its opening night on 3rd June 1929.

Johnston's daggers struck home. The play aroused a good deal of controversy; but there were no riots, no protests from the auditorium. Whether this was because of the growing tolerance of Dublin audiences since the early productions of *The Playboy of the Western World* and *The Plough and the Stars*, or because of the complexity, subtlety, sophistication, and occasional obscurity of reference, must be matter for conjecture. One thing, however, is certain: the brilliance of Hilton Edwards' production. Johnston – no easy man to please concerning his own or anybody else's work – has stated that this production 'has become an integral part of the play as is the text, and is not likely to be bettered.'[5] He was lucky in his producer; lucky in his leader actor, Micheál MacLiammóir, who also designed the settings and costumes; and lucky in the 'timing' of his première. Everything clicked together as everything must if a production is to be a memorable one. And this was! I didn't see the original production but was fortunate enough to see a Hilton Edwards–Micheál MacLiammóir post-war revival at the *Gate*. An unsung opera; a three-dimensional film; a pageant of history and myth; a romantic story killed at birth; a costume play; a contemporary play; an omnium-gatherum of lyricism and bombast, parody and plain speaking; what *was The Old Lady Says 'No!'*? I was unable to classify this theatrical experience and still am, thank goodness, unable to do so; for Johnston's first play resists classification (at least for me) just as much as Joyce's *Ulysses* does. If classification is to be called for (and I think that outside textbooks it is seldom necessary) Johnston's own phrase can hardly be bettered: 'an expressionist gesture of dissent.'[6]

The term 'expressionist' was originally a pictorial term which was coined – as an antithesis to 'impressionism' – about the beginning of this century. Its transference to drama took place a decade or so later and until the thirties it was the dominant avant-garde drama form in Europe, and especially in Germany. It is not surprising that an iconoclastic young Irish dramatist should have been attracted to it; indeed it would have been remarkable if he had failed to be so. According to Eric Bentley, 'it reflects the anxiety, the soul-searching, the sense of crisis and insufficiency, sometimes the hysteria of a generation . . . though it was offered to the world as the drama of the future it was more obviously an aftermath.'[7] Whether or not it was to be the drama of the future wouldn't have much concerned Johnston either then or now. But what would have concerned him was the challenge of the new techniques: the sense of excitement, of exhilaration, of exploration: all that would be irresistible to a young man fresh from Cambridge and Harvard. Bentley, writing in 1946, might well pronounce that 'theatre maniacs were the making of expressionism . . . They needed a drama without substance, so that light and colour and design could have pride of place . . . The result is recorded in all those lovely picture-books of the drama, dated between 1918 and 1930, in which a New Theatre is ecstatically announced. Poor Expressionists!'[8]

But Johnston wasn't working with maniacs but with highly skilled artists. And his first play had too much substance rather than too little. Indeed he wrote an essay in 1929 denying that *The Old Lady Says 'No!'* ever should have been called an expressionist play, and affirming that he had attempted 'to evolve a thematic method based on simple association of ideas.'[9] His approach to playwriting was, I imagine, more practical than theoretical. *The Old Lady Says 'No!'* was written very much in the spirit of 'Let's see what would happen if we did this or that . . .' which is the normal method of a dramatist setting out on the voyage of discovery of how best to display his wares. Johnston's *donnée* was the quality of life of the young Irish Free State of the twenties, contrasted with the idealism of his hero, the most romantic of all Ireland's heroes – the young Robert Emmet. The juxtaposition and contradiction of youthful idealism with shop-soiled materialism, of fresh aspiration with dull philistinism, called out for the new techniques once the 'dream'

160

notion had been accepted. The associative technique was simply the best way of communicating the theme that had fired Johnston's imagination.

His technique – a collage of colour and scene, choral speaking, argot, cliché, quotation; swift 'cutting' between scenes; timeshifts; the shattering of illusion; the unconventional use of the stage itself, the unexpected tempi of the action – all this mélange contributed to the total effect of sheer dramatic excitement of presentation. The multiplicity of means orchestrated the sought-for ends. John Whiting in his essay *Statement for a Play* may convey something of what in *The Old Lady Says 'No!'* Johnston felt impelled to reproduce:

> I want to achieve something very raw; not coarse in texture, no, raw in the sense of the agony of an exposed nerve. As such it must carry at its beginning the sob of pain, the half-laugh, and then, in progress, rise through the crescendo scream to a finale of realization and awe.[10]

The Moon in the Yellow River, Johnston's second play, though very different from, is complementary to his first. In *The Old Lady Says 'No!'* romantic Irish mythology is splintered in the mirror of twentieth century Irish reality. In *The Moon in the Yellow River* the splintered reality itself is mirrored. C.P. Curran has clearly stated what the content of the play is and is not. It 'is not a play on the Shannon Scheme, nor of the conflicting ideals of the Republic and the Irish Free State, nor of an indignant spirit outraged by a sudden vision of robots. Its interest is the interlocking of these themes with the neurosis of Dobelle and the resolution of his bleak nihilism into a renewed harmony with life.'[11]

The themes interlock. So do the three acts. The play takes place in an old Fort, now used as a dwelling-house, near the mouth of a river in Ireland. The action is confined to a single evening in late September. Act One is set in the living-room. Act Two is set in the armoury and overlaps Act One by about five minutes. Act Three returns to the living room, several hours later. Johnston's acceptance of the Unities certainly contrasts with the romantic indulgence of time and space in *The Old Lady says 'No!'*. Restraint replaces freedom; a linear story is tautly related in the traditional manner. Johnston may not have been aware of Yeats's injunction of a surprise every five minutes, but he has certainly written this play as if Yeats were leaning over his shoulder during its composition.

In *The Moon in the Yellow River* the action is indirect as well as direct. The direct action culminates with the shooting of Darrell Blake, the Republican, by his former friend, Commandant Lanigan, now a Free Stater and bitter political foe. But this shooting – the climax to Act Two – is foreshadowed in Act One by the farcical little scene when Willie interrupts the Tausch-Dobelle supper and acts the part of a gunman until his mother Agnes, the servant, enters:

DOBELLE: Oh, Agnes, here's somebody who says he wants to search us all for arms.

GUNMAN: (*gruffly*) Everybody ought to put up their hands.

AGNES: If I put up my hands, it'll be to take you across my knee and give you a good skelping where you least expect it.

DOBELLE: An excellent suggestion.

AGNES: Take that old rag off your face at once, Willie Reilly. And who, may I ask, let you in here with them boots on?

GUNMAN: (*sheepishly removing his mask and displaying an honest pink face*) Aw, I didn't know you knew me.

AGNES: Do you hear me asking who let you in with dirty boots?

GUNMAN: I have me orders, Ma.[12]

Willie Reilly, who a moment before looked as though he might be the ruthless killer of the young girl Blanaid, is revealed as an 'ignorant yuck' terrified of his mother's tongue. By contrast Lanigan, who accepts the taunting of Blake and the scorn of Aunt Columba without protest, shoots Blake dead just after Tausch has declared that Ireland is a country where everybody talks and talks and nothing ever happens.

The indirect action (by which I mean the action which we are told about) is of special importance in this play. It counterpoints the direct action we see on the stage and encourages the audience to exercise its own imagination. It is the action that has happened before the play began or that is happening at the same time but placed beyond our field of vision. For instance, the play begins with an account by Agnes of the accouchement of Mrs. Mulpeter, but Mrs. Mulpeter doesn't appear and the result of her accouchement is not given. But the importance of this unseen suffering is evident. Birth is violent just as Death is violent. And little Blanaid, who is listening to Agnes, is now suffering in her own life from her mother's death in childbirth. Rejected by her father, she seeks substitute fathers in both Tausch, the German visitor, and Darrell Blake, the IRA leader whose mission is to blow up the Hydro-electrical Power Plant. The other listener to Agnes's story is Aunt Columba, the spinster whose only serious love affair ended in a row over a mowing-machine, and whose emotional life is so desiccated that she cannot bear to have her 'things' touched. Aunt Columba too is a woman of violent emotions expressive of many frustrations. For her there is no natural suffering of childbirth; nothing but abortive political action by means of pamphleteering, her care of her bicycle, and her skating championship to defend. This poor eccentric lives on the volcano of her pent-up emotions; as she confesses to Dobelle 'if anyone inferferes with my skates I won't be answerable for the consequences.' And his comment is a story of a bungled shooting incident from the past which has suddenly surfaced into his mind. 'A most peculiar thing! I had quite forgotten the incident, it's so many years ago. I was driving with my uncle in one of those old-fashioned high dog carts. We were coming back from duck-shooting and a rabbit ran across the road directly in front of us. I remember it distinctly now. My uncle rose from his seat, took careful aim, and shot the horse through the head. It was a most surprising incident at the time.'

Another story of a bungled death occurs in the middle of Act Two when Captain Potts is encouraged by Blake to tell the story of how Mrs. Potts was 'rescued' by lifebelt from the apparently sinking *Mermaid*, but had the misfortune to meet her death in the most undignified manner 'floating a cable or two off Salthill. The wrong ways up'. Whereupon Blake raises his glass:

BLAKE: To Death, Herr Tausch, that makes the whole world kin. (*He drinks*) There's nothing cruel about her. (*He sits*) Quite the reverse.[13]

The Moon in the Yellow River displays Johnston's technique at its best; though one of the most philosophical of Irish plays it is at the same time one of the most swiftly paced. It is never static, thought and action being unified to a remarkably effective degree. Johnston's characters may be men and women of action; they are also contemplatives, Dobelle and Blake especially, but also Tausch and Aunt Columba. If in structure *The Moon in the Yellow River* is traditional, in content it is speculative, and as a dramatic experience wholly memorable.

Johnston's third play *A Bride for the Unicorn* (1933) is seldom staged and I have never seen a performance. This handicap should make for caution; but as caution is hardly characteristic of Johnston's dramatic practice it would be misplaced in any critical comment on what is certainly his most complex experiment. Rashness is all; this *pons asinorum* has somehow to be crossed. After all, the play has been performed in Ireland, England and in America, though it is omitted from the Collected edition of 1960. This omission does not mean of course that it is outside the Johnston canon (as *Storm Song* is reckoned to be); it merely means that Johnston, 'an inveterate reviser', still hopes that this play can be rewritten. For as it stands *A Bride for the Unicorn* is not fully alive. Structurally daring, speculatively far-reaching (and perhaps far-fetched), *A Bride for the Unicorn* tells the questing adventure-story of John Foss and his seven alliteratively-named companions – Leonard the Learned, Bernard the Brave, Percy the Prosperous, Egbert the Eccentric, Lewis the Loving, Albert the Acquisitive, and Harold the Helpful. It is an Imaginary Adventure of Everyman – the most perilous of quests.

The play is prefaced by an Argument which summarizes the action:

This is the story of the strange adventure of John Foss; of the proposal that was made to him one Christmas Eve; of the manner of his acceptance, and of his subsequent transformation; of how he lost his love in the morning and with his seven doughty companions set out into the world to find her once again; of what befell them there; of his despair at the march of the seasons and his ever-growing fear that death would overtake him while his quest was still unfinished; and of how at last, upon another winter's night, he found again the object of his desire and learnt her secret.

Now taken down from the authentic sources by the present author, transcribed into play form, and humbly offered to the voice of the turtle.[14]

The matter of the twelve parts (or scenes) of the play is admirably stated in this argument; but the literary self-consciousness is far from reassuring.

A dramatist cannot learn the limits (and limitations) of his own talent unless he takes risks and advances not only as far as these boundaries but beyond them. Good drama is exploration of new content as well as of new form. And in this formal experiment Johnston has ventured on an artistic voyage of discovery (and of self-discovery) and returned if not empty-handed at least not triumphantly. It would be wrong to damn *A Bride for the Unicorn* as 'an interesting failure', but certainly it is not wholly a success – though its effectiveness in the theatre must be far greater than a reading of the text suggests. Hilton Edwards found it a thrilling play to produce, but 'what a brute'.[15] Technically it is Johnston's most complex play; and unfortunately on its first performance the Gate could not provide the revolving stage which the action almost demands. But revolving stage or not, this play is overloaded with a symbolism which would be better jettisoned at the outset. It would of course be a different play but perhaps a more satisfactory one. It suffers from excess of method as well as excess of matter. In an unpublished Preface Johnston writes that the text of this play might well be that 'the greatest illusion of all is that we fear the End.' That is to say, his subject is the profoundly philosophical one of the nature of immortality. And it is this counsel that is discovered at the deepest layer of his play: John Foss, the Everyman protagonist, embraces at last the lady of his dreams and thereby gains life in the arms of death.

This play begins with a Prelude and ends with a Coda, and throughout is conceived both in musical and in mythological form. But the dramatic machinery is much too heavy and complicated to be borne by the puny protagonist whose name was John Phosphorus in the original version – a too obviously symbolic naming for a character who only sporadically flames into life. Johnston himself has admitted to a violent dislike of the published version of *A Bride for the Unicorn*, an admission that is understandable. For the potential greatness of this play must be as evident to the author as it is to anyone else. It is Johnston's *Emperor and Galilean*. Still the conclusion that *A Bride for the Unicorn* is not wholly successful is no reason for devaluating it. It is an ambitious play and a memorable play. That it is not performed in Ireland is a comment on the Irish theatre today, not a comment on this particular work. Of course it is a 'difficult' play and requires that its audiences think as well as feel. But it is certainly a play that should be revived (perhaps rewritten) so that Irish audiences may be aware of the range of Johnston's achievement. The only other play written by an Irishman with which *A Bride for the Unicorn* has close affinities is *One for the Grave* by Louis MacNeice which was given its première in the Abbey during the Dublin Theatre Festival 1966. MacNeice's play follows the basic pattern of the medieval *Everyman*; and, like Johnston's play, makes use of music and chorus to buttress the story line. *One for the Grave* is set in a television studio (where the floor represents the Earth and the production gallery Heaven); but Everyman's life is revealed in a series of flashbacks which cover his married life, his youth, his first love, his war experience, and his conflicts with conscience. MacNeice's play, has a much more closely knit texture than Johnston's; the television studio serves as the central image and gives the play a cohesion that is essential for the working out of the theme – the quest of Everyman for life, until his final encounter with Death.

Although both dramatists are concerned with Time, MacNeice is not burdened – and I think it is a burden – with a philosophical or mathematical theory. J.W. Dunne's once popular ideas as expressed in *An Experiment with Time* certainly deeply influenced Johnston's thinking while he was writing *A Bride for the Unicorn*, and I am not convinced that the influence was dramatically necessary or useful. Indeed I think it made for confusion and a sense of clutter. Without such clutter *One for the Grave* has been given a much cleaner, fine-cutting edge. Yet I consider that Johnston's play is the more memorable; that the 'felt' experience is more profound. In the end, however, both dramatists reach not dissimilar conclusions, though they are arrived at by different routes. MacNeice's Everyman ultimately discovers that:

The bright daylight is here for all to see
Whatever it may mean of storm and strife,
The new freedom we shall find when we are free
And the chance of each man's lifetime is his life.[16]

The final chorus of *A Bride for the Unicorn* is also one of joy:

Sing, oh children of triumphant Zeus
To him who tunes his lyre upon the snow-capped heights.

Sing, fair-armed daughters of the trumpeting Gods,
Sing of your brother, Phoebus, of the golden hair
Who rules Parnassus and the Delphic stream
Flowing from the fair Castalian hill.[17]

Johnston's next two plays cannot be regarded as *dans le vrai*:
Storm Song was 'a sad little attempt at the popular market'; *Blind
Man's Buff* was written because Johnston 'didn't bother to say no to
Toller'; so from my point of view both plays are not essential.

The Golden Cuckoo, which followed *Blind Man's Buff*, was given
its first production in 1939. It is Johnston writing at the height of his
powers. Having come across the true story of a One-Man-Rebellion
which ended with the protagonist being sent to the asylum instead of
to jail, a story which deeply moved him, Johnston wrote a play
which allowed him to deploy all his dramatic skill and express all his
compassion and anger. In its three-act structure it resembles *Blind
Man's Buff*; but otherwise the plays have little in common, though
both excoriate the workings of the Law and reveal the helplessness
of the individual caught up in its machinery.

The Golden Cuckoo is of course a very serious play, dealing with
one of the deepest of moral issues: the rights of the individual
conscience in society. It is a play concerned with freedom as well as
with justice, the protagonist being an eccentric little man living on
the fringe of society and scraping his livelihood as an obituarist. The
ordeal of the well-named Mr. Dotheright (pronounced Duthery)
ends with his incarceration in an asylum, and Dotheright may well
be mad. Perhaps; but perhaps not. He may well be a saint; which is
the conclusion that Letty Golightly arrives at. But whether saint or
lunatic, he is certainly one of Johnston's finest creations. 'As a saint,
I am a failure. But as a Madman – ah, there at least, I am in the
forefront of the field. So let us all be happy in the facts, whatever
they may be. For to be otherwise is to die twice.'[18] 'The Chivalry of
Christendom' gives no succour to this 'outsider' without a place –
even a stable – in society. And Dotheright's residence is hardly
fortuitous; neither are his 'voices'. His conscience is as uncom-
promising as that of the Maid of Orleans, and his fate not far
removed from hers. If a literary influence has to be mentioned it is
clearly that of Bernard Shaw; for *The Golden Cuckoo* contains a
great deal of the heartbreak, humour and irony of *Saint Joan*; the
dialogue shares the Shavian cutting edge; each scene has the
Shavian dynamic force; and the protagonist obeys the voices.

The play is supposed to take place 'somewhere in the British Isles', but the whole atmosphere is definitely Irish (which is hardly surprising in view of the genesis of Dotheright's ordeal). And though the action is situated in Dotheright's residence, a newspaper office, a street outside a small shop-cum-Post-Office, an ante-room in a Police Court, and finally back at Dotheright's residence, Johnston – the most accommodating of dramatists – states that the play can readily be performed in a single, permanent structure, if the usual objection to more than one set is valid.

If in structure and language *The Golden Cuckoo* contrasts with *A Bride for the Unicorn*, both plays share the story of a pilgrim's progress: John Foss's journey to his cave with its rock guarding the porch where he and his friends sleep; Mr. Dotheright's journey to his lunatic asylum, where he finds company he prefers. Both are Unicorns 'without whom nothing can be done out here in this echo-chamber of conflicting messages.'[19]

'A lonely, contradictory, bemused creature that is difficult to ensnare, except by the bait of an Ideal, and that can turn and rend the Ideal when it proves to be a fraud . . .'[20] Such a description of the Unicorn also fits Jonathan Swift, the subject of *The Dreaming Dust*. If Yeats, in his introduction to his Swift play, could write 'Swift haunts me; he is always just round the next corner',[21] Johnston could echo *a fortiori* Yeats's cry. Yeats wrote a preface to *The Words upon the Window Pane*: Johnston a biography *In search of Swift*, as evidence of the theory on which *The Dreaming Dust* is built – that Swift was Stella's half-uncle, and therefore he could not marry her.

The rightness or wrongness of this theory does not concern me here. All I know is that Johnston is well able to defend it against either academic or literary opponents; and I remember with pleasure the spirited defence he put up when faced with Frank O'Connor, a redoubtable opponent, in a BBC discussion that I arranged during the fifties. But true or false the theory adds a dramatic dimension to Swift's life; and it is little wonder that Johnston – with his keen scent for a literary mystery story – was fascinated by the riddle of Swift's relationship with his two women, Stella and Vanessa.

It took Johnston nineteen years to put his biographical theory into a dramatic shape that finally satisfied him (if indeed it did satisfy him). *The Dreaming Dust* began as a Radio Feature programme and ended as a play 'Designed for Performance or Public

Reading, not necessarily in a Theatre.' It went through three versions from 1940 to 1959 and I have read – and heard broadcast – only the final version; and so my comments are made about it. By 1959 the play had not only undergone structural changes but had also changed its thematic emphasis, as Johnston admits in 'Period Piece', his introduction:

> Theatrically, it has long since ceased to be as much concerned with the personal problems of Swift, as with the seven deadly sins, their relative deadliness, and the curious phenomenon that it is our own particular sin that we find really unbearable in other people.[22]

In other terms, *The Dreaming Dust* had changed from a who-was-who mystery play to a morality play, or perhaps it is best viewed as a fusion of a psychological study with a tragedy in which a man's greatness is measured not only by his virtues but by his flaws. For Swift's faults (or sins) are but part of the whole man and every bit as important to his magnificent wholeness.

Technically *The Dreaming Dust* is a remarkable achievement. The action begins in 1835 in St. Patrick's Cathedral, Dublin, where a miracle play has just ended and the masked players – Pride, Anger, Envy, Gluttony, Avarice, Sloth, Lust – begin to discuss with the Dean the character of Jonathan Swift; and then come the flashbacks to Swift's own lifetime when the Seven Sins assume the costumes and characters of Swift's entourage, the Dean becoming Swift. Structurally, a play within a play. But Johnston, not content with that well-worn convention, brings back the Seven Sins at appropriate moments to comment on the action, thereby deliberately breaking up the dramatic flow and in effect 'distancing' it as it were in the best Brechtian manner. Alienation of character occurs throughout the play:

(PRIDE *walks down the forestage, and stands there for a moment in silence.*)

DEAN: (*following her, in some surprise*).
              What is wrong?

PRIDE: The rest of the scene makes no sense.

DEAN: Stella . . .

PRIDE: I'm not Stella.

DEAN: (*relaxing into* THE DEAN). Maybe not – but for the purposes of our . . .

PRIDE: I am not Stella in any sense of the word. I'm not even a credible woman. What woman in her senses would behave like this?

DEAN: (*nervously*) Your behaviour is perfectly reasonable. A very wonderful woman.

PRIDE: Perfectly reasonable!

DEAN: It has satisfied generations of biographers.

PRIDE: (*scornfully*) Swift's biographers – not hers . . .[23]

The Seven Sins have consequently a multiple role: they make up the seven characters of the masque of 1835; they provide the chorus to and commentators on the Swift-Stella-Vanessa story; they interrupt the story to allow the audience to think about what is happening before their eyes and to shatter the illusion; and, finally, as seven actors and actresses, they have to have their roles made credible to them. As Johnston rightly remarks: 'while biographers can be intimidated by authorities, playwrights are even more intimidated by the need to make sense that can be explained to a cast.'[24]

In *The Dreaming Dust* the complex, enigmatic and paradoxical life of Jonathan Swift is compacted into a play which with minor cuts makes a broadcast of an hour and a half, a public reading of about an hour and three-quarters, and (presumably) a stage play of about normal duration, that is to say, about two hours and a quarter. And it is also 'an exercise for actors and actresses with a flair for character, who seldom get enough opportunity to display their versatility in the course of one play.'[25]

Nikolai Leskov says in one of his letters: 'Writing to me is no liberal art, but a craft';[26] and in this all-purpose play Johnston displays his mastery of craftsmanship adapted both for broadcasting and stage performances. This is undoubtedly a superb feat of technique and proves – if proof were needed – that a drama composed for the stage can be readily adapted to radio and television; that the dramatic form in these three media can be interchangeable to a very great extent. But while Johnston's practice validates this theory, it is not a practice to be followed by lesser dramatists. Radio drama is one thing; television drama something else; and stage drama something else still. They have much in common; that is undeniable and all too obvious; but their differences are equally undeniable and sometimes not at all obvious. Each of the three media has its limitations and it would be an interesting experiment to experience *The Dreaming Dust* as a radio, television and stage play, and to balance the gains and losses of each medium (particularly if the same cast and director were used). This experiment, however, will hardly take place; if it did I have little doubt that the stage performance would be the most rewarding. And I agree with Johnston that its ideal presentation would be as an Interlude in Saint Patrick's Cathedral, Dublin.

The Dreaming Dust was given its première at the Gate in 1940; *Strange Occurrence on Ireland's Eye* opened at the Abbey in 1956; sixteen years had passed without a new Johnston play in Dublin, and many thought that he had long given up writing for the theatre, probably in despair. After all, his success, measured in financial terms, had been modest. Professional managements and film producers showed little interest in his work; his plays continued to be popular only with amateur companies, Little Theatres and Drama Leagues. And although this amateur interest was gratifying, Johnston still (naturally enough) cherished the hope that economic success would eventually come his way. Possibly *Strange Occurrence* was a bid for popular success. It was a play about a murder trial, which is a reasonably good recipe for success; as Johnston had been a lawyer authenticity would be assured; and the story itself was based on a well-known Irish court case which took place about the middle of the nineteenth century. All the characters were real people appearing under their own names; and for the purposes of the play the trial was updated to 1937. In view of all this it may seem surprising that *Strange Occurrence* has made so little impact after its initial run of seven weeks in the Abbey. But when *Strange Occurrence* is examined more closely surprise at its relative lack of commercial success becomes readily understandable.

Despite its conventional trappings this play is far from being a conventional commercial vehicle of rising suspense for the fate of an unfortunate hero. Johnston, as usual, has something important to say – here his message is that the Law and Justice are sometimes two entirely different things – and the accused 'hero' is more of an 'anti-hero' who plays an unimportant role throughout the action. If there is a 'hero' it is the middle-aged Chief Superintendent Henry J. Brownrigg of the Garda Siochana; if there is a 'heroine' – and Dr. Teresa Kenny earns that title for herself – she is far from being the pure and innocent young woman usually given that role: instead she is a young dispensary doctor who has had her illegitimate child aborted – something hardly likely to endear her to a Dublin audience. In addition Johnston explodes what Teresa calls the 'silly old Love Motive' and then, right at the end of the play, holds out this carrot tantalizingly for a brief moment before withdrawing it when the audience had been wooed towards accepting it. All in all, a dramatist who appears to be quite willing to give his customers what they want, and then changes his mind and leaves them instead with a feeling of frustration. With the church bells pealing out the advent of the New Year and Teresa's renunciation of her former lover as a 'cheap Narcissus', the way is made clear for the conventional happy ending. But no, that would be too much. Hero and heroine have to be content with sharing a drink rather than a bed.

Like *Strange Occurrence*, Johnston's next play *The Scythe and the Sunset* has an historical background. Produced in the Abbey in 1958, it is Johnston's most recent play and in his introduction he writes that it 'shows every sign of turning out to be one of those elusive phenomena – a play without a public. Apart from whatever intrinsic demerits it may have – and I must confess that I like it very much myself – an anti-melodrama on what has now become a sacred subject is distasteful to the sea-divided Gael, and is concerned with a matter that the Sassenach has chosen to forget.'[27] Because the matter is the Easter Rebellion of 1916 (perhaps a less sacred subject now than when this introduction was written) Johnston's play can hardly avoid comparison with O'Casey's masterpiece *The Plough and the Stars* whose title it parodies. But Johnston rightly discourages any such comparison, 'as it would be the act of an idiot to measure his play against such a yardstick as the *Plough*.'[28] So I shall refrain from comparing what are certainly two of the greatest plays to come out of Ireland, and concentrate on *The Scythe* which is by far the lesser known play; a play which has never received proper recognition, either inside or outside Ireland. Once again, this is hardly surprising; for Johnston takes all *les idées reçues* about the Easter Rising and turns them upside down, just as Shaw upturns all les idées reçues about war in *Arms and the Man*. The difference is of course that Shaw sets his comedy in Bulgaria in 1885 and debunks war in general while Johnston sets *Scythe* in a seedy restaurant opposite the General Post Office in Dublin during the Easter Rebellion. If *Arms and the Man* had been written a few years later than it was, and been set in Belgravia and played during the Boer War, its popularity might have been somewhat delayed. In Ireland 1916 is still the year when a terrible beauty was born, a beauty which went almost unnoticed in Dublin at the time and which Johnston himself, then a schoolboy, could hardly have been aware of. His memories of the rebels are of 'their charm, their civility, their doubts, and their fantastic misinformation of what was going on.'[29] And these schoolboy impressions have probably contributed a good deal to the antimelodramatic tone of his play.

Structurally *Scythe* is written in the conventional three acts; the time-duration is confined to Easter week from Monday to Friday; and the dialogue, for the most part, is the sharp witty pointed speech characteristic of *The Moon in the Yellow River*. Though realistic it is carefully cadenced to such a degree that a transition to verse form (as in the speeches of Endymion, the harmless lunatic) can be effected quite smoothly:

ROISIN:	Tell us what's happening to the rebels.
ENDYMION:	They, too, are doing their best to earn unpopularity Out near Ballsbridge, a few old men With wooden guns that will not fire Have been shot down.
ROISIN:	I don't believe it.
ENDYMION:	The issue's knit, And every fellow plays the other fellow's game. The Green makes murder and the Crown makes martyrs. And the great and unwashed Liberated loot. Victory's the crown, my friends, for him With the least power to engineer his own defeat. In short, the situation's normal.
PALLISER:	Marry, here's grace and a codpiece; That's a wise man and a fool.
ENDYMION:	(*staring at him coldly*) No, I will be the pattern of all patience;

> I will say nothing.
> I am Endymion – beloved of the Moon.
> I wear my cuffs upon my ankles.
> So in a world that's upside down.
> I walk on my hands.
> Good afternoon.[30]

Even the prosaic Volunteer Maginnis, the beloved of Roisin, is transported into the 'heroic' mode of verse after the experience of actual battle. But self-deflation soon enters his soul once he has recounted his part in the fighting:

MAGINNIS: . . . The gun was red-hot in me hands
              An' I cooled it off with oil from a tin a sardines.
              The smoke'd catch me by the troat
              And tear the eyeballs from me face.
              But it was them went back – not us . . .
              Back an' then on agin,
              Till all the terrace was a hell a flames
              And the lead was rain runnin' from the gutters.

ROISIN: Glory be to God, how could flash an' blood
              stand the like a that?

MAGINNIS: (*matter of fact*) I declare te God, I dunno. I
              wudden' reckernize meself.

And his non-recognition of himself expresses Johnston's own philosophy of Man's potentiality for perennial joy:

ROISIN: It would a put the heart across me. Were ye not
              scared te death?

MAGINNIS: At first I was scared, Roisin . . . scared that I was
              goin' to be afeared. D'you know. But when it all
              got goin', I forgot. An' then when I re-
              membered, I sez to meself, 'Begob, I forgot to
              be scared.' An' at that, God forgive me, I started
              to laugh, an' the most unholy joy came over me,
              for I knew then I was a soljer, an' nuttin' could
              ever take that from me. (*Pause*) Has no one got
              a Woodbine?[31]

174

Those sentiments are echoed by Johnston himself when under battle, as he relates in *Nine Rivers from Jordan*:

> . . . From somewhere in amongst those earthworks, somebody was shooting at us. There was no whine or whuffle because it was coming at short range, and beating the sound of the gun that was firing it. On the ground to both sides of the road little whirlpools of dust and metal rose and splashed about. Then I noticed that the others were no longer standing by my side, but were lying on their bellies in a sandscape . . . And as I stood there watching those ugly little particles spurting about my feet, I suddenly made the most surprising discovery of all – a most enlightening and exhilarating discovery. It was the fact that although I was apparently being shot at from comparatively short range with anti-personnel shells, it was not particularly scaring.
>
> I think that the most frightening thing about war is the fear of being frightened . . .'[32]

Self-realization through the defeat of fear is central to Johnston's philosophy. It recurs throughout his plays and receives possibly its most memorable statement at the end of *The Brazen Horn*:

> So, when Forgiveness reigns
> As the cut worm forgives the plough
> And the smith absolves his hammer,
>
> I cast forth from my mouth the fruit of the Tree of Peril
> And with it both Fear and Remorse
> And the mortal Ills that are bred of Evil . . .[33]

I have made this apparent digression to underline a point that should always be kept in mind when discussing Johnston's work. That is, that his work must be viewed as a whole; plays, autobiographies, radio and television, films, criticism, all express different facets of a many-sided man. And I am of the opinion that *The Scythe* reveals more of Johnston's vision of life than any other of his plays. It is about a revolt, and Johnston is a man unafraid of 'stepping unwisely into No-man's-land while it is still too early for comfort'. It is about Dublin, and Johnston is almost as obsessed by his native city as James Joyce was. It is about heroism and the challenge of death, and Johnston has deeply concerned himself with both. It is Johnston's most mature dramatic statement.

175

But *The Scythe* was written over twenty years ago, and no full-length play has followed it. Johnston, in the general introduction to the new edition of his work, states that it is fairly clear that he has not moved with the times as far as Dublin's Theatre is concerned, 'Indeed, having been somewhat out of step at both ends of my career, it might be questioned as to whether any of my plays can be classified as 'Irish' at all. Maybe they belong to some unclassified underworld in which problems are presented from which there is no solution and questions are asked that had better be ignored.'[34] Perhaps the best reply to this is that the plays certainly defy most efforts of classification; but it is impossible to deny that they are 'Irish' plays, and uniquely so. The Irish tradition in playwriting is wide enough to include Shaw as well as Synge, Beckett, as well as Yeats. And it is undoubtedly wide enough to include the extraordinarily stimulating and moving plays of Denis Johnston.

NOTES

1   London, 1954, p. 9.
2   'Preface,' *Collected Plays*, Vol. 1, London, 1960, p. 10.
3   Ibid., p. 11.
4   Ibid., p. 17.
5   Ibid., p. 18.
6   Ibid., p. 9.
7   *The Modern Theatre*, 1948, p. 62.
8   Ibid., p. 63.
9   'A Note on What Happened,' *The Dramatic Works*, Vol. I, Gerrards Cross, 1977, p. 76.
10 *The Art of the Dramatist*, London, 1970, p. 146.
11 'Foreword,' *The Moon in the Yellow River*, London, 1934, pp. 8–9.
12 *Collected Plays*, Vol. 2, p. 35.
13 Ibid., p. 55.
14 *Storm Song and A Bride for the Unicorn*, London, 1935, p. 157.
15 'Denis Johnston,' *The Bell*, Vol. XIII, No. 1 (Oct. 1946), p.13.
16 *One for the Grave*, London, 1968. p. 89.
17 *Storm Song and A Bride for the Unicorn*, p. 300.
18 *The Golden Cuckoo and Other Plays*, London, 1954, p. 129.
19 Denis Johnston, *The Brazen Horn*, Dublin, 1976, p. 189.
20 Ibid., p. 189.
21 *Wheels and Butterflies*, London, 1934, p. 7.
22 *Dramatic Works*, Vol. I, p. 252.
23 Ibid., p. 296.
24 Ibid., p. 252.
25 Ibid.
26 Quoted by Walter Benjamin, 'The Storyteller: Reflections on the Works of Nikolai Leskov,' *Illuminations*, New York, 1969, p. 92.

27 *Dramatic Works*, Vol. I, p. 86.
28 Ibid.
29 Ibid., p. 87.
30 Ibid., p. 123.
31 Ibid., pp. 153–54.
32 London, 1953, pp. 88–89.
33 Pp. 201–2.
34 *Dramatic Works*, Vol. I, p. 9.

THE PLAYS OF DENIS JOHNSTON*

ROGER McHUGH

One of the declared aims of the Irish Dramatic Movement was the production of international masterpieces. The failure to fulfil this caused trouble from the beginning. Joyce's pamphlet *The Day of the Rabblement* (1901) complained that the Irish Literary Theatre was 'surrendering to the trolls' by including no such plays during its third season. His phrase reveals the committed Ibsenite. Edward Martyn and George Moore were of the same way of thinking. Both had contributed Ibsenish plays to the first two seasons but they were weak plays; they would have done better to stage the masterpieces themselves. Both had severed their connection with the central movement by the time that the Abbey Theatre opened in 1904. The Fays advised Yeats along similar lines in 1907, shortly before they departed also. By that time it was clear that Yeats and Lady Gregory were determined to concentrate on the heroic play and the folk-comedy, which, said William Fay, 'would mean first stagnation and ultimately, when we found no more pots to boil and no more news to spread, death.'

The results were far-reaching; between 1906 and 1928 only about a dozen translations of international plays of merit had been produced by the Abbey Theatre Company. From 1918 to 1928 the Dublin Drama League tried to fill the gap but as the Abbey was available only on Sunday and Monday nights, their excellent and well-attended productions of the masters were decidedly restricted. Then in 1928 the Gate Theatre, with its opening of *Peer Gynt*, changed the Irish theatre scene for at least a decade.

Denis Johnston linked these events. He worked with the Dublin Drama League and his play, originally called 'Shadowdance', was rejected by the Abbey, with the words 'The Old Lady says 'No!' scribbled upon the envelope which contained it. So Johnston's play had a new title and the Gate Theatre gained a new playwright, almost its only Irish playwright of any lasting distinction. 'Lasting' is a relative term in the theatre, of course. Outside Ireland *The Moon*

* *The Dramatic Works of Denis Johnston* Volume 1 (Gerrards Cross: Colin Smythe and Toronto: Macmillan of Canada, 1977); Volume 2 (Gerrards Cross: Colin Smythe and Atlantic Highlands: Humanities Press, 1979).

in the Yellow River has publicly proved his most enduring play; and it is perhaps his best, if one can judge by the number of times it has been translated. Although it has a framing-theme about alienation between father and daughter, its real concern is the struggle between an elected government and an extreme group which claims to be carrying on the national tradition without compromise. To state the problem in local terms, had the extreme republicans a right to take up arms against the Irish Free State Government of 1922, and had the latter a right to execute republican prisoners in retaliation for acts of assassination? The summary murder of the extremist Blake by a Free State officer, Lanigan, which abruptly terminates the second act seems to reduce the issue to its simplest terms; but it really settles nothing. Blake had intended, on the most idealistic principles, to blow up a power-house (substitute Shannon Scheme) under Government protection. But Lanigan knows that he has signed his own death-warrant by the shooting, motivated by his feeling that 'inspiration always ends in trying to blow up something' and that the gunman is usually called in to protect something, whether it is an institution or a power-house. In this case his logic is upset by chance, for the power-house is blown up by accident when two eccentric scientists (also idealists) dispose of their last shell. So the product of science applied to industry is destroyed by the product of science applied to armament. This is not a 'problem play,' though it touches disturbingly on several problems which are still with us in Ireland and in the world at large. The reconciliation of the engineer, Dobelle, and his young daughter, the only happy solution which it presents, suggests that in man's unhappiness, unique in nature, lies both his greatest danger and his greatest glory, and that none of his problems can be settled without a consciousness of human values.

In Ireland *The Old Lady Says 'No!'* has proved more popular. It is a dream-play about Robert Emmet's romantic conception of Ireland, set against the social and political pretensions of Dublin society in the nineteen-twenties. Emmet's surrogate, called The Speaker, wanders through a motley maze of publicans, diehards, rugby players, hostesses, symbolic types (an Old Woman, a Blind Fiddler), who treat him as a hero, a murderer, an honoured guest, a seducer and a crackpot. Yet at the end of the play he is still an idealist, who echoes Shaw: 'Every dream is a prophecy: every jest an earnest in the womb of time' and who proclaims his faith in Dublin, 'strumpet city in the sunset', and concludes that he was right to go on. In 1929 this play's satire hit the prevailing mood of reaction against the drab political and social realities of the time. A recent revival showed that the play still has life but that it is somewhat dated. One puzzling thing about it is that in 1929 its author stated decisively that it is 'not an expressionist play and ought never to have been mistaken for one' but in his Introduction to the same volume he refers to its expressionism and to several expressionist writers to whom he is in debt. Strindberg is not among them and, as one who has always admired *The Old Lady*'s expressionistic technique, may I suggest that *The Dream Play* may have been an influence as well? Mr. Johnston may deny it but clearly, as his numerous revisions of these plays also suggest, he is capable of changing his mind.

'It will be fairly clear from the present collection that I have not moved with the times so far as Dublin's Theatre is concerned,' wrote Denis Johnston, retrospectively. 'Indeed, having been somewhat out of step at both ends of my career, it might well be questioned as to whether any of my plays can be classified as "Irish" at all.' The question seems to me to be irrelevant. Whatever the answer, certainly the bulk of his plays are concerned with Ireland. *The Scythe and the Sunset*, for example, is about the Easter Rising. Its title is obviously derived from *The Plough and the Stars* but it is very different from O'Casey's masterpiece; it does not take an anti-heroic or anti-war stance; its women are not victims but killers; much of it consists of logical argument between a Republican leader and an Irish officer in the British Army, who is his prisoner. The former, Commandant Tetley, knows that the Rising has failed but foresees that his execution will ensure its success; Captain Palliser wishes to save him by testifying at his trial and by telling a few lies in his defence. When Tetley turns down his offer and goes out of a burning building to surrender, Palliser by choice remains in it, heroically playing Ravel as the curtain falls. This play deserves more attention than it has received; it has some excellent minor characters and the hostility/affinity of the two soldiers is interesting, but the ending needs revision, possibly excision; for Palliser's death is a bit of inept melodrama under the circumstances.

The Dreaming Dust (once entitled *Weep for the Cyclops*) was first produced by Edwards and MacLiammóir in 1940. In its revised form it has been considerably altered, probably for the best. The triangle of Swift, Stella and Vanessa presents an enigma that has never been resolved by scholars, who have concluded, on somewhat slender grounds, either that Swift was secretly married to Stella (Esther Johnson) and broke the heart of Vanessa (Esther van Homrigh) rather than tell her so; or that he knew that he was mad and avoided intimacy with either of them, since he refused to pass insanity on to his children. Lord Longford's play, *Yahoo*, as far as I remember, was based upon the first theory, Yeats's *The Words Upon the Window Pane* upon the second. Denis Johnston researched the material very thoroughly and came up with the theory that Swift and Stella were related by blood through Sir William Temple, who was certainly Stella's father and may have been the half-brother of Swift who was ostensibly a posthumous child.

Although Johnston's theory is not conclusive, it fills in more of the gaps than any other. His play, which is presented in a manner reminiscent of Pirandello's *Six Characters in Search of an Author*, portrays a Swift who knows that he is Stella's half-uncle, that the penalty for incest is death, that he cannot marry Stella; nor can he marry Vanessa without giving Stella the reputation of a discarded mistress or without revealing the whole truth. The play is set in Saint Patrick's Cathedral, near the graves of Swift and Stella, Faulkiner's bust of the Dean and Swift's magnificent epitaph. It is one of Dublin's most dramatic places; in my opinion *The Dreaming Dust* does it justice. Has it ever been played there? It is an obvious choice for a Dublin Theatre Festival.

A Bride for the Unicorn and *The Golden Cuckoo* are best described as fantasies. The former is a rather undergraduate effort based on the story of Jason's Quest, which in this case is to solve the riddle of woman's mystery. *The Golden Cuckoo* is chiefly a comedy about a Mr. Dotheright, who symbolically breaks the window of a post-office and declares himself a one-man Republic; it really has a serious theme, the duty of the individual to oppose the tyrannies of democracy, a theme which in these days when dockers, postal workers and bank clerks can legally sabotage the workings of democracy itself, seems decidedly topical. Like most good fantasies, including Strindberg's, this play has a zany quality which makes people laugh but then makes them think hard about some of the zany qualities of modern civilisation and of some contemporary leaders. Mr. Johnston continually seems to hover between the idealist, the moralist and the satirist.

The moralist is predominant in *Nine Rivers from Jordan,* an operatic libretto based upon his autobiographical book about his experiences in World War II and the moral problems they raise. It is about Don Hanwell, a British soldier who becomes a pacifist and allows Otto Suder, a Nazi prisoner, to escape. When an allegorical court decides that Suder shall bear all mankind's guilt for the atrocities committed at a prison-camp where he was a guard, and deserves death, Don takes a Mills bomb and sets off to find him and kill him. He does capture him but Suder captures the bomb, with which he accidentally kills himself. The moral, according to Mr. Johnston's synopsis, is 'that though we must accept all of life, both good and bad, we ourselves have the personal responsibility for making the choice between right and wrong and, though we are all "dirty", we are not all damned.' This will doubtless be a great consolation to the victims of Buchenwald, Hiroshima, Vietnam, Arab-Israel conflicts and any other wars that have happened along since! The libretto will need very good music.

Ireland's epic, *The Táin*, has had great attraction for creative artists from Ferguson, to go no further back, to Thomas Kinsella. Johnston has written *Táin Bo Cuailgne*, a pageant, printed for the first time in the second volume of his *Dramatic Works*. This pageant keeps mainly to the established story-line, preserves its most dramatic incidents and makes excellent use of crowd, sound and visual effects. Fortunately *The Táin* has no moral whatever.

The idealist and the satirist perhaps are two sides of the same coin, impossible to distinguish when Denis Johnston spins it, and as liable to turn up heads as harps. His idealism about Ireland is often signposted with satirical indirections which, pointing towards our follies, are often mistaken for mere whipping-posts or even more mistakenly, for notice-boards on which are posted proclamations about the shortcomings of the natives. Shaw once asked a relevant question: who is Ireland that her good writers should not satirise her? It is particularly relevant in view of the fact that Johnston once sat at Shaw's feet, listening to his advice and then, he says, did the exact opposite. Despite this assurance – perhaps because of it – I venture to think that Johnston carries on two Shavian traditions in most of his plays: one is that of the argument, which he uses in a less extended form than Shaw; Blake and Lanigan, Tetley and Palliser, even Dotheright and his counsellors state their opposing viewpoints with Shavian clarity and something of Shavian wit. Another is the Shavian trick of inflating a conventional or institutional absurdity until it blows itself up. It is interesting to see how often the law is the victim; in the fantasies, in *Nine Rivers from Jordan,* and in *Strange*

Occurrence on Ireland's Eye, where it brays most realistically.

Finally, Denis Johnston's talent in the theatre, although sometimes diffuse, was always remarkable; he had a courage in experiment that resulted in a great variety of theatrical styles. If he was often out of step with Dublin Theatre twenty or more years ago, that was a bad thing for Dublin Theatre; for, during that period, when the Abbey was in the doldrums and the Gate suffered from the results of the 'Longford split,' what Ireland needed most was good directors. It did not get them, for Edwards and MacLiammóir trained no successors. In general Johnston's plays, like Continental masterpieces, would have forced their development.

DEAR DENIS!

CYRIL CUSACK

Yes, well, let me think . . .

He is my neighbour (I should be caring) and, furthermore, a neighbourly neighbour (I should be more caring), but also closely neighbouring: therefore should I be careful?

The Johnstons live just around the corner from me, in one of a row of quiet, tall, pale-faced houses on Sorrento Terrace, Dalkey. Sorrento, Vico, Nerano, Milano, Padua – where do all those names come from? Nostalgic recollections of the Grand Tour perhaps. The long windows look back dreamily over sea, along a sandy shoreline towards Wicklow hills – the Silver Spears, the Golden Spears – cone-shaped, in sea-misted mornings distantly resembling a Japanese landscape. Dalkey is a coastal townland ascending in slow retreat some ten miles from the Irish capital. A proud and formidable community, as yet it eludes the prodding fingers of the city speculator. Possessively it commemorates Dowland, the poet someways in communion with Will Shakespeare; Shaw, living in Torca Cottage, the young visionary citing the Wicklow Hills as 'eternal' against the passing materiality of man; O Faolain, your gimlet-eyeing Cork observer, uneasily perched up high on the Vico; Hugh Leonard, to-day Ireland's most successful playwright, in his own lighthouse down by the harbour casting a clear yet compassionate eye around on the contemporary scene. It is apt that Johnston should take his place, himself betimes an inferno of white-hot creativity, amongst these lively spirits of past and present.

While now only scratching and snatching at shreds of memory, on reflection I surprise myself that I have held our acquaintance, almost simultaneously intimate and remote, for close on a half-century. So should I like to think of my neighbour, not as a mere personality, the popular fabrication much cultivated in Ireland both as a home comfort and a tourist attraction, but as that disappearing rarity, a person. To see Johnston as a person is to point towards his value as an artist, as part of our theatre heritage; in the person one might espy the essence of his work as a playwright.

Set down in the records as British, he should rather be described as Irish – Irish of the North. The tinge of dialect is in the voice, a sudden directness of expression, a disconcerting contrariness in tone. For me, always there was – still is – something of the unexpected in his appearances. I first became aware of Johnston, an El Greco-like figure gracing it over me, in the Gate Theatre. Behind me I heard the voice, icy-sweet: 'Did you write that?' it said, sharply.

In his hand he held a copy of the National University magazine, *Cothrom na Féinne*, which – the call to arms and honour of the ancient Fianna – may be translated as 'Fair Play'. My contribution, with 'Pages from a Mad Student's Diary' – an attempted parody of Gogol's *Diary of a Madman* – had twisted in a few quotes and some near-plagiarisms from Machiavelli and Victor Hugo. I could not be certain as to whether the speaker was impressed or appalled. Here, as ever since, I could take it either way. Thus began a quiet, if distant, nevertheless constant relationship in the experience of professional theatre.

Johnston spilled out a generous flow of plays for the Dublin Gate Theatre. There was, of course, *The Old Lady Says 'No!'*, a title popularly supposed to have derived from Lady Gregory's rejection of the play for the Abbey Theatre. This had its benediction from the deep glow and glamour of MacLiammóir's rendering of the Actor-cum-Robert Emmet character at the core of the play ('Glamour' is the particular credit the playwright accords this actor), on top of its baptism from the vigour of Hilton Edwards' highly professional production, along with an almost idolatrous devotion from the rest of the cast. Came *Storm Song* and, with a bubble of schoolboy prankishness but out of a maelstrom of anguish and anger, *A Bride for the Unicorn*. The Abbey found room at last for his adaptation of a play by Ernst Toller, performed at that theatre in 1936 under the title of *Blind Man's Buff*. More than any other Irish playwright, Johnston was open to the influence of the European theatre, to the genre of drama then operating on the Continent, and for this he found a ready venue and vehicle in the Dublin Gate, of which he was now a director.

Johnston's plays, in the theatre of his time, produced a sense of adventure; they provided for the actor opportunity for creating theatrical excitement. But also, aside from the artist's sometimes many-coloured wash of equivocation – in Ireland part of the several-sided, double-edged backward thrust of the Anglo-Irish in retreat from the charge of assaulting nouveau Gaeldom – did I detect a brush of mischievous, even malicious humour of the brand described in those English schoolboy magazines – as the jape!

Denis – for now, as my neighbour, so do I speak of him – sharp-visaged, sharp-witted of the North, incapable of deceit, always with an eye to adventure, always ready to be amused, now stepping firmly beyond the seven ages of man he has held fast to the spirit of youth. I sense that early presence still, looming, with a little irony but by no means in mockery, over my juvenile Republicanism; still I regard him as Senior Boy.

Internationally his most successful play, *The Moon in the Yellow River* – like O'Casey, he had a turn for titles – even this, in my opinion, sprang from a youthful mind well disposed towards his country but at a crossroads between idealism and affectionate derision.

What next –? Ah, yes – entering the cinematic field I find myself with Denis in the Dublin Mountains directing a film version of Frank O'Connor's great story, *Guests of the Nation*, a compassionate study of a relationship growing in warmth between the insurgents and their British prisoners, the Tommy played by the Irish comedian, Barry Fitzgerald. Fortunately, it was a silent film. Alas, apart from the happy direction, what do I remember most of that? Sean Brady, one of the old brigade, deftly twirling a rifle with one hand as we were shown drilling in Rocky Valley; and later, myself, as the Kevin Barry figure, feeding crumbs to a bird through the bars of a cell-window in Kilmainham Jail.

Some months afterwards I had a telephone-call to the Peacock Theatre – Denis! Could he have a showing there of his *Guests of the Nation*? Well, why not! As successor to MacLiammóir I had just concluded a season of plays in Gaelic – mostly translation from the French – on the stage of this little theatre, sister of the Abbey, and now, the season over, quite penniless, I shared with Brady one of the dressing-rooms, where at night we slept on the floor. During the day the ballerina Ninette de Valois had her little cygnets thumping around in an adjoining room, but at evening the theatre itself was free. Most certainly my director should be accommodated for the showing of his film! And so with Denis I sat in state to view the result of our mountainy labours. Even in retrospect I can say that the film had verisimilitude, better by Irish miles than Hitchcock's eccentric version of O'Casey's *Juno and the Paycock*, and by many miles more the lamentable attempts at filming Synge.

Came a brief interlude in television – Denis, with perfect aplomb directing Sheridan's frenetic pantomimic trifle, *St. Patrick's Day;*

Dear Denis!

or, The Scheming Lieutenant. In those pioneering days with the
B.B.C. at Alexandra Palace, technically it must have taxed his
ingenuity to the utmost, but, accepted by that austere corporation as
an authority, Denis directed with a calm and gentle precision.

So too in the theatre; and in those late 'thirties crescendoing
towards the holocaust, with a production of O'Neill's *Ah,
Wilderness!* under the aegis of Edward, Earl of Longford, moving
successfully from the Gate over to London's Westminster Theatre
and thence to the Ambassadors, I remember the light and delicate
touch weaving like a zephyr amongst the actors. Invited, Shaw
came to see the play – I caught sight of the great white head in the
stalls – and he announced afterwards that he 'never went to sleep
once!'

When was it that Johnston went almost obsessively searching into
the enigma of Swift with his ladies, Stella and Vanessa? About now
the world was splintering into war. A million marital barques were
listing towards the rocks. Perhaps, with those sad shadows lingering
still in St. Patrick's Cathedral, straining, through the sighs and
whispers he might hear some answer to man's dilemma, to his own,
and a play emerges out of the dreaming dust and bones, out of the
savage indignation of the gloomy Dean.

Soon bombs were falling on London. Johnston's sally into
Churchill's war entourage will, I'm sure, be dealt with elsewhere.
What I remember best of him from that time is the quiet concern for
Betty, now his wife in the home overlooking peaceful Killiney Bay.
I, a neutral, having volunteered for the Irish Army, was about to be
dispatched back to Ireland. Would I take Betty with me? Standing
in that house at Mill Hill, I waited. But who has authority over a
woman's deep affections? I returned to Ireland alone.

After the long emptying-out of war, out of the nightmare, almost
somnambulistically we straggled back on to our various stages. Into
the fifties now, I invited Denis to direct his play, *The Golden
Cuckoo*, at the Gaiety Theatre, Dublin, to my mind, with the
Christ-like figure of Dotheright (an actual name, pronounced
'Duthery'), not the Man of Sorrow but a man of joy, pitting an
inspired innocence against the forces of darkness, a most significant
contribution to the theatre of that time. Critics were baffled with the
Golden Cuckoo's egg, before the final curtain, dropping from
the 'flies', from Above, as it were, and smashing on to the head of the
Golden Calf – the jape again! But there, through the strangeness,
the antics of Dotheright moves the questing spirit of the author,

187

with a smoulder – something of the Dean's *indignatio* – ready to flame out upon the Father of Lies.

I have tried to treat of Denis Johnston, the person, the person revealing but also at times concealing the playwright. To take part in that production of *The Golden Cuckoo* I had brought from Belfast the actor-playwright, Joseph Tomelty. Tomelty had not long before been involved in a dreadful car accident, resulting in long hospitalization. With the start of rehearsals it was easy to see that as yet he had no means recovered. A member of the cast, Niall Maginnis, remarked that, seeming to have lost a sense of direction on the stage, Tomelty appeared to be punch-drunk. What on earth should we do? My thought, as actor-manager, was to replace him. But no – it was decided, on the author's suggestion and with the agreement of the cast, that we should 'nurse' the actor through his performance for the run of the play. And there we see the genuine humanity of the person taking precedence over the playwright. Nevertheless, the play presents that very person.

But gossip prattles up and down and around Dublin still; reputations sway and fall; only genius may survive, perhaps to deal out fearful retribution. Local rumour whispers with a flash of jokey malice – never one of your anti-clerical Irish, that Johnston, surrendering to the riddle, attends service at St. Patrick's Cathedral, and the tattler tells of a Johnston theory that the orgasm is a foretaste of heavenly bliss – and so on.

On one of my neighbouring visits recently, amidst chatter about theatre and acting, looking down at me with that curious look of appraisal – 'You're a natural, of course!', he said. Was it a tilt or a compliment? Again, as Betty and I joined in a minuet of reminiscence, which took in relations in the theatre, including Brefni O'Rorke, my stepfather, suddenly the lofty figure leaning towards me, eyes gleaming, with a wide grin, said: 'At lunch you never mentioned Brefni once!' Still the elusive intonation, the ambiguous note – was it a sardonic compliment or meant in affectionate reproach?

Yes, well, let me think.

Johnston is a man of war and peace, a man both proud and humble, essentially a *person*, and that to-day you might say, is to be a man of genius – my neighbour, dear Denis!

DENIS JOHNSTON'S SPIRITUAL QUEST

HAROLD FERRAR

I first met Denis Johnston fifteen years ago, when he was a professor of drama at Smith College in Massachusetts and I was a graduate student completing a dissertation on his plays. I had written to Johnston asking if I could visit him and look over his memorabilia. His answer immediately endeared him to me. 'I consider myself very much alive,' he wrote, 'and I don't have any memorabilia. But you're welcome to examine my clippings and scrapbooks.'

I arrived in Northampton with a cumbersome, ancient tape recorder, a great deal of eagerness and a marked obliviousness to the obvious irony of the situation. I was a naive graduate student about to interview a renowned writer so that I could explain him to the world. My life had been an academic one, spent mainly in university libraries; his life had been active – he had known civil war, world war and a full lifetime of creativity and thought. It was so typical of Denis Johnston that he welcomed me with utmost graciousness, and that I never felt for a second that we were meeting on any but the common ground of our humanness. In professorial tweeds, he was warm, witty, alert, energetic, utterly honest, keenly intelligent, and master of timing the telling of an anecdote or opening up a new angle of vision. I was in the presence of a happy, compassionate man.

I spent about a week in scholarly bliss with a goldmine of materials and with breaks always at the right moment when Mrs. Johnston (the Irish actress Betty Chancellor) would bring refreshments and we would sit around discussing their theatrical experiences. How it brought to life the archives I was exploring! And how different from the bitterness, anger and disappointment one so often associates with Irish writing. I realize now, thinking back, that much of what I saw and felt that week were also the dominant qualities of Denis Johnston's work. I don't think of him as an angry writer. One calls to mind Yeats's insistence that greatness in Ireland goes hand in hand with bitterness or Synge's description of the 'whole passionate rage' of Irishness. Johnston's first play, *The Old Lady Says 'No!'* (1929), does have its fair share of disillusion and hopelessness. But, as Johnston said in an interview a few years

189

ago, 'I know . . . that since writing *The Old Lady* I have had no further complexes or heart-burnings about Ireland or her damn politics . . . because, in that play, I had given public expression to all I had to say on that subject.' Johnston's two subsequent Irish history plays, *The Moon in the Yellow River* and *The Scythe and the Sunset*, stand as incontestable proof that he hadn't exhausted his involvement with Ireland and her 'damn politics' in *The Old Lady*. But he did vent much of his native son's spleen in that early work. Johnston doesn't suffer from what Brecht calls 'a long rage . . . a big anger.' He strikes me above all as a man at home in the world, walking the earth with confidence that he belongs here. You wouldn't include him among the modern *angst* writers. He has tremendous detachment; so that his plays don't insist that anything has gone wrong with the world in some irredeemable way.

I don't mean to suggest that Johnston avoids political reality; on the contrary, his work and life confront it unflinchingly. He has personally been in the middle of the agony of contemporary history, and that agony is in the middle of his plays. Without this confrontation, his work would be negligible. What's important, however, is that in the face of devastation he maintains and reaffirms the joyous acceptance of life that is at the root of his vision. The horror is faced, known, survived and transcended, not denied. Rather, it is a factor that is incorporated into a mature spirituality that acknowledges and rejoices in the universe as it is.

Denis Johnston's best work is characterized by compassionate detachment, by fairness and a long view. Interestingly, with one exception his work is grounded in fact, in events that have really happened. His writing is pervaded by objectivity, decency, integrity and a steady impulse towards clarity. One feels safe in the worlds of his best plays, trustful that he will wrest from his interpretations of history a balanced, humane view without sacrificing artistic or factual complexity. Johnston writes to understand more, not to purge his private nightmares or his personal demons. He is a reflective writer. I felt, as I worked in his home and sometimes talked with him about his grandchildren or his daughter's budding career as a novelist, that he didn't write to survive, but to make sense. It's a quality in his work that I admire and enjoy; it helps us all hold on to the essential sanity of life beyond the tragedy and irony of history.

One thing that continues to intrigue me is Johnston's habit of not considering his work as finished – of not treating it as complete for eternity. Much to the scholar's consternation, Johnston periodically changes his plays, and particularly the endings ('finalities' he calls them). If he sees differently over time, he simply makes changes to accord with his new vision. His autobiography, *Nine Rivers from Jordan*, has two different endings; *The Moon in the Yellow River* has several conclusions; *A Bride for the Unicorn* is still, according to Johnston, a play he's working on nearly half a century after its première; and he just recently revised the ending of *The Scythe and the Sunset* eighteen years after its first production. It's possible, though, instead of considering these changes as evidence of uncertainty (as several commentators have), that we can see them as representing, very simply, a free attitude towards art. Nothing is so perfect or so sacred that it must exist for all time in unaltered form.

Actually, this iconoclastic view is in accord with one of Johnston's important philosophical tenets. He is fascinated by the nature of time and posits multiple time dimensions. We live in a linear past, present, future time scheme but we simultaneously exist as witnesses to this linear scheme. He asks: How could we even perceive this linearity if we weren't outside it or beyond it in some way? Thus, only in linear time, which is a very limited and incomplete approach to the nature of time, does an event have a fixed beginning, a conclusive end or an unalterable meaning. However, Johnston's philosophy of time does not completely explain his organic and open view of the artistic process. I see the alterations and revisions of his work as expressions of his own deepening understanding of life. It's wonderful that as Johnston sees more deeply and truly, he feels the freedom to alter his work and not to view it as finished and inviolable.

Johnston is nearly eighty and death is clearly a more paramount consideration now than it was twenty years ago when he first wrote *The Scythe and the Sunset*. So, a few years ago, in preparation for a new production of the play, he changed the original ending. One of the main characters, who originally elects to die rather than participate in a series of events he considers evil, decides in the new version to live. The change reflects Johnston's changing view of people's behaviour in the face of death. Underlying this alteration lies a persistent attempt on Johnston's part to be true to his own understanding of human nature.*

* It has recently come to my attention that Johnston has dropped this revised ending in favour of the original ending. It remains to be seen which ending will ultimately stand, but I personally think the original ending has more power in the context of the historical themes of the play, and I'm glad Johnston has returned to it.

191

Another way of thinking about Johnston's habit of changing plays, and particularly endings, is that instead of writing a new play (say *The Tempest* ten years after *Hamlet*) to express personal change, he rewrites *Hamlet*. This tendency leaves him vulnerable to the accusation that he lacks a firm philosophy (what is the value, anyway, of a 'firm' philosophy unless that philosophy is utterly true?). Actually, his 'fiddling', as he puts it, is to me an exciting artistic outlook. At the very least, this fiddling helps one to take the business of criticism with a healthy grain of salt.

There is still another way to look at this issue of changes. One of Johnston's main subjects is modern history and the violence of our times. He asks, in effect, who can make sense of human destiny in the twentieth century? How often has it been called 'a madhouse'? 'hell on earth'? 'an absurd joke'? Who can be sure of what any of it means? To write an immutable ending, especially to plays that examine historical events, is to say 'this is what it means.' Even in an early work like *The Moon in the Yellow River* (1931) there are alternative endings because there is a sense that we don't know the final score; we don't understand history. Who can explain *why* the holocaust happened? All you can know are your own reactions, and these change over time. Johnston always takes the long perspective; it's characteristic that he wrote about Easter, 1916 (so vividly!) forty-two years after it happened and then eventually changed his conclusions (to The *Scythe and the Sunset*, 1958) some years later. Johnston likes to stand back and see how things shift over time, how perspectives broaden. He's always aware that 'objective reality' is a matter of inquiry, not just of public record. Surely, events *happen*, but even while they're happening they are subject to varying interpretations. An Irish rebel and a British conservative would see the Easter rebellion rather differently. Perhaps there is a certain diminution of intensity in the 'long perspective,' but there is no reduction of truth. There is great value in stepping back from the drama and melodramatics of an event and absorbing the shadings and ambiguities. Time modifies our understandings, and even, on occasion, reverses them.

This ability to step back and reflect and to know the temporariness of conclusions is a dominant quality of Denis Johnston's talent. He is a writer with great detachment. We tend to think that a twentieth century writer, to be meaningful and authentic, cannot be detached, but has to be *angst*-drenched and shattered by the awfulness of human suffering. Johnston, however, works from a core of awareness that lends measured acceptance to passing events; he doesn't feel responsible for history, but witnesses its play. Johnston is not an engaged activist. He is full of understanding for his characters, whatever side they're on. It's not a matter of simple-minded evasion of issues of right and wrong, but a very clear-headed awareness that there can be two wrongs in any given situation, or two rights, or that what's wrong at one point in time may be right later on. This balanced conviction makes for great compassion and it's very life-enhancing.

* * *

Denis Johnston isn't the only one who changes his mind when he looks at his material from a new vantage point. My appreciation of Johnston has also changed over the years. When I first began to read him seriously, I was lost in admiration for his irony, his urbanity, his literary and dramatic complexity and mostly for his profoundly beautiful grasp of Ireland's contemporary history. I was immensely impressed with his contribution to Irish drama and his expansion of the possibilities of the Irish history play. I relished his relentless *exposé* of melodrama and his commitment to the investigation of the complexity of the historical process. All of these qualities were embodied in ultra-modern experimental theatrical forms that I found exciting. Now, some fifteen years later, all of these still remain major accomplishments to me. But, as I continue to ponder, teach and write about Johnston's plays, I find myself involved increasingly with another dimension: the spiritual inquiry which is at the centre of his vision. Just as surely as he is a tireless inquirer into the arena of Irish events and their impact on the nation and its people, he is also unceasingly concerned with the basic questions that underlie history, the spiritual questions.

Johnston's third play, *A Bride for the Unicorn* (1933), is the first one in which he overtly probes these underlying questions in a context beyond Irish history. *Unicorn* is Johnston's most densely philosophical play; the central issue is how to cope with death. As Johnston said once to an interviewer, 'I'm inclined to speculate about death.' The guiding idea of this play is that our fear of death, if looked at logically in terms of the rhythm and basic choices of life, is really an illusion. Everything we do, every choice we make to attain our maturity or fulfil our desires, denies the mind's fear of death. Each voluntary step we take to fulfil ourselves is literally a step towards death. When we get up from all fours to walk, when we

193

marry, when we work and put funds aside for retirement – always there is an implicit acceptance of death as the goal. If Johnston persistently refuses in his plays to tell us what's right and wrong, he does at least comfort our minds, telling us not to be afraid of death because we're really running after our death as we live. Johnston makes an interesting point about shaping the form of a play with such an esoteric theme: 'I was trying to do something that I still don't believe is possible on stage –. . . to deal with an idea that is not already – consciously or subconsciously – in the mind of an audience. In this case it was that the fear of death is an illusion and does not really exist at all.' It is not like writing a play about unhappiness, or the anguish of change, or the loss of love – experiences and feelings familiar to any audience. Rather, it is a kind of hyper-drama of ideas – to make the audience ponder something previously not in their mental vocabularies – and to push them to a logical conclusion based on evidence. Johnston's compassion is nowhere more evident than in this play; not only, as usual, for his characters, but for us as well. He helps us to ease our anguish about death by dissolving its hold on our minds. In teaching us how to die fearlessly, he actually presents an ethic of how to live fully and intensely at every moment; the fear of death once dead, we are free to truly live.

In addition to Johnston's bountiful respect for the role of intelligence in happiness, there is in the play a spiritual dimension that transcends the limits of reason. For, in the last analysis, logical solace is necessary but not sufficient. It cannot predictably calm or wipe out terrors in the night. The only true comfort against the fear of death is an unshakeable awareness of immortality. The play raises some fascinating possibilities along these lines. One way to attain awareness of immortality is through perfect fulfillment in life. The main character's initial experience in *Unicorn* awakens him to the reality of perfection as inner experience. For a moment, he is immersed in a state of being and consciousness that satisfies all desire. This momentary perfection is so powerful that he continuously yearns, throughout his life, to recapture and dwell in it again. The experience, originally a sensual one, is far more than that. It is a revelation of the absolute unity of body and spirit, a moment of timeless oneness in a realm of consciousness beyond logic; in short, a 'visionary gleam' which motivates a lifelong quest. This overwhelming experience, deep enough to shape a lifetime, is apparently a gift of grace, of divine dispensation.

The play begins with a kind of 'prologue in heaven', or at any rate in an infinite space of timelessness and ominiscience. There is a supernatural figure, a deity of sorts, who initiates the action in ordinary time and who grants the protagonist John Foss the extraordinary moment of completion. This character reappears periodically as a guide and moves John through his mundane life to maturity and ultimately to the ripeness of re-discovery. The physical needs of the dramatic medium demand that the guide be embodied in human form and separate from the main character. But what this guru-like guide suggests is that within us and inseparable from us there is a pure unchanging awareness of our own nature as consciousness. The guide, who sets the play in motion with a 'yogi clock' (a symbol of the realm of conscious awareness beyond ordinary linear time) and who knows John's entire destiny in advance, suggests that we exist not only on a physical plane in linear time but that we also exist in a state of consciousness from which we witness our existence on the physical plane as it unfolds in ordinary time. In the play, this witness state is called the Ultimate Observer. Johnston's Ultimate Observer is virtually identical to what in Indian philosophy is called the *atman*, the Self which is the permanent consciousness that underlies all change, which experiences and is the knower of all that which changes. The goal of Indian philosophy (or Yoga) is the unbroken immersion of the limited mind in unlimited consciousness, the merger of the individual self with the absolute. It is precisely this state of continuous merging that John seeks after he has been awakened to its existence. Although he is granted a revelation of his own true nature, after he returns to ordinary life he seeks to recapture the experience outside himself in outer subjects. John is like the musk deer who exhausts himself chasing an exquisite fragrance on the wind and finally collapses only to discover that the fragrance he has so desperately pursued emanates from his own navel.

John's 'initiation' is the first step of his coming to know the truth of his own immortality. Throughout his life he suffers because of his ignorance of that truth. In the end, he attains the desired liberation from his limited concept of his own nature. The play ostensibly traces John's life through its seven ages; but the real action is his inner journey back to the awareness of what was always there.

The mind's fear of death can only be finally conquered by union with the witness; the only enduring solace lies in absorption into changeless consciousness. As John learns, external gratification is fleeting and partial. Metaphorically, his quest is everyone's search for the knowledge that releases us from suffering. It takes John a lifetime to discover the key to release. As Lord Krishna says in the Sanskrit scriptural epic, the *Bhagavad Gita*, 'The world outside is constantly changing, nothing lasts. If you live continually with external things, your life will be sorrowful. Therefore you must discover the space within and begin to live there . . . One who lives there does not know misery or sorrow.' We contain within us all the knowledge that we ever need to understand the purpose of our lives; we already contain our own immortality in the form of the Ultimate Observer, the Witness. We live our lives, Johnston suggests and Eastern scriptures insist, on two levels at once. One level consists of daily activity and is measured by linear time; it is here that mental activity predominates and suffering abounds. On the second level, a level of timeless consciousness, we register our daily lives, we witness our suffering but we are, in fact, free from that suffering. On this second level we are like a movie camera which may record a painful scene but is not itself in pain. When we are able, as we move through the daily level, to merge with the Witness or the timeless level, we become detached from our suffering. Daily events take on an evenness and we live in a full-ness, desirelessness and equanimity like that which John knows initially for a night, yearns for during his lifetime and eventually recaptures.

As I read the play now, I see that the crucial episode is not the final acceptance of death (which I originally thought was paramount) but rather the awakening at the beginning to the knowledge that perfection and utter fulfilment are not some Edenic fantasy but are actual realities that reside always in us quite simply as our own true nature. John glimpsed, in that awakening, that true happiness and fearlessness do not come from the achievement of impossible dreams but that they are available to us at any moment when we recognize the essence of our being, when we dive past personal histories and mentally-constructed value systems to the inner realm of pure consciousness. We have all experienced the merging of the mind in the absolute; we have all known, at least for a moment, our own perfection. Perhaps we have experienced this merging during instants of love, creativity or inspiration: during periods of oneness with nature; during moments of unselfconscious joy in some activity like playing with a child; during spontaneous responses to great art. *Unicorn* begins with an act of grace that leaves the hero yearning for a continuous experience of perfection and which leaves him dissatisfied with less. The action of the play is not aimed at the accomplishment of an external goal but at the removal of obstacles to the recognition of the unchanging inner truth.

Separation from the Witness, from an ongoing fusion of the mind with consciousness, causes the mind to desire that union and to be discontent with anything less, and therefore to suffer. There is plenty of suffering in *A Bride for the Unicorn* – loneliness, disappointment, desolation, greed, anger, competition, violence – it comes in many forms. Suffering is so pervasive in the play that we are inevitably led to contemplate its very nature and its place in the scheme of things, particularly the suffering that stems from fear of death. What Johnston implies is that suffering is not ineradicably built into the nature of existence, but that it is conquerable, certainly on an individual basis. We *can* overcome the fear of death. This suggests that suffering is a mental attitude toward experience, a creation of the mind. Two people in the same situation might react very differently. For example, one person faced with a terminal illness might become severely despondent or suicidal; another might decide to fulfil some long-held dream, like travelling. There is no suffering necessarily inherent in the situation. Often suffering depends upon deeply-etched mental concepts. King Lear, for instance, believes that children should show overt gratitude to parents. He holds a *concept* of filial obligation and when it isn't satisfied he suffers intensely. The source of all emotional suffering is the mind's reaction to failed expectations – expectations, of course, of its own making. Suffering is the result of a vicious cycle of the mind, a cycle that can be broken.

Implicit in the action of *Unicorn* is the understanding that the union of the mind with the Witness, of the individual ego with universal consciousness, is itself the transcendence of suffering. John actually exists in this blissful state for one night; it colours the rest of his life. Subsequently, while he seems to suffer from the dissatisfactions of imperfect relationship, what he really yearns for is this oneness. He suffers from separation from the Ultimate Observer; next to that oneness, ordinary life seems paltry and joyless. What John really quests for, as he searches for his 'lost bride', is an inner state of non-separateness. His search is reminiscent of the path of *bhakti yoga* in which the *bhakta* loves the Divine with such singleness of purpose that separateness is agony.

197

Bhakti is not the exclusive possession of Indian tradition. The Christian poet George Barker describes it as:

Love that sorrows
In separation, the desire in the heart of hearts
To come home to you.

The divine beloved is an exterior form of the indwelling Witness, the Self, the 'heart of hearts' that is journey's end, the Kingdom of Heaven which lies *within*. What we seek, says the great Indian poet-saint Kabir (in Robert Bly's modern version):

is inside you, and also inside me . . .
We are all struggling; none of us has gone far.
Let your arrogance go, and look around inside.

The blue sky opens out farther and farther,
the daily sense of failure goes away,
the damage I have done to myself fades,
A million suns come forward with light,
when I sit firmly in that world.

John has had an initiation into 'that world' and spends his life, in Wallace Stevens' words, 'still feel(ing) the need of some imperishable bliss.' He had that bliss for a night and 'lost' it, but he never doubts for a second that what he apparently lost is the truth, the meaning of his existence. From time to time in the play, Egbert, who seems permanently established in the state John has tasted, appears and reminds John about what's real (just as all the enlightened beings throughout history have appeared to remind us of the possibility of union with immortality, with 'the Witness of living and dying'). John comes to know that we are born to realize this immortality; that liberation into that realization is our birthright.

After so many years of reading plays about suffering ('Aren't we ever going to read a *happy* great modern play?' my students often beg) I find *A Bride for the Unicorn* bracing in its spiritual awareness. The possibility of realizing perfection seems to be a much more truthful and uplifting approach to reality than are endless chronicles of pessimism and complaint. Joy is also the human condition.

* * *

198

Denis Johnston's spiritual quest

In *Nine Rivers from Jordan*, Johnston's complex account of his adventures as a World War II correspondent for the BBC, there is an autobiographical moment which expands the spiritual perspectives we've been considering. The scene is Buchenwald. Johnston finds himself outside the Nazi concentration camp just after it has been liberated by the American army. He is gazing at a multitude of corpses and emaciated survivors. Before him stretches the technology of mass murder, the gas chambers which have not yet been dismantled. The scene becomes unbearable to him, despite his long exposure to war. He feels that all his life he has searched for meaning, that he has been able to love life with all its violence and greed, that he has managed to hold onto some credo of acceptance. But this steadiness is finally shattered at Buchenwald. Despair overwhelms him and he acquiesces to an ethic of vengeance which has always in the past seemed to him to be the antithesis of civilization, reason and justice. He had in fact written two major plays repudiating vengeance in Irish history (*The Old Lady Says 'No!* and *The Moon in the Yellow River*), but now as he confronts the horror of Buchenwald he is on the verge of losing his most cherished ideal:

> Cruelty I have known, and sadism, and the rascalities of red-hot anger. But mass dehumanization as a matter of planned policy has so far not come my way . . . good will is a mistake – . . . destruction is our only means of preservation . . .
> Oh Christ! We are betrayed. I have done my best to keep sane, but there is no answer to this, except bloody murder . . .
> And if nothing remains but the stench of evil in ourselves, that cannot be helped!
> How horrible that this should be the place that I have been seeking all these years.

Johnston is in the midst of his 'dark night of the soul'; the hard won idealism he has maintained throughout the war is mocked by the actual sight of Hitler's handiwork. He is thrown into a spiritual crisis that has only two exits: despair which would force him to accept what he has always hated, a life without value or final distinction between good and evil; or else a new 'leap into faith' that would somehow incorporate the absolute evil he has now encountered. The Buchenwald experience is of fundamental importance in understanding Johnston and his work for the Irish theatre. The moment of radical confrontation did not spring from

199

nowhere; as Johnston points out, it is 'the place I have been seeking all these years.' It is a *necessary* moment, for what use is a philosophy or faith, however deeply felt, that hasn't faced the tests of history and unconditional evil?

Johnston emerged from the Buchenwald test not an absurdist nor a revenge-seeker, but a believer in the essential value of human life and in a divine principle, a believer whose faith had been tempered in the worst the twentieth century had to offer. The Buchenwald experience solidified Johnston's long-developing acceptance of the world *as it is*. This acceptance isn't disguised pessimism; it is embracement. He digests the ultimate horror and transcends it, a process which allows him to come to a joyous affirmation. Johnston is full of pity for suffering, but is not paralyzed by it. He says of his renewed and deepened faith – for it *is* faith, a 'spiritual centre' in Tillich's phrase – that the meaning of 'life is life itself.' It is possible to be a realist *and* a lover of divine principle. The man of faith and compassion is, in the final analysis, the true realist.

Johnston presents the dynamic process of acceptance in theological terms. He offers us, in the British edition of *Nine Rivers from Jordan*, two endings. The first ending, a talonic ethic based on the limitations of human justice, demands vengeance, shuns pity and calls for the punishment of war criminals (the conclusion enacted by history). The second ending is 'an alternative from the bag of possibilities that Heaven has provided.' Johnston casts it as a liturgy, 'a service in which each man is his own celebrant.' The bitter tone of the Buchenwald scene is gone, replaced by a mood of grief, indignation (at the cruelty of a God who can create the 'wreckage' of the holocaust) and frustrated pity that gradually shifts to understanding, awe and joyous celebration of God's world just as it is:

Let the measure of my tribulation
Be the measure of my joy in being alive.

The book ends with 'my act of faith' that

. . . all things, future and past
Hidden and revealed,
Are in His gracious hands.

Disaster is understood as grace. Surrender into love of the creation and to the creator's hand that manifests in every cataclysm of history, every pang of human life as well as every blessing, is the only alternative to despair, to absurdity. I think of Johnston's image of Swift in his play *The Dreaming Dust*, ending a life of lacerating anger in madness and pain; the embodiment of despair, alone, unbelieving. 'Without belief,' says Isaac Bashevis Singer, 'we are lost.' *Nine Rivers* ends with a massive affirmation, an exhilarating emergence from the long tunnel of war into the light of a living faith.

Nine Rivers reminds me strongly of the dilemma of the warrior Arjuna in *The Bhagavad Gita*. Arjuna is involved in a family war and on the morning of battle finds himself paralysed with horror at the prospect of killing his kin. Arjuna's charioteer, the god Krishna in human form, leads Arjuna to right understanding, to the knowledge that he must surrender his own limited will and vision to the divine will. When Arjuna finally transcends his limited view, he unites with his *dharma*, his destiny. This union, via complete acceptance, is Arjuna's liberation into grace, into love and into true humility. It is, he perceives, no different to battle against his family than against anyone; only from a limited perspective is it worse to kill a kinsman than a stranger. Arjuna ultimately accepts a karmic universe in which all human beings are in the process of evolving towards their own divinity. He realizes that he is an actor in God's play and not in his own. Similarly, the Mass that concludes Johnston's war autobiography ends in a communion, a oneness of creator and created, a new 'innocence beyond maturity' that is a grand acceptance and rejoicing. If we look back over his work, from the anguished questioning of the violence-filled world in the early Irish plays through *A Bride for the Unicorn* to *Nine Rivers from Jordan*, we can see that Johnston has been on a steady quest for inner certainty. He has been asking the question all along, 'What do I do with history?' and he finally answers, 'history belongs to God'.

Johnston's latest play to date, *The Scythe and the Sunset* (1958), is a return to the Irish scene of his great early plays, but this play is now fully imbued with the acceptance of 'loving all that lives'. Sacrificing none of the irony of human miscomprehension nor his empathy for the pain of men trying to mould their own destinies, Johnston ends the play with a splended affirmation. What had been possibility a quarter of a century before has become a firm belief: 'Winter gives back the roses to the frost-filled earth.' It is an affirmation wrested from the edge of apocalypse, as it must be in a world of Guernicas and Dresdens and Hiroshimas. Like Blake, Johnston finds God in the tiger as well as in the lamb; and he emerges from his quest a

201

great yea-sayer, singing the song of God. On a level far beyond the logic he adores, he repudiates the wasteland vision, the *nada* of the modern perspective. This beautifully affirmative spiritual dimension of Johnston's work is inspiring and, unfortunately, still utterly necessary. To encounter this stirring vision is to move a step closer to living it.

JOHNSTON IN ACADEME

B.L. REID

The century and his own life were in their late forties when Denis Johnston decided to leave London for a new career in the United States. He had had an early taste of American life in 1923-24 when, on leaving Christ's College, Cambridge, with a degree in law, he had spent a year as a Pugsley scholar at the Harvard Law School. He never lacked the nerve to take up a new challenge. His ten years at the bar in Dublin had been followed by ten years with the BBC in Ireland and England. His BBC service had come to a high plateau during World War II in his three years as a correspondent in the Middle East and the major European theatres of action. That complex experience he would harvest ten years later in the best known of his non-dramatic works, *Nine Rivers from Jordan*. A new peak seemed to have been reached after the war when the BBC made Johnston Director of Programmes for its television service. So the move to America was odd on the face of it and not easy to explain. But Johnston was congenitally energetic and restless. He was depressed by the meanness of life in post-war England; on the other hand, he was now happily married to the former Gate actress Betty Chancellor and they had two new children; the time seemed right to shake up his life.

Johnston spent the better part of two years in and out of New York writing for NBC's 'Theatre Guild of the Air' and on assorted freelance scriptwriting assignments, and the experience was sufficiently desultory to induce him to listen hospitably when he received his first offer of a formal academic appointment. Curtis Canfield, head of the theatre program at Amherst College in Amherst, Massachusetts, was a long-distance acquaintance of Johnston's and an old admirer of his writing; in 1935 he had directed the American première of *The Old Lady Says 'No!'* at his college. When Canfield proposed to Johnston that he replace him at Amherst during his coming sabbatical leave in the second semester of 1949-50, Johnston accepted at once and made the move with his family to the pretty New England town where the spacious century-old campus adjoined the central green. During his half-year's tenure he directed *The Old Lady* and *The Moon in the Yellow*

River, this being his first opportunity to present his own work under his own hand.

The president of the college, Charles Cole, took a friendly interest in Johnston's career, and when Canfield's return was imminent he introduced Johnston to Roswell Gray Ham, a Shakespearian scholar who had come from Yale to be the rather embattled first male president of the oldest women's college in America, Mount Holyoke College, standing ten miles to the south over the Notch in South Hadley, another small town in the Connecticut River valley. The two men took to each other at once, and Ham now offered Johnston the only endowed visiting appointment in his gift, a Purington lectureship, for the academic year 1950-51. It was at about this time that I first laid eyes on Denis, when as a marginal young instructor of English at Smith College, in Northampton ten miles to the west, I screwed up courage to attend a luncheon at the Faculty Club because Denis Johnston was to speak on the modern Irish theatre. I was impressed by his burly good looks, his strong clear baritone with its Irish tuning, his general cosmopolitan air of ease and knowledgeableness, the way he surmounted, by ignoring, the fairly intimidating solipsistic atmosphere of the Smith faculty.

Mount Holyoke was to become Johnston's favourite American academic place, and he was to spend ten mainly happy years there; but his professional function at the college never became the one President Ham planned for him or the one Johnston naturally anticipated. Ham had assumed that Johnston would 'take charge' of and bring order to a theatre programme that had been in disarray for some time after a long period of early strength. The official academic theatre, Laboratory or 'Lab' Theatre, had been conceived primarily as a device for bringing out of the closet and onto the visible stage examples of the standard plays being taught in English and in the other modern languages, hence as an adjunct to courses in dramatic literature. For many years Lab Theatre had been run as something of a private preserve ruled tyrannically by Jeannette Marks, protégée and intimate friend of Mary Woolley, the very durable president who preceded Ham. Miss Marks tended to treat the theatre as the vindicating arm of her course in playwriting, which in turn partly expressed her illusion that she was herself a playwright. This division of emphasis, depriving the theatre of free-standing stature, actually epitomized a curious but long-lasting division within the department of English, which for many years had compartmentalized itself into what amounted to two rather jealous autonomous departments: Division I, 'English,' meaning mainly language and composition, and Division II, 'English Literature'. Miss Marks's power and vanity were such that she had managed to keep the theatre under the umbrella of Division II, implying higher kudos; but the programme was really a poor relation of both divisions Both sides of the department had long done distinguished work, but the relationship between them was unavoidably awkward and occasionally tense.

Poor physical facilities also made it hard to do good theatrical work. The Laboratory Theatre on Morgan Street was a pretty little white frame crackerbox with wide porches and minimal interior space: a stage the size of an ordinary kitchen and a tiny auditorium stuffed with hideously straight-backed wooden benches with virtually no knee room – perhaps the most uncomfortable theatre in America. To this the only alternative was the big Chapin Auditorium with an over-large and stiff proscenium stage, much more suitable for formal academic functions than for intimate amateur theatre. It was this stage that was used by any visiting players who appeared on campus; by Junior Show, an annual musical comedy production of the junior class, more or less original, more or less satirical; by Faculty Show, in which the faculty made willing fools of themselves once in each four-year college generation; and by the unofficial branch of college theatre, the Dramatic Club, run by students who wanted a free hand to do their own plays, one each in fall and spring, the second repeated for the graduation audience in June. As things worked out, it was the rather ramshackle productions of Junior Show, Faculty Show, and Dramatic Club that were to receive most of the benefits of Denis Johnston's highly professional skills in the theatre.

On the more official academic side, after the retirement of the dragon-lady Miss Marks in 1941, Lab Theatre had drifted gradually downhill in charge of a series of transient young directors and technical people, mostly male. Meanwhile, in the late 'forties, a small palace revolution had taken place in the bifurcated English department when the jockeying 'sides' had pulled themselves together into one theoretically seamless fabric. When Denis Johnston appeared on the South Hadley scene in 1950 this rapprochement in the department was new, and in its way of confronting him far from perfect. Old stiffnesses and parochialisms were still alive. A problem for all hands was the fact that President

Ham had presented him to the department, as a Purington lecturer to be attached to them, as a *fait accompli*, virtually without consultation. Then his credentials looked so queer to a solid old American department of English: an Irish free lance, trained in the law, a gifted but sporadic playwright, a world wanderer who had conducted long flirtations with popular media. Entrenched survivors of the old Division II, 'English Literature,' in particular found the whole idea hard to swallow. They would not hand him their theatre, whatever Ham had supposed. It was then wallowing more or less peacefully under the direction of the wife of a full professor of the department, and waiting in the wings was a well-qualified academic, Nadine Shepardson, who had come from Northwestern University by way of New York; her primary training had been in speech and oral interpretation, but she had stage experience as an actress and lecturer, and her service at the college eventually came to include all these areas. These assorted entrenchments would be very hard to penetrate.

Yet to any objective view Johnston's general theatrical experience made him even over-qualified to head a college theatre programme; and by the common terms of academic ironic comedy that fact worked against him. Whereas Ham had undoubtedly taken a longer view of the case, the Purington appointment was ostensibly a visiting one, covering 1950-51, and that at first made the issue appear only a passing one. But something had to be found for Johnston to do. In many colleges and universities, the writer-in-residence kind of thing would have seemed the natural solution. But Mount Holyoke's puritan instincts had always resisted anything resembling a sinecure; for example, W.H. Auden, who also held a Purington during the first half of 1950-51, worked very hard in standard courses of the English department. Nor did Johnston seek a position in which he did not earn his keep by services. College documents of his first year refer to him politely but vaguely as 'director-at-large'. That year he directed, for Dramatic Club not Lab Theatre, his own adaptation of Pirandello's *Six Characters in Search of an Author* and *The Constant Nymph* by Margaret Kennedy and Basil Dean.

He also agreed to teach the course in playwriting which continued from the old Division I offerings, and to fill out his programme with – of all things – two sections of freshman English. Having been judged dubiously qualified as an academic, he was now installed in a thoroughly academic, and a fundamental if fairly elementary, regimen of teaching. Johnston must have felt ironies in his situation, but typically he accepted it without visible resentment and with evident good grace. He taught his young women how to read and write, and neither he nor they found any cause to complain. He and Miss Shepardson reached not only an accommodation but a friendship, and he helped her cheerfully in the work of the little college radio station, then new. He let it be known that he was willing to accept directing assignments in any of the campus branches of amateur theatre, but he did not require to run anything whatsoever. When he directed *A Change for the Worse* by the Scot James Bridie and Christopher Fry's *A Phoenix Too Frequent* for Lab Theatre in February 1951, the programme carefully designated him as 'visiting director.'

Before the year was out President Ham had joined the issue again by renewing the Purington appointment for 1951-52. By the second year the Johnstons' situation had grown firmer and more comfortable. The family occupied the two lower floors of a rambling, roomy grey stucco house on Jewett Lane, an easy walk to campus. Their neighbour Sydney McLean, one of the most difficult women in town, found them easy to like. Denis and Betty liked the quiet unpretentious town as a place to bring up their two boys, Rory and Jeremy, who were interesting polyglot small figures in themselves. Betty became one of the kindest of the necessary friends of Lotte Rox, the sculptor's wife, an enchanting but pitiable figure in her wheel chair, paralysed and nearly speechless but still humorously percipient. The Hams and Johnstons became good friends, and Denis also formed quick and firm friendships in the department, especially with Joseph Bottkol and Alan McGee, and in the faculty at large. Department members got over their suspiciousness about his worldly and journalistic past when they saw that he did his straight academic work willingly and well. Before the second year was out he had completed his probation as a visitor and had been confirmed as a full Professor of English with permanent tenure. He was to fill out the decade at Mount Holyoke.

The department chairman's report for 1951-52 referred to Johnston as 'general head for dramatic activities,' and under him Dramatic Club gave in December the American premiére of *God's Gentry* by Donagh MacDonagh. But his position remained somewhat equivocal, and his special expertness in the theatre was less adequately used than it ought to have been. Henceforward he regularly taught sections of freshman English and playwriting at

Mount Holyoke, and he soon began teaching Irish literature in summer sessions at Harvard University. Within a couple of years he was able to install a new elective course in the Anglo-Irish writers at his home college. Occasionally he directed the work of honours students in one or another of his subject matters. In May of 1952 he directed *The Winter's Tale* and in December *A Bride for the Unicorn*, the only work of his own to be performed at Mount Holyoke.

In his work as director of the fairly informal and lighthearted productions of Dramatic Club, Junior Show, Faculty Show, Johnston invested solid effort as well as high talent. The files of Dramatic Club preserve, for example, his commentary on one production running to several pages of single-space typing – witty, pointed, pragmatical, and tasteful, a document designed to teach. Together with Nadine Shepardson, who had succeeded Louise Wallis as Director of Laboratory Theatre in 1953, he was able to break down the hampering old tradition that Mount Holyoke's young women were to play all parts, male and female, in student plays; and now male faculty members, students from Amherst and other colleges, and occasional townspeople began playing male roles with considerable advantage at least to the realism of campus productions. In May, 1954, Johnston himself acted the part of the king in Jacinto Benevente's *The School of Princesses*. Over the next few years he directed Dramatic Club performances of such plays as Pirandello's *Right You Are If You Think So*, Ibsen's *Peer Gynt*, Shaw's *Heartbreak House*, Synge's *The Playboy of the Western World*, Barrie's *Dear Brutus*, William Inge's *Picnic*. The general note might be described as fresh and energetic, bold and nervy but solidly grounded stuff. Perhaps his most ambitious and impressive undertaking at Mount Holyoke was his production on two occasions of Mary Manning's dramatic adaptation of *Finnegans Wake*, with Alan McGee of the English department playing the bravura role of Earwicker's son Sean. This was appropriately uproarious, and satisfyingly incomprehensible to the parents at graduation time.

As a director Denis Johnston at Mount Holyoke was a fairly easy rider, his touch being light but not slack. He did not flourish his ego, did not impose personality or will, but patiently, solidly, sensitively led young actors to use their own intelligence to find their way to a persona and a voice; gradually he wove the collective amateurism into a fabric that gave off harmony and light. On the technical side, in matters of costume, lighting, settings, his patient professionalism brought a new coherency and finish, a new stageworthiness to the formerly slapdash Dramatic Club productions.

When I joined the Mount Holyoke faculty in the fall of 1957 Denis Johnston was an established but still odd feature of the scene. He had recently come back from a year's leave on a Guggenheim fellowship to continue work on his lifelong interest in Jonathan Swift, to bear fruit in 1959 in *In Search of Swift*. His book *Nine Rivers from Jordan* had been by far the most interesting piece of writing to emerge from the English department, but it had by no means turned him into a familiar academic type. I wondered what this distinguished middle-aged Irish playwright was doing teaching freshman English. But then the Mount Holyoke English department, to its honour, was one in which hardly anybody held himself superior to the most basic work of the discipline. Nothing came easy there. We met often and long, and every question was resolved or at least confronted by a kind of excruciating democratization in which every member, top to bottom, took part by performance and endurance. The preparation and adjudication of the general examination, for example, which every major in English had to pass to receive the degree, involved a score or more of meetings, of committees and of the whole department, from September to June. I often wondered what Denis Johnston could make of such processes of American puritanism; but it dawned on me after watching him in a few meetings that what he made of us was the best. He sat, he listened, he offered judgments. He not only respected but shared the general honorable commitment, in which there was no prospect of cash or acclaim.

In their house on Jewett Lane the Johnstons were generous hosts to students and colleagues, and one evening my wife Jane and I were pleased to be included in a group of ten or so gathered for dinner and a first reading of the manuscript of *The Scythe and the Sunset*, Denis's version of The Matter of Easter 1916. It was all a surprise to me; I had not even known he had been at work on the play, though he and I talked often that year about Irish writers and writing in connection with some work of my own. Such reticence about his own work was typical of his personal style. I confess I found the play baffling in that first oral reading by many unprepared voices, and I can't imagine that Denis learned much from our amateur efforts. The chief pleasure of the evening was the visible evidence that Denis Johnston still had plays in him, that our academic exploitation of him had not dried him up as a writer.

Denis Johnston: a retrospective

Smith College, the largest of the American women's colleges, situated ten miles northwest of South Hadley in the larger town of Northampton, had put on Johnston's *The Golden Cuckoo* in 1958, and he had been going over to Smith for several years to teach their course in playwriting, travelling by the winding valley road that he loved, Route 47, along the Connecticut River past Hockanum and Hadley. The Connecticut was in a fair way to become his Tenth River from Jordan. In 1960-61 Smith was looking about for a chairman for their theatre department, and they sounded out Denis Johnston as to his interest in the post, which carried certain obvious attractions: autonomy as head of a larger, more concentrated programme, directly specified to his training as a professional theatre person; a small but firmly established graduate programme; a pleasant house on the central campus. The offer came at a time when Johnston's stomach had been turned by a minor crisis into which he had been drawn at Mount Holyoke. One of his advisees was an officer in the Student Government Association and as such she was a leader in a student campaign to do away with compulsory attendance at chapel, an ancient institution which was being stubbornly defended by the new president of the college, successor to Roswell Ham. The young woman told Johnston that she was being subjected to pressures by the administration, backed by threats such as that of the loss of her scholarship grant. He advised her to hold fast, and promised that if reprisals were taken against her he would see to it that a legal suit was brought and national publicity arranged. The student stiffened her back and her anti-chapel party eventually won its point. Johnston assumed that his Mount Holyoke copybook was thenceforward blotted, and he felt that in any case the new administration was one he did not wish to serve. When he decided to close with the offer from Smith, the new president must have been the only person at Mount Holyoke who was glad to see him go.

In February of 1961 Denis and Betty moved into the charming white-frame Victorian cottage at 7 College Lane, with Paradise Pond down the small hill behind them, which would be their home until the spring of 1966. Denis was in his sixty-first year but in good health and vigour for this late movement in his long professional career. In the Smith Student Center, adapted from an outgrown Victorian gymnasium, his physical theatre, as at Mount Holyoke, would be small and ungainly; but better things were promised and he could look ahead with interest and optimism. He quickly formed a close harmonious working relationship with the theatre's new

210

technical director and designer, William Hatch, and the two families became warm friends. Among his first undertakings as a director at Smith was a production of his old favorite, Pirandello's *Six Characters in Search of an Author*, and I remember driving over to see it along Route 47 on an icy white winter night when God's sky offered such a glorious display of Northern Lights that Jane and I pulled off the road, coming and going, and stared at it for a half-hour, trying to comprehend the mere stunning possibility of it all. Man's theatre, even Johnston's Pirandello, seemed pretty pale.

In subsequent years at Smith he staged such plays as Tennessee Williams's *Camino Real*, Shaw's *Arms and the Man*, a double bill of Yeats's *The Player Queen* and *Purgatory*, and the play of *The Innocents* made from Henry James's haunted and haunting novella, *The Turn of the Screw*. He also lent a hand to the music department in staging operatic performances. Bill Hatch remembers occasional conflicts between American idiom and Denis's European sensibility, as when he read Tennessee Williams's 'desert rat', meaning a wandering prospector, in the light of his own experience of British soldiers in Africa. His relationship with students and colleagues continued to be relaxed and warm and civilized, humane but firm. He was serious about his work but never solemn. In directing he was always willing, even eager, to test his own sense of a role or a dramatic situation against the actor's own conception. His conduct of department affairs, formal meetings and such, was economical and efficient, humorous, unpretentious. In all he showed the divine gift of making the unpleasant or onerous or merely necessary a matter of forgiving amusement. His formal classroom teaching involved his standard course in playwriting and a course in modern European drama. One of his many admiring student friends, Carol O'Brien, was later moved to endow in his honour an annual prize for the writing of an original play. Recognizing that by his work at Amherst, Mount Holyoke, and Smith, Denis Johnston had made himself a regional resource, she stipulated that the competition should be open to students of all five of the valley colleges.

Smith College was planning to build at a cost of several million dollars a big new Center for the Performing Arts on Green Street bordering the campus. The old Student Center housing the existing makeshift theatre was to be torn down to make way for a new science building. Doris Abramson, who had been asked to come over from the University of Massachusetts to fill a part-time position, taking a short cut out of the Student Center via a metal fire escape, slipped on an icy tread and broke her arm. When Johnston filled out the official form reporting the mishap, he enjoyed answering the question 'What is being done to correct the condition leading to the accident?' as follows: 'We are razing the building.' It was a chance he never expected to have again, he told Hatch. He took a very active part in planning the new complex on Green Street, and it was owing to his insistence that the new main theatre was given a 'shuttle' stage, a cruciform shape that allowed a set to be assembled on a platform at one side, moved onto the central stage for playing, then drawn off onto a platform on the opposite side. Ground was broken for the Center for the Performing Arts in the fall of 1964, but the structure was not completed until after Johnston's retirement in the spring of 1966. Hence he was barely spared the double disaster which seemed to lay a curse upon the first days of the new theatre: a junior student, involved in a 'treasure hunt' as part of a bit of mild hazing, stumbled into the still unshielded opening of a deep air shaft and was fatally hurt; three days later a young male technical assistant in the theatre, tinkering with an unfinished bit of machinery, was crushed to death by a falling paint frame.

No curse attended Denis Johnston's tenure at Smith College. Bill Hatch remembers the period as 'pleasant years', a good time. Their friendship has been warm and abiding. When Denis returns to the Connecticut Valley nowadays, in what has to be called, reluctantly, old age, he stays with the Hatches out in the country in West-hampton. He was an unpersuaded retiree. For years after he left Smith in 1966 he treated his back-home homes, first in Alderney in the Channel Islands and finally on Killiney Bay in Co. Dublin, as mere sally-ports for new American academic incarnations, typically single-year 'visiting' appointments: at Amherst College once more, at the University of Iowa in Iowa City, at the University of California at Davis, at New York University, at Whitman College on the west coast in Walla Walla, Washington, at the Graduate Centre for Study of Drama, University of Toronto. He appears to have enjoyed all of these institutions, and I am sure they have all profited by his presence. In the quarter-century of his American academic life, as in the rest of his life, he showed himself an able and honorable man, one who never said the thing that is not, one who earned his keep by hard and intelligent and tasteful work. I happened to be involved marginally in one of his late appointments, that at New York University, when the chairman David Greene telephoned and asked for a character for Denis Johnston, whom they were in the process of considering. I took pleasure in giving him a clean bill, even a shining one.

Editor's Note:

Carolyn Buracker wrote in the Mount Holyoke *News* of 13 May 1955: 'Mr. Denis Johnston is a figure well-known on campus. His praises are sung for his proficiency each year in the role of 'Commander-in-Chief' of Junior Show. As director of all the productions of Dramatic Club each final curtain earns him another round of applause which never seems to fade out, and as teacher in compositional English courses his experience and knowledge as a professional in that field serve as a constant guide and source of advice for the potential creative writer.' He was known by students as Mr. J.

WITH DENIS JOHNSTON IN THE WESTERN DESERT

MARK CULME-SEYMOUR

When Denis Johnston arrived in Cairo in June 1942 as a BBC war correspondent Field Marshal Erwin Rommel, commanding the combined German-Italian army, had just won what was to prove his last victory in the Western Desert.

After three weeks of ferocious fighting he had broken through the Gazala line, a string of self-contained 'boxes', interspersed with minefields, running some thirty miles south from a point west of Tobruk. In the centre was the box known as Knightsbridge, manned by the British Guards Brigade, and at the southern end was Bir Hacheim, to become famous for its epic defence by the Free French.

The allied forces had lost virtually all their armour and had no option but to withdraw and reorganise if the 8th. Army was to remain in being. The withdrawal became a race towards the Egyptian frontier and beyond, with Rommel's forces often level with, sometimes even ahead of the retreating columns, until in the last days of June Rommel was stopped at El Alamein by General Dan Pienaar's 1st. South African Division.

Perhaps it was difficult to foresee that by pushing his exhausted army into the area of El Alamein, the only bottleneck between Tripoli and Cairo, Rommel had sealed his own doom. Even with the captured supplies from Tobruk, which he had taken in a day, he could get no further, nor could he safely extricate himself. With the massive reinforcements available close by in Egypt and more arriving by sea the 8th. Army would quickly build up an overpowering force which would inevitably inflict total and final defeat on the Afrika Korps and the Italians, and Rommel soon realised it.

* * *

Up to this point the war that had swung back and forth across the Western Desert since 1940 might well have been described, with only small exaggeration, as a Boy Scouts' war.

This magnificent arena, stretching westwards from the delta of

214

the Nile across the Egyptian border and into Libya for nearly 1,000 miles, could have been expressly designed for war games on a grand scale.

For newly arrived men the need for improvised skills in coming to terms with the desert itself was immediately apparent. They had to learn how to manage on a ration of one gallon of water per man per day for all purposes – very easy, once you knew, and you could even keep shaved and clean. You made a cooking stove from a cut down British petrol container, half filled with a layer of sand and soaked with petrol, and had to practise the drill of getting it going in seconds so that even a ten-minute halt during a manoeuvre was enough to make a 'brew-up' of tea and drink it.

The unfortunates assigned to making meals had to find a dozen ways of inventing concoctions from the eternal tinned bully beef and hard tack – I remember 'Bully Rissoles' and 'Biscuit Burgoo' among them – and somehow make each of them taste different, at the risk of violent abuse from the eaters.

Above all a newcomer had to learn how to find his way. There was only the one coastal road stretching from Alexandria round the bulge of Cyrenaica southwards from Benghazi to El Agheila, where it turned west towards Tripoli. Near the coast too were a few well-worn tracks, but for the rest the desert was totally empty. The few place names on the map meant nothing more than a grid reference. Navigation across this territory was by dead reckoning, using a compass and the mileage shown on your vehicle. When you thought you had got to where you were meant to be you still couldn't be sure it was the right spot – compass errors were common. If the speedometer wasn't working a rough-and-ready calculation of distance based on petrol consumption had to be made, and you could be wrong by many miles.

At night, if within striking distance of the enemy, the open day formation closed up into a night leaguer with an all-round guard. Some men dug themselves a shallow trench to sleep in. More often one merely wrapped oneself up in blankets or a sleeping-bag and slept on the desert floor.

The desert itself was of great beauty. There was something about the silence and the distances which gave one a feeling of complete freedom. The sunsets were magnificent but short lived, and from a blazing sky came sudden darkness, faintly illuminated by the brilliant stars. The nights were often bitterly cold.

The universal rule was to 'stand-to' at first light, well before

215

sunrise. One of the greatest joys of that life was the first mug of scalding tea drunk in the half darkness, huddled in greatcoats, sometimes warmed by a bonfire of scrub and thorn.

The fact that our war games were played with live ammunition for the most part merely added excitement to an already fascinating life. Only a very small part of the time was spent in real fighting. Between the sudden full scale excursions of whole armies or the set piece battles the majority of the forces were in reserve or rear positions. We were constantly training or taking part in large scale manoeuvres, but sometimes we were just 'resting'. During these latter periods, which could last for a couple of weeks or more, the desert, which had seemed so utterly featureless, became very soon as familiar as a corner of Salisbury Plain. The shape of the slightest elevation on the horizon, a few rocks a couple of miles away, often marking the site of a well of unknown antiquity, a crashed plane or burnt out truck – such landmarks served to guide you over quite long distances and were more reliable than the compass.

The live ammunition soon turned out to be a good deal less dangerous than one had expected. A few days after my battalion of the Rifle Brigade had relieved our 2nd. Battalion at the foremost of our positions, El Agheila, Rommel emerged from round the corner in strength and there was nothing for it but to drive like hell if we were not to be cut off (the start of the 'Msus Stakes' as this race eastwards became known).[1] After going for a few hours our column, completely without air defence, was attacked by a group of some 20 planes. We jumped from our trucks and Bren carriers and lay on the ground watching the circus helplessly as they machine gunned us at leisure, and being new boys expecting death at any moment. They finally flew off and I can't remember hearing of a single casualty and only one of our vehicles was hit. Unfortunately it was our Company HQ truck with the rum ration on board. It burnt with a beautiful purple flame.

Another feature of those desert war games was the ease of escape if one got cut off and on one's own during one of these desperate chases in which each side took turns in being the pursuer and the pursued. All it needed was to turn south into the empty desert for 20 miles or so, stocking up with petrol, water and food from abandoned vehicles of either side, head east or west according to the direction of the race, and with a bit of luck and common sense one could turn north again after two or three days and expect to join up with one's friends.

* * *

Life when the battles began was of course very different. Those vast distances contracted into a comparatively small area in which armies hurled themselves at each other in deafening, dusty confusion by day, gathering themselves together at night to reorganise as best they could. Now live ammunition was used in earnest and in vast quantities. Very seldom did anything go according to plan. Whole brigades got themselves into the wrong places, orders and counter-orders were sent to commanders who weren't where they were thought to be, and who in any case were already busy doing something else.

In the earlier confrontations the allied tanks were outranged by the German tank guns, so that for the British to engage an enemy tank force they first had to charge in old fashioned cavalry style to get within range. This made for some spectacular set pieces even if they ended, as they mostly did, in expensive failure.

Nor was there any lack of Beau Geste incidents – Brigadier Jock Campbell leading his tanks into battle in his staff car, and similarly General Gatehouse, a Divisional Commander, having a canvas chair fixed to the top of the command tank of his main force so that he could see what was happening. What happened was that he was the first to see an enemy tank force approaching on his flank and was able to manoeuvre his own tanks in time to get the best of the encounter. His tank was hit nine times, but the General was unscathed.

There were some bizarre occurrences as well. For example, there was the British field hospital which was overrun, but didn't realise it until they began to receive German casualties instead of British. The medical staff carried on and the Germans accepted their instructions with great correctness. After four days the tide of battle turned, the Germans removed their own wounded, and very soon the hospital was taking in British casualties again.

At the battle of Alam Halfa a British officer was captured, escaped, and the next day re-captured by a group of German officers hunting gazelle behind the lines.

The main trouble about the battles was that we kept on losing them.

* * *

When Denis came on the scene he found Cairo in a state approaching panic. The people there understood nothing of Rommel's increasing supply difficulties, nor the strength of the Alamein position. They could see for themselves that the 8th. Army was in full retreat and to them it seemed that the whole Afrika Korps, commanded by a General of apparent genius and invincibility, would be upon them in a matter of days, if not hours. There was talk of the Germans overrunning Egypt, the Canal, Palestine and Syria, and finally joining up with their armies in Russia. Many of the foreign population had been evacuated officially, others were using any means they could find to get out to Palestine, Kenya, South Africa, no matter where. The BBC office itself was under notice to move to Jerusalem.

The King said he was going – he wasn't going to be a puppet king (what else had he ever been?). The British Ambassador said he was staying, though the bonfire in his garden showed that he was burning the Embassy documents. The Egyptians in general appeared mainly indifferent: they would doubtless do just as well for themselves under the Germans as they had under the British.

British habits die hard. In every military establishment the siesta was observed as usual and from noon until 4.30 p.m. everything closed down.

From Mena House, the hotel near the Pyramids, Denis watched the chaotic retreat go by, a roaring confusion of battered trucks, huge transporters carrying broken-down tanks, field kitchens, ambulances, and everywhere dirty men, but men who were singing their favourite songs, and who looked in no way depressed, merely rather bored. This extraordinary caterpillar of retreat (by now christened the 'Gazala Stakes') stretched all the way back to the desert; and in the other direction there seemed no indication where it would stop.

Denis had been instructed that for the moment he should do no broadcasting at all. In any case hard information was impossible to come by. When Public Relations finally decided to hold a Press Conference and admit that all was not well their communiqué began: 'Developments in the battle have resulted in certain areas losing their former tactical importance. Accordingly the garrison of Knightsbridge has assumed a mobile role.'

Finally exasperated at the total lack of information that could be believed Denis decided to go into the desert himself and find out what he could. Struggling all the way against the unending stream of a retreat that at times seemed unpleasantly like a rout – the garrison of Knightsbridge in their 'mobile role' – he eventually found the

218

BBC's Conducting Officer, at that moment the Marquess of Ely. Together they found near Alamein station a small line of dugouts in which was installed the HQ of General Dan Pienaar, commanding the 1st. South African Division.

As Denis recounted it they found Pienaar on the telephone, himself in search of information. Why had his troops been shelled from the rear yesterday? Which side was he supposed to be on? His father had fought the British in the Boer War, they had only to let him know and he would have Rommel in Alexandria in 12 hours.

When this little discussion had ended he discovered that Denis worked for the BBC and another storm blew up about the BBC's report that there had been air cover at Gazala. Indeed the sky had been full of planes, said the General, but not one of them was ours. He was not mollified by George Ely's explanation that this was a different correspondent.

Finally he answered some questions with remarkable honesty. They were in the Alamein 'box' all right, but the question was who was caught in it? There was a gap of 7 miles to his south, which left the desert route to Cairo wide open. He didn't know who was going to stop it up, although some New Zealanders and some Indians were supposed to be on their way. Would he have to retreat then? Certainly not, said the General, he'd had enough of retreating and so far as he was concerned he was staying there.

Denis could hardly have got material out of this interview which would cheer up the Home Service, his first priority.

* * *

In mid-July a second BBC correspondent arrived, Godfrey Talbot. Denis persuaded him to take over the Cairo office so that he himself could go up to the desert again. At that moment too, after a minor wound which made me temporalily unfit to rejoin my battalion, I had been posted to Cairo PR as a Conducting Officer and had been ordered to take over from George Ely and look after the BBC.

Denis and I met in Cairo and got on well from the start. We agreed completely about Denis's plans, which were to explore thoroughly for ourselves the now more or less stabilised position at Alamein, and in particular to get up as far forward as possible – Denis was among other things fed up with remarks about 'reporting the war from the bar of Shepheard's Hotel'. We decided also that we would insist that PR should give us the facilities to which we were

219

entitled, and especially so as the BBC was the only source of news for the men in the field.

Denis could be a formidable and determined character, with a useful streak of cunning too, and we got everything we asked for. Indeed we set out not only desertworthy but almost luxuriously so, with a staff car and driver, Presley, and a recording truck with driver Pretswell and Denis's old friend 'Skipper' Arnell as recording engineer. We were lavishly equipped with maps, compasses, towing chains and sand tracks for getting ourselves out of soft sand, a proper cooking apparatus and even folding beds.

We first went to Alexandria and dined on quails at the Union Bar with 'Red' Freeman,[2] with whom I had shared a cabin during the three-month voyage out in the 1st. Armoured Division convoy. He had rather swiftly risen to be a Brigade Major and as I expected knew a good deal about what was happening.

For the first time in the desert war the two sides faced each other on a line with a southern flank. This was formed by the impassable Qattara Depression, only some 30 miles from the sea at the narrowest point and not more than about 40 miles where the opposing positions formed a rough line further to the west. To our enquiries about where to go for some excitement and interest, and especially where to reach the most forward of our positions, Red suggested we aim for Hemeimat, a sandstone peak at the southernmost end of the line, and overlooking the Qattara Depression itself. We asked him who was holding this part of the line and Red replied that so far as he knew there was nobody much there, 'except, of course, Jimmy'.

This was good news, as Jimmy was Jimmy Bosvile, my own Colonel commanding 1st. Bn. Rifle Brigade, and my C.O. until I had been forced to retire from the field, and I should be certain of a welcome and every sort of help. He was now a Brigadier, commanding 2nd. Motor Brigade. We could find their B Echelon on the Diamond Track, said Red.

We set off the next morning steering for the Diamond Track by compass – this was simply a track of wheel and caterpillar marks like any other, but provided at intervals with posts carrying a diamond shaped sign. We found 2nd. Motor Brigade's rear Echelon without difficulty and were hospitably welcomed and fed and shown where to sleep.

I was delighted to find within the first 24 hours with Denis that he accepted our desert routine without complaint, in particular our rule of getting up at first light. (Not so his colleague, who was to join me later. A thoroughly good fellow, Godfrey seemed not to have left his desk in London, and considered it perfectly normal to keep his usual office hours. He got our two drivers to rig him up some extra little piece of privacy and from it he would emerge with shining morning face sharp at 9 a.m., flexing his muscles and practising his leg breaks with an imaginary cricket ball, while our long suffering drivers made a second breakfast for him. We became good friends, however.)

We turned south the next day until we hit the Barrel Track, which led straight to Cairo and was an alternative route there to taking the road from Alexandria. It seemed incredible to us that so far we had seen nothing whatever to stop Rommel using it himself whenever he felt like it.

We turned west again and pretty soon saw a jagged, brownish lump some miles ahead. I reckoned this must be Hemeimat, but before swanning ahead into the blue thought it as well to make sure of our position. We found the HQ of one of the Motor Brigade's battalions, who confirmed our position. Again we were given outstanding hospitality and pressed to stay for dinner and spend the night. However, somebody remarked that of course if we wanted to get into the picture properly we ought to push on and not hang around a rear HQ. This was enough to get Denis leaping into the saddle and off we went, spending the night on our own near a crashed Stuka dive-bomber.

We were all discussing the apparently total lack of defence in what seemed a vital sector when, just before sunset, a vast fleet of British Grant tanks appeared to the north, completing some manoeuvre and preparing to go into night leaguer. The Barrel Track was not as defenceless as it appeared.

The next morning we reached a Company HQ, only a mile or so from the Hemeimat peak. Ahead of us we knew there was empty desert and then Germans, and it seemed to us we had come about as far forward as we could get. Not so. A visiting young gunner officer called Bowman, commanding a forward artillery observation post, piped up with 'Of course we wouldn't see anything from where we were, why didn't we come up with him to his OP, called "July", it was much more fun and wouldn't we like to see some Jerries?' I myself was not too pleased at this Lieut. Bowman's exuberance. I didn't particularly want to see any Jerries, I had seen plenty. Besides, if I could see them it meant that they could see me. But of course there was no holding Denis.

Lieut. Bowman was keen to take us to 'July' and then on to what he called his 'pimple'. To get there, he said, we'd have to go in an armoured car. Actually, said Bowman, it didn't have a top, but it didn't really matter, we'd be going pretty fast. So we set off, leaving the recording truck behind, and sitting most uncomfortably on the rim of the armoured car where the turret should have been. Within 20 minutes we stuck in soft sand.

When we got going again we went through a lane traversing a minefield and emerged into what Bowman described as a sort of no-man's-land. His people occupied it by day, but the Jerries often came snooping round at night, and he pointed out with delight some tracks which he said hadn't been there the day before and were certainly Jerries'. I began to get mildly uncomfortable. But at least I was grateful for Bowman's local knowledge because after the confused fighting earlier in July there were odd minefields all over the place, unmarked and unmapped, and a nagging anxiety if you didn't know the ground well.

We came to a wireless truck in a hull-down position behind a small ridge and got out. 'This is "July",' said Bowman. 'Let's walk around a bit.' 'Not bloody here, you don't' came a voice from the wireless truck. 'Go somewhere else if you want to be shelled.'

'OK,' said Bowman, and suggested that we should walk up to the top of a hummock a little further off. We'd still get a good view, but perhaps he'd better go ahead and make sure everything was clear. At this point I decided that I was not only lazy and didn't enjoy walking up hummocks, but also that it seemed a good moment to have a sleep and let Denis and Bowman get on with it. So I relaxed in the shade of the wireless truck while they went off to the hummock. I managed to justify my craven behaviour to some extent by reminding myself that the fewer people showing themselves on the skyline the better pleased would be the gunners manning the OP, who would obviously be disgusted by a group of sightseers drawing fire on themselves.

Denis indeed saw Jerries from the top of the hummock, many of them, engaged in various humdrum activities, cooking, washing, digging, working on elaborate strong points. Bowman insisted, however, on going on to his prize pimple, from where, he said, there was an even better view. According to Denis the view was very similar and Bowman's main idea was to dash in the turretless armoured car across some open ground and hope to get the Jerries to open up and provide some excitement. He'd managed to put on a jolly good show for some R.A.F. types that morning, he said. A few odd shells did come over but burst a mile away.

We started back towards Burg-el-Arab on the coast, where TAC Army HQ was situated next door to Air Marshal Coningham's RAF HQ. On the way we heard rumours that Churchill himself, accompanied by Montgomery, was going to pay a visit to the desert. We knew that he had arrived in Cairo with his CIGS,[3] Brooke, and that there had been a lot of shuffling around of generals, culminating in the appointment of Alexander as C. in C. Middle East and Montgomery commanding 8th. Army. We managed to intercept this important little convoy at a convenient point where it had stopped to let the troops have a look at them.

The Old Man in boiler suit, topee and pale blue umbrella looked very bad tempered. Denis, however, approached him and got him to make some fairly banal remarks into his microphone. The surrounding troops seemed rather indifferent to the proceedings. For months their inferiority in war material generally had been compounded by muddled and indecisive generalship and they wondered what difference still another, and unknown, Army Commander was going to make.

Denis also made himself known to Montgomery, whose only remarks were: no, he wouldn't record anything and how did Denis like his new Australian hat?

We slept whenever we could at Burg-el-Arab. The dunes between the road and the sea were clean and white and here and there were green groves of fig trees. There, too, we could plunge into the most gorgeous sea and wash off the sand of the day's travelling. Being so close to both Army and RAF Headquarters made it possible to have off-the-record conversations with the senior staff of Montgomery and Coningham, from which we could deduce what was likely to happen later on.

Our proximity to these two HQs had occasional inconveniences, since their approximate location was known to the enemy. I strolled off one morning with a spade – 'taking a spade for a walk' it was known as – and chose a pretty spot behind a young fig tree. At the exact wrong moment I saw three Messerschmidts come roaring in just above sea level and as they crossed the beach they opened up with their machine guns. The centre one seemed to be aiming at me personally (it always seemed like that) but I was hardly in a position to take avoiding action – there didn't seem much point anyway. Within seconds they had gone and not a fig leaf fell. Denis had some ribald remarks to make when I told him of this episode.

*   *   *

Godfrey Talbot came up to the desert to switch places with Denis who was to go back and man the Cairo office. It was some time before I was to see Denis again. Apart from his work in Cairo he had thought up an assignment which left the Cairo office in the hands of an assistant and took him to Jordan and Palestine. He baptised himself in the River Jordan; visited the Dead Sea; spent some time in Jerusalem; went for a 12 hour bombing trip over Benghazi in an American Liberator; survived with credit a ceremonial dinner given by the Arab Legion; and returned with a huge white sheepskin coat.

He and Godfrey switched places again and Denis arrived back in the desert at the final moments of the battle of Alamein, when the break-through had been successful and the chase was on.

*   *   *

I was delighted to see again my tall, lanky friend, with his black hair, his loose-limbed stride and his rather mixed up clothes, which were always practical but always managed to look slightly untidy.

He told me that on his way up he had attended a press conference given by Montgomery to announce to the world his total victory at Alamein. Montgomery's opening words were: 'Well, gentlemen, as you see I have got a new hat.' Denis was a little cynical on the subject of Monty and his hats.

Meanwhile I myself had been in Alexandria and got information not generally known that an armoured column was to start straight for Tobruk in an attempt to cut off the entire Afrika Korps before it got there. We had permission to go with it. At first we were mightily excited about this news which we kept quiet about, as we hoped to be the only correspondents with this column. It soon appeared however that this news was spreading rapidly, that there was a good chance of it already being too late to reach Tobruk before the Germans, and in that event we would be out in the blue with little to report and miss the main action. (The operation was in fact cancelled.)

We decided then to do the obvious thing, to get going as soon as possible and catch up with the van of the advance, already two days ahead of us. We started off along the coast road, passing prisoner-of-war cages near Alamein station, but soon turned south, threading our way through the marked gaps in the minefields and making better time than was possible on the traffic-jammed road.

On every side tanks and vehicles were still burning. In the distance we could see long columns of prisoners from the Italian divisions, left without transport, shuffling back towards the POW cages.

Once past the minefield areas we made good progress, at times out in the desert, at others rejoining the road or driving along parallel to it. The advance of the 8th. Army was strangely reminiscent of its retreat – a seemingly confused and endless stream of vehicles of every kind. Just as the men in the retreat had shown no sign of dejection, so now they showed no sign of jubilation, only that rather bored look that it was all in the day's work.

By our second night we were clearly coming up somewhere near our leading units. The jam on the road had thinned out, as we had seen before we went off into the desert again. The trucks, tanks, Bren carriers we could see on either side appeared more organised and more like an advancing army. Although we knew we had passed Daba and had seen Fuka airfield already being cleared for our fighters we had no idea of our exact position. As it became dark we saw fewer and fewer of our own units and it seemed sensible to stop where we were for the night.

With the onset of real darkness this decision seemed all the more sensible as Very lights began to shoot up all round us. These were used far more by the Germans to maintain contact at night than by ourselves. So far as we knew we might be not only at that moment the leading unit of the 8th. Army, but could well have got ourselves mixed up with stragglers of the retreating Afrika Korps. We decided to make ourselves as invisible as possible, closed all chinks in the windows of Belinda, our recording truck, and settled down with a bottle of whisky to wait for morning.

The next day there was heavy rain, turning the desert into a bog and virtually halting all movement, except on the road. As soon as we could unbog ourselves we got onto the road, no longer jammed, and during the rest of that day and the next made good progress, passing halted unit after unit, until we felt sure we must be near the head of the advance. No one could tell us, however, just what the position was, not even whether or not we had got ahead of our leading armoured units.

We soon found out for ourselves. As we approached the top of a slight rise we saw a truck ahead of us suddenly turn round and come haring back, shouting out that they had been shelled. We had reached the perimeter defences of Mersa Matruh, manned by a rearguard of the German 90th. Light Division.

Pretty soon a group of Bren carriers arrived and dispersed on each side of the road, followed by a number of tanks which also dispersed into hull-down positions. We ourselves cautiously drove forward, got our two vehicles off the road and walked on to the top of the rise to see what was happening.

Only about half a mile ahead was a long slope rising to the skyline and at the bottom of it an obvious minefield, surrounded by barbed wire, an anti-tank ditch and other obstacles with the railway line running through them.

Quite a lot of gunfire was coming and going from both sides, the shells passing over our heads. Suddenly there were bangs of a quite different and very characteristic kind and those of us who recognised them for what they were, anti-personnel shells, were soon down on our faces. Only Denis continued on his feet. He looked round to see with some puzzlement that we had all taken what cover we could find. Then he noticed the sand around him erupting in sharp bursts, comprehension dawned on his face and he took cover with the rest of us.

This, I am sure, was a moment Denis had been waiting for. Everyone going into action knows, if he is not a fool, that he is going to be frightened. What no one knows – and has to wait to find out – is how frightened he will be and how he will behave. Denis hadn't had any luck at Hemeimat, despite the best efforts of Lieut. Bowman; his hair-raising experiences in the Liberator over Benghazi might, I would have thought, have been enough, but apparently not. Now, however, he was being shot at in person and at close range. This was it. As he took in what was happening and joined us on the desert floor his moment of self-discovery had arrived and predictably he hadn't been as frightened as he had expected.

At last light we saw the German rearguard disappear up the slope over the skyline, but we had to wait until morning to clear a way through to Matruh.

We didn't linger long there but drove on towards Sidi Barrani, being machine-gunned by a couple of German fighters on the way. They made two passes along the column on the road, their machine guns rattling, and everyone out on the sand firing back at them with any available weapon. No harm seemed to be done to anyone.

226

Near Sidi Barrani there was another rearguard action which promised again to take at least a day to clear up. Denis had been worried about his recordings, which had not been coming through, so we decided to use this delay in going back to Tac. Army HQ, now near Mersa Matruh, to find out why not and also to pick up any mail or messages.

For Denis there was a cryptic request from the BBC to interview some Greek artillery, which no one had ever heard of. How he dealt with this odd instruction I never knew, because my own single message was much more explicit – I was to return to Cairo forthwith and report back to my regiment.

So came to an abrupt end, and much too soon, my days with Denis Johnston. He had been the most satisfactory of companions: we had worked well together, he was full of enterprise and energy and had a wonderfully ironic scepticism about the conduct of the war and those responsible for it, and not least about the point of the whole thing. At night, with a bottle of wine under the stars, we found we could converse freely and easily.

For my friend this was only the first chapter of his Dioniad. He followed the business through to the end, with many diversions and excursions by land and sea and air, and out of it all devised his magical book, *Nine Rivers from Jordan*. Reading this book again today, some 36 years after the events I have recounted, I am at once brought back vividly to my time with Denis, with whom I spent some of the most enjoyable and stimulating weeks of my war.

August, 1978.

NOTES

1   Msus was a place in the desert of some importance at that time and there was a race on between us and the Germans to see who could get there first. All the important horse races in England are sweepstakes, abbreviated to 'stakes', hence the name of this chase.

2   Rt. Hon. John Freeman, P.C. Labour M.P. and junior minister 1945-55; Editor of *The New Statesman*; High Commissioner in India; British Ambassador in Washington. Known as 'Red' at that time because of the colour of his hair.

3   Chief of the Imperial General Staff. Field Marshal Sir Alan Brooke, CIGS 1941 to 1946, and Churchill's chief military adviser. Created Viscount Alanbrooke. Died 1963.

PERFECTION OF THE LIFE, OR OF THE WORK?

VIVIAN MERCIER

The late Herbert Howarth suggested that every important Anglo-Irish writer of the period 1880-1940 wanted to write a sacred book; indeed, he proved the thesis – to his own satisfaction, at least – in a remarkable critical work, *The Irish Writers* (1958), which dealt with George Moore, Yeats, Synge, Lady Gregory, A.E., and Joyce.[1] Undoubtedly *A Vision*, *Finnegans Wake*, and more than one work by A.E. were sacred books in the eyes of their authors and some of their readers. But Howarth went further: as the subtitle of the London edition, *Literature Under Parnell's Star*, indicates, he felt that his six writers all regarded Parnell as a crucified Messiah, for whom they wished to play the role of the Evangelists. (As it turned out, their sacred books, except perhaps *Finnegans Wake*, touched only peripherally if at all upon the life, death and miracles of the Uncrowned King of Ireland.) Howarth also put forward an even more startling paradox: each of these very different authors was prepared to offer himself or herself – in however oblique and symbolic a manner – as an alternative Messiah for Ireland. Had Howarth, an Englishman, been more familiar with Irish history, he would have found a powerful reinforcement of his views in the plays, speeches, and death of the 1916 leader Patrick Pearse.

The two decades gone by since the publication of Howarth's seminal work suggest that living Irish writers have not abandoned the aspirations of their predecessors. In 1953, five years before *The Irish Writers*, Denis Johnston had published his first sacred book, *Nine Rivers from Jordan: The Chronicle of a Journey and a Search*. Many of us Irish, accustomed to thinking of Johnston as a satirist and ironist, failed to recognise its true nature. We had forgotten, or perhaps never known, his third play, *A Bride for the Unicorn*, which aspired to be a sacred drama. It was not until the appearance of Harold Ferrar's *Denis Johnston's Irish Theatre* in 1973 that this play received proper attention. The sumptuous publication of *The Brazen Horn* by Dolmen in 1976 finally confronted us with a sacred book that *looked* like a sacred book, even though it was little more than an extended commentary on *Nine Rivers*. It forced some of us

228

to take a new look at the earlier book and to realise that, despite all
the parody and persiflage, it meant what it said – including the death
and resurrection of Dionysius (or Dionysus) Johnston. The American edition of *Nine Rivers* bore the more evocative title *Dionysia*,
meaning on the one hand 'the rites of Dionysus' and on the other
hand 'the doings of Dionysius (the Latin form of the name Denis)'.
Perhaps if the same title had been given to the English edition, we
Irish might not have missed the point, but I doubt that: we would
probably have laughed at the title as pretentious. Johnston himself
is partly to blame; he quotes in *Nine Rivers* a criticism of himself
(perhaps written by himself?) that explains why:

> Whenever he stooped to deception, it was usually by means of the
> irritating trick of telling the truth, while insinuating that it was
> really a lie. Whenever he invited one to join him in a laugh at
> himself behind his own back, it was usually because he meant
> what he said, but did not want others to believe so.[2]

We might also plead, as an excuse for our obtuseness, that *Nine
Rivers* is a difficult book to grasp as a whole, operating as it does on
so many levels, successively and often simultaneously. The biggest
component, undoubtedly, is reportage of World War II in various
African and European theatres by a very privileged observer: a
BBC radio correspondent from a technically neutral country who
thinks himself sufficiently above the battle to be justified in by-
passing all petty regulations, and even some that are matters of life
and death. Over forty, well over six feet tall, with ten years of the
law and seventeen years of acting, directing and writing for the
stage, the films, radio and even embryo television behind him, he
combines an authoritative manner with a flexible mentality en-
compassing artistic and legalistic modes of thought. In short, a man
capable of browbeating, bluffing, wheedling or evading the average
Public Relations Officer with consummate ease. This is not the
place to record all the 'firsts' that Johnston scored in his new
profession, including the first broadcast commentary on a bomber
raid from a participating aircraft and the first visit by a Western
newsman to Tito's partisans. Despite his taste for anecdotes
belittling the earnestness of both sides, Johnston never lets the
reader down when describing a crucial scene or episode – Buchenwald, for instance. Like his compatriot Francis Stuart in the more
portentous *Black List, Section H,*[3] Johnston offers credible tes-

timony about the traumas of modern war to that great majority of his fellow Irish who escaped them.

On a more subjective level, this autobiography partly resembles both a *Bildungsroman* and a *conte philosophique*. In the first of its three parts, Johnston tends to present himself as an innocent rather like the title character of Voltaire's philosophical tale, *Candide*:

> I had imagined that I was going to be entrusted with some pretty serious work out here. Knowing what was wanted under our system of free and objective reporting, I was not going to concern myself with propaganda. I was going to describe soberly and sensibly exactly what I saw, and give the people at home the Truth, the whole Truth, and nothing but the Truth, whether happy or unfavourable.(8)

This forty-year-old Candide, however, has undoubtedly read *Candide*, as well as *Faust* (sometimes quoted in German), the *Odyssey*, and the *Divine Comedy*. Because he has read these works and much else, he sees his travels as a quest, but it would be unfair to assume that he knows to start with what he is going to find. True, he is the author of *A Bride for the Unicorn* (first performed 1933), in which the age-old questions about good and evil, life and death, time and eternity, are asked and answered by a Johnstonian version of J.W. Dunne's time theories. The main objection made to *A Bride for the Unicorn* in its 1933 and 1935 versions concerns its protagonist:

> John is too much of an abstract everyman and not enough of an individualized three-dimensional character to carry sufficient conviction in performance.[4]

Although Johnston maintained to Harold Ferrar that it is possible to create an everyman character who is also psychologically individualized ('Look at Faust and Peer Gynt'), the 1978 version of the play is still vulnerable to the same criticism as its predecessors. In sharp contrast, *Nine Rivers* has for its protagonist the idiosyncratic man of many wiles already sketched, who, along with some highly specialised experience, shares the lot of Everyman in a number of ways. He has been a husband and father, and finds that the most painful aspect of his impending divorce is estrangement from his first-born son. He is deeply in love with the woman who will become his second wife before the book ends, and suffers the normal pangs of separation from her. He remembers his dead father with affection and regrets that he has left his mother to die alone. He is untypical only in his attitude to money worries: having hinted that divorce is expensive and war correspondents are underpaid, he drops the subject, although, like most writers in wartime, he must have been very glad of salaried work to compensate for lost royalties. On the whole, he suffers the horrors of war only vicariously, quickly imitating the apparent indifference to fear of the British officer class, to which, by education at Merchiston and Cambridge, he belongs. Finally, he would have us believe, he undergoes the most universal experience of all – death.

Before investigating this staggering claim and analysing in more detail the *Bildungsroman* and Quest Romance aspects of *Nine Rivers*, let us look at one more of the book's levels, that of stylistic imitation and experiment. It would be an immense relief to at least one reader if all modern writers with ambitions as vast as Dante's would also share his frankness, making themselves without equivocation their own heroes and speaking in a reasonable approximation of their own voices. Marcel Proust and Ezra Pound come nearest to doing this, I suppose; James Joyce, after promising well, became more and more embarrassed as he strove to compose first the epic and then the myth of himself. Perhaps because so many readers believed he meant what he said in *A Portrait*, he began to adopt Johnston's strategy of inviting them 'to join him in a laugh at himself behind his own back.' I call it Johnston's strategy, but of course Joyce, nineteen years his senior, used it first. The chapter of *Nine Rivers* entitled 'A Catechism' will remind, and is intended to remind, any keen Joycean of the Ithaca episode in *Ulysses*. The preface to Book Three of *Nine Rivers*, 'A Critical Exagamen by E.W. Tocher', rather unskilfully parodies academic criticism: the title is clearly suggested by *Our Exagmination Round His Factification for Incamination of Work in Progress*, a collection of twelve essays on *Finnegans Wake* published ten years *before* that work reached its final form. The critic's name, however, happens to be the pseudonym employed by Johnston as actor and author until he gave up the law in 1936. Johnston teases me by name in a footnote (296) for claiming that many of the overtones of *The Old Lady Says 'No!'* appear to be drawn from *Finnegans Wake*. Nevertheless, I still stand over what I wrote in 1948:

This fantasy . . . owes at least as much to *Ulysses* as Thornton

231

Wilder's *The Skin of Our Teeth* does to *Finnegans Wake*. In Johnston's play there is some attempt made to keep up a parallel with Dante, as Joyce did with Homer, but it is not worked out very thoroughly. The Dublin voices that mock Emmet come straight out of the Circe episode in *Ulysses*; Johnston *may* also have seen what had already been published of *Work in Progress*.[5]

This 'Exagamen' concludes with a perfectly genuine paragraph of author's acknowledgements for assistance rendered in the writing, editing and publication of *Nine Rivers*. The paragraph immediately before this one consists of a single sentence, 'In such a Rite, Everyman is reconciled to the Deity.' (297) It too is to be taken literally, as we shall see.

The most successful of all the parodies, to my mind, is 'The Back Garden of the Hesperides', an account of Denis's return to Ireland in March 1945 for his second wedding, after which he hurried back to the war at once. It takes the form of an Old Irish *echtrae* or adventure in the Celtic Otherworld, translated fairly literally into Victorian English by someone like Kuno Meyer or Whitley Stokes. Its hero, Donnachada, is unwilling to linger in the island of Hy Brasail among the people of the Sidhe, however pleasant life there may be. Instead, 'mounting up on the back of his silver bird he . . . flew off towards the east where reign strife and decay . . .'(380) Another chapter, 'The High Court on the Brocken', prophetic of the Nuremberg Trials, combines the *Walpurgisnacht* from *Faust* with the Circe episode of *Ulysses* and the trial in *Alice in Wonderland*, not quite successfully. All of these parodies and pastiches have value as satirical commentary upon such matters as war crimes trials and Irish insularity, but their chief intent, I feel, is to convince the reader that Johnston is tough-minded, unsentimental, able to case aside at will the persona of a hero of romance. The danger of such a pose is that when *Nine Rivers* reaches its liturgical climax and conclusion 'in the guise of the Canon of an unknown Mass' (441), the reader may regard this as simply the most accomplished of all the pastiches, mingling reminiscences of Catholic liturgy and the Book of Job. Never has Johnston come closer to true poetry than in this passage, but it is possibly still open to the self-criticism he pronounced while reviewing a revival of *The Old Lady Says 'No!'*:

But what a pity it was not written by a Poet instead of by a Half-Coherent who, whenever he finds himself staggered by the

232

gigantic issues he has raised, has nothing better to do than to fall back upon Dante and the Holy Writ!⁶

II

Thinly disguised as E.W. Tocher, Johnston gives us a half-joking, wholly serious guide to 'the varying levels of analogue, in the text' of *Nine Rivers*:

> For example: (1) the biological structure moving from Birth (Cunt of the World) and Baptism (Jordan) to Senility (Snows of Hafelekar), (2) the liturgical format proceeding from Introit to Ite Missa Est, (3) the temporal span from sunset (Mena House) to sunrise (Innsbruck), and (4) the dialectical parallelism revolving from Homer through Blake and Goethe back to the Book of Job. These indicia are by no means exhaustive . . .(296)

By doing so, he once again undermines his readers' belief in his sincerity, while at the same time annoying the critics, who like to win credit for detecting allegories unaided. Given Johnston's temperamental bias toward mockery of himself and others, and the degree to which his work has been misunderstood or neglected – especially in Ireland – I refuse to blame his adoption of this strategy. Nevertheless, it contains an element of cowardice: if the critics take him seriously but deny that he has written a masterpiece, he can always use the bad child's lame excuse – 'I only meant it as a joke.'

For me, the biological and liturgical patterns have most importance. Combined, they naturally suggest a rite of passage – or, rather, a succession of such rites – dramatising the transition from one stage of human growth to another. *Nine Rivers* is divided into three parts with liturgical titles: Book One, 'The Catechumens'; Book Two, 'The Ordinary'; Book Three, 'The Epiklesis'. These are prefaced by a brief 'Introit' (a psalm or antiphon sung while the priest approaches the altar to celebrate Mass), spoken at high noon from the Dome of the Rock above Jerusalem. In a little over two pages (1–3) we are given a bird's-eye view of the entire book, including four possible starting points for the narrative; the whole passage is beautifully written and replete with hints of what is to come.

The titles given to the three books all refer to the Mass but involve some overlapping. The Mass of the Catechumens is an old name for what is now called the Liturgy of the Word, based ultimately on the

233

service in Jewish synagogues: the catechumens were converts under instruction before baptism, who must leave the church before the Mass of the Faithful, the Eucharist properly so called, began. They therefore could not be present for the Epiklesis (or Epiclesis), which is the invocation of the Holy Spirit to consecrate the elements (bread and wine) of the Eucharist. The Ordinary of the Mass, however, includes both the Mass of the Catechumens *and* the Mass of the Faithful: it consists of those prayers which are always used no matter what the feast may be, as opposed to those which vary with each Sunday or feast in the liturgical year. The correct opposition is Ordinary/Proper, not Ordinary/Catechumens or Ordinary/Epiklesis. Johnston was born into a Presbyterian family, but this does not mean that he errs through ignorance: he may be punning on a more familiar meaning of the word 'ordinary', for in the middle section of the book, the élan of youth is over:

> In the desert, I think as a child; in the Pontine slough, I practise the artifice of middle age . . .(2)

The title of the entire book is due to a prediction allegedly made by an Egyptian dragoman who read Johnston's palm on the way to the Great Pyramid:

> Before long you will start on a journey – a journey over earth, over fire, over air, and over water. I do not know where this journey will lead you, but I think that it is from where it is white to where it will be white again. It is from a depth to a summit. And here in your hand I see nine rivers that you must cross . . . When you have reached the last river, you will be at the end of your journey, and there you will find what you have been looking for.(27)

The first river is, of course, the Jordan, where Johnston 'baptises' himself but sees no dove. For the record, Baptism comes before Birth, as he proceeds from the Jordan crossing to the Valley of the Dead Sea, which, borrowing from Joyce, he calls 'this wrinkled cunt of the world'. (60) The next river in his westward journey from the east bank of Jordan is the Nile. The rest of 'The Catechumens' in effect portrays childhood and adolescence. Johnston, by his own account, enjoyed the Battle of Alamein, in which Montgomery defeated Rommel, especially the pursuit of the retreating German and Italian forces. He drank 'the heady wine of real, anarchic freedom – another topic quite unsuitable for a Press despatch!'(92) At the conclusion of this part of the book he seems willing to accept 'the creed of the fighting men – that War is not really such an evil thing at all.'(119) Earlier, he has declared, 'I am not oppressed by any particular feeling of evil in myself.'(64)

Not until the second chapter of Book Two does he learn from an Irish Catholic chaplain that this involves him in the heresy of Pelagianism. (141-42) The slow progress of the British forces in Italy leads him to a more realistic view of war:

> This is war – the thing I used to say was quite a good thing in its way. That's the trouble with the world. Too many liberated adolescents thinking of war in terms of the desert and excitement and pursuit and loot. But war isn't really like that.(152)

Later, he has reached the threshold of middle age, where all he wants after the War is 'to have a good regular office job, to go to the pictures a couple of times a week with a comfortable wife, and to study the Bible from Saturday to Monday.'(231) Although he bought his King James Bible in Jerusalem, it is in 'The Ordinary' that he begins to read it seriously, along with St. Francis of Assisi's *The Mirror of Perfection* and some New Testament Apocrypha. He visits Assisi himself at the end of Book Two and thinks of founding a Fourth Order of Saint Francis, 'open only to Protestants, Sceptics, the Unbaptised . . .'(289) Prior to this, he has entered Rome with the Allied Armies, recorded a broadcast talk in the empty Coliseum, and sung 'The Old Orange Flute' in tipsy Protestant defiance on the steps of St. Peter's. (The two rivers crossed in this Book are the Sangro and the Tiber.) It is at Assisi that he first comes upon 'the words of an unknown Prophet. . . . A startling revelation. . . .'(285) The 'unknown' prophet is usually called 'Second Isaiah' by biblical scholars, and the words that startled Johnston will be found in Isaiah, ch. 45, vv. 6-7: 'I am the Lord, and there is none else. I form the light, and create darkness: I make peace, and create evil: I the Lord do all these things.' This unfamiliar text brings Johnston to a new phase in his recurring meditation on the problem of evil:

> If I cannot have the Church's God without its Satan, maybe I need not deny them both, because according to this, they are the same person. There is no God but God, the Father of Night and Day,

Creator of Heaven and Hell, who sends us the frost and the flowers. If he freely confesses to Evil as well as to Good, I can believe in him again, and honour him, for that makes sense. Why he should have created Evil, I do not need to know. . . . But I can take it, because it is not a trap set to destroy me. (285-86)

He then goes through the remainder of the Apostles' Creed to see what in it he can or cannot believe, reaffirming the conclusion about immortality reached in *A Bride for the Unicorn*:

> . . . although Life Everlasting would be too intolerable to contemplate, I do nevertheless believe in the physical eternity and indestructibility of this life. For Death is only a boundary, not an End – a trick of bodily consciousness, and not of annihilation. (286)

In the second chapter of Book Three, Johnston, finding himself in Belgium, quickly reviews his travels since he crossed the Jordan; once again, he stresses the biological analogy:

> The milestones of this journey are like the footsteps of the race. In some odd and rather mystical way they seem to parallel the course of life itself, from childhood to maturity – a journey, maybe, in search of its own meaning. (306)

These ideas are developed further on the next page. As we have seen, in the 'middle age' of Book Two Johnston began to think about religion; now, 'here in snowclad old age', he accepts the idea that religion has a meaning and hopes to find out just what that meaning is. The first half of Book Three becomes rather diffuse, however, as Johnston's new west-to-east course doubles back on itself, first to the River Seine – he is a patient in a Paris hospital with his only war wound, a chipped elbow caused by a fall downstairs – and then further back still to the River Liffey in Dublin; soon after that, however, he has crossed the Rhine. Finding himself near Naumburg, he remembers the love letters written by a girl from a neighbouring village that he had found in the desert in an abandoned German staff car. (They are quoted extensively in Book One.) He goes to look for Annaliese Wendler in Eckartsberga but does not find her; as he is leaving, an American officer suggests that he take another road out of the village: 'I guess you don't know much about this war until you've been down that way.'(391) Thus, almost accidentally, Johnston finds himself at Buchenwald.

Up to this point he had been sceptical about stories of atrocities – had indeed seen very few dead bodies on any front – but he saw a truck at Buchenwald 'piled high with emaciated yellow naked corpses' and was told by two English-speaking ex-prisoners that this was 'just a day or two's collection.'(393) They brought him to the torture cellar and then to the worst block in the camp:

> As we entered the long hut the stench hit us in the face, and a queer wailing came to our ears. Along both sides of the shed was tier upon tier of what can only be described as shelves. And lying on these, packed tightly side by side, like knives and forks in a drawer, were living creatures – some of them stirring, some of them stiff and silent, but all of them skeletons, with the skin drawn tight over their bones, with heads bulging and misshapen from emaciation, with burning eyes and sagging jaws. And as we came in, those with the strength to do so turned their heads and gazed at us; and from their lips came that thin, unearthly noise.
>
> Then I realised what it was. It was meant to be cheering. They were cheering the uniform that I wore.(395)

Only the artist can offer convincing testimony on such horrors. The 'queer wailing', the 'thin, unearthly noise' that turns out to be cheering – no artist could have invented that detail, yet none but an artist could have seized on it and progressively revealed its full obscenity. No Irish person, however prejudiced, could any longer deny the existence of such camps after reading this passage among the excerpts serialised in *The Bell*. The experience led Johnston to ask himself, 'How did I ever doubt that there is not an Absolute in Good and Evil? . . . I have done my best to keep sane, but there is no answer to this, except bloody murder.'(397) Symbolically, as he left Buchenwald, he accepted a Lüger pistol as a souvenir, thus breaking the vow never to carry a weapon that he had superstitiously kept ever since becoming a war correspondent in 1942. It is to this breaking of this vow that he attributes his 'death', for he was killed with his own pistol by a Nazi, Otto Suder, to whom he had lent it as a suicide weapon. (438) And so he pronounces the final words of the Mass:

Ite Missa Est.

Or would you prefer a different ending?

On the assumptions of Newtonian Determinism, such a question is a ridiculous one. But mathematics have already proved these assumptions to be untenable, so perhaps it is not too outlandish an idea to suggest that we pick an alternative from the great bag of possibilities that Heaven has provided.(441)

The book – except for a brief postscript (456) giving a version of events in which Johnston sees the Nazi's car on the Brenner Pass highway but does not get into it or speak to Otto Suder – then ends with 'this alternative, in the guise of the Canon of an unknown Mass.' The Mass (441-55) is untitled, but one takes note that the chapter in which it occurs is named 'Uz', after the homeland of Job. This Mass is divided into two parts, 'Preface' and 'Epiklesis'. The Acolyte represents a Job-like Johnston, who reproaches God and is answered by a Voice from the Silence recalling the voice from the whirlwind in the Book of Job. If we are still conscious of Faustian overtones, let us remember that *Faust*, like Job, begins with a prologue in Heaven; furthermore, the mature protagonist of the Second Part of *Faust* reminds one a little of the Man of Uz.

The 'Preface' takes the form of a duet with chorus: Acolyte carries on a dialogue with Pieta, Pity personified, who is also the Blessed Virgin and the German girl Anneliese, whom Johnston thought he caught a glimpse of mourning over her dead fiancé. (427) Acolyte promises to avenge her, but she begs him to 'cast out/The knowledge of Good and Evil'(443) and throw away the pistol which is the forbidden fruit. Instead, he should seek 'an innocence that lies beyond maturity.'(445) In the 'Epiklesis', the dialogue is between Acolyte and The Voice, presumed to be that of God. At first, Acolyte is abashed and fears to speak what is in his heart, but the Voice says,

> you must first accuse the Lord
> Before he will lend his ear.
> Speak up, therefore, and confess my sins. . . .(448)

Acolyte replies,

> You have created Man –

238

In whose image of frailty I do not know –
And set him in the way of temptation.
You have bidden him to fight for his existence
And plagued him with a Pity for the things he has to kill. . . .

You have created me to long for life
When death is all that is intended for me.(448-49)

He ends by firing a shot from his Lüger in the general direction of
Heaven. Nevertheless, God spares his life: he is not to die in the
sedan on the Brenner Pass after all. As foreshadowed in an earlier
passage (427), Johnston in his turn forgives God and agrees to do
His will. In response to insistent questioning by the Voice, Acolyte
finally gives his reason: 'Why does the hammer do the will of the
smith?'(453) Man is a necessary implement in the hand of God. As
the symbol of his maturity, he throws away his gun, proclaiming
with the choir,

And this is my act of faith–
That I cast forth the Knowledge of Good and Evil,
And the deadly sins that are bred of sin,
Secure in the promise
That all things, future and past,
Hidden and revealed,
Are in his gracious hands.(455)

But the Voice has the last word, a rather ironical comment:

I have harnessed the Unicorn to the plough.
The range of the mountains was his pasturage
But now he shall bend his back to the furrow.
In Famine he shall save you from starvation
And in War from the power of the sword.
But keep him hungry till his work is done.
Will the wild ass bray while he has grass?(455)

III

The unicorn, 'the most virile of animals and at the same time . . .
one of the most chaste,'[7] only tameable by a virgin, has become
Johnston's favourite emblem in recent years, decorating the dust

239

jackets of his *Dramatic Works* and *The Brazen Horn*. It appears to symbolise among other things Man's creativity, his questing spirit, which God seeks to harness for His own purposes. Johnston seems to share one of Bernard Shaw's fundamental ideas, that God (the Life Force, Shaw calls Him) needs the help of Man, in fact of all living creatures, to accomplish His ends. As Johnston had promised us, 'Everyman is reconciled to the Deity.'(297) But note that the problem of Evil is not solved; it is simply handed over to God. Let me complete a quotation given earlier in this article:

> Why he should have created Evil, I do not need to know. I may not like it – I shall do my best to avoid it, as I avoid the winter's wind. But I can take it, because it is not a trap set to destroy me. It is clear that he is neither a bungler nor a demon, and in praising him for all his works, I am praising Creation as he has made it.(286)

Whether he realises it or not, I think Johnston has returned to the Pelagian heresy – named after Pelagius, who may have been an Irishman. He is denying the doctrine of original sin, which says that every human being is born guilty of the sin committed by the first man, Adam, and can only be saved from damnation by the grace of God and the sacrifice of Jesus Christ on the cross.

Confirmation of this view will be found in the creed, 'An Approach to an Absolute Statement,' which concludes *The Brazen Horn*. The tenth article of this statement of belief runs as follows:

> I cast forth from my mouth the fruit of the
>   Tree of Peril
> And with it both Fear and Remorse
> And the mortal Ills that are bred of Evil.[8]

One is reminded of Yeats's poem, 'A Dialogue of Self and Soul,' which ends which these lines:

> When such as I cast out remorse
> So great a sweetness flows into the breast
> We must laugh and we must sing,
> We are blest by everything,
> Everything we look upon is blest.[9]

240

The Irish Protestant, no matter how emancipated from traditional beliefs he thinks himself to be, carries on an almost life-long struggle against guilt. He is lucky if he can free himself from it at any age. Yeats was nearly seventy, Johnston seventy-five, when they thus affirmed their freedom from remorse.

But there is also a symbolism in Johnston's unknown Mass that has little to do with personal redemption from sin. When he accepted the pistol at Buchenwald, he was in a sense accepting the responsibility to avenge the Nazi atrocities. How are we to interpret his being 'killed' with this very weapon by an acknowledged Nazi leader? 'All they that take the sword shall perish by the sword' is part of the meaning, undoubtedly, and gains special relevance from the fact that Johnston prided himself on his Irish citizenship and therefore on his technical neutrality. Some 'hawks' would say that Ireland, by not declaring war on Germany, incurred part of the responsibility for Buchenwald and therefore Johnston's killing was an act of poetic justice. Again, by recognising the existence of absolute evil and agreeing that only the unconditional surrender of Germany and the execution of war criminals could satisfactorily end the war, Johnston was committing the sin of Captain Ahab in *Moby Dick*: vengeance and the abolition of evil should be left in God's hands – especially if one believes that He created evil in the beginning! But the final meaning of the unknown Mass is probably this: Acolyte/Johnston is, like Job, an innocent victim; the traditional Catholic interpretation of the Old Testament sees Job as a 'type' of Christ; therefore Johnston himself is in some sense Christ and by his death redeems the Allies as well as himself and the Nazis.

Thus Howarth's Hypothesis is vindicated, as all truly ingenious critical theories ought to be. It would be a lame and impotent conclusion to add that Johnston's death occurred in a dream – though that is in fact what I believe. Johnston has since written *The Brazen Horn* to prove, with the help of theories about time drawn from J.W. Dunne's writings and modern physics generally, that he did in fact die on the Brenner Pass the day the war in Europe virtually ended – all appearances to the contrary notwithstanding. (For example, he was a dinner guest at our house in Dublin on 10 January 1980).

In all honesty, I feel that the writing of *The Brazen Horn* was a waste of valuable creative energy. As John Lighton Synge warned Johnston at the very beginning, it is impossible to discuss physics today unless you have mastered the mathematics which provide the only language in which it can be meaningfully discussed. It was, however, as useless to warn Johnston off physics as to warn his greater exemplar, Bernard Shaw, off biology. We may legitimately complain, however, that while *The Brazen Horn* is no doubt equivalent to the preface of *Man and Superman* or *Back to Methusaleh*, there is no new play by Johnston for which it can become the preface. Shaw himself once wrote Johnston a postcard asking, 'Why don't you write more plays?' I can only echo the question. The revision or even total rewriting by Johnston of his earlier plays at intervals of up to forty years has proved no substitute for writing new plays: the later versions may show greater technical expertise, but the original élan is missing. I remember being surprised and delighted by the 1939 première of *The Golden Cuckoo*, yet I felt some disappointment at the première of the 1956 version; the author doubled as director on both occasions, thereby eliminating one possible reason for my differing reactions. There now exists a 1978 version, as yet unproduced, and I suspect that the 1971 Proscenium Press edition represents a fourth version, or rather a third, which differs materially from the second.

As Hilton Edwards wrote in 1946,

> He will work at the same script, correcting, developing, fundamentally altering, with what at first appears to be infinite patience, until one discovers that it is infinite impatience.[10]

Despite the fact that Edwards is partly paying off old grudges, dating chiefly from Johnston's brief stint as drama critic of *The Bell* (1941-42), it is hard to say anything about Johnston's career, before or since 1946, that has not been touched on in this prophetic article. For instance,

> He is now an important person in Television, but I dread the next scientific invention, or the next artistic craze; if there is anything that Denis can do about the Atom Bomb he will be off and away, and on to it within the hour . . .

The Brazen Horn is not exactly about the atomic bomb, but it will serve to illustrate the tendency in Johnston that Edwards had in mind. Edwards qualified his remark by adding,

> Heaven forbid I should plead with him to stay put; on the contrary, it is his spirit of adventure that I admire. . . .

242

Elsewhere in the article he complained that although Johnston has had 'a variety of experience . . . he has made very little use of it in his work . . . Like Wilde, perhaps, he puts his genius into his life.' Nevertheless, Edwards hoped that 'Some day he may write the play or the novel or do the thing that will bear the fruit of his wanderings.'

What I have been suggesting, of course, is that in writing *Nine Rivers from Jordan* Johnston has done the thing that Edwards was hoping for. 'Who touches this touches a man', as Whitman said. Into it has gone as much of Johnston as can be put in any book. What is more, I consider that *Nine Rivers* is a work of art, in the tradition of what Northrop Frye calls the Anatomy or Menippean Satire, comparable with *Moby Dick* and *Tristram Shandy*, *Ulysses* and – perhaps the closest analogy – *Hail and Farewell*.

Yeats insisted that

The intellect of man is forced to choose
Perfection of the life, or of the work . . .[11]

meaning that one cannot be both an artist and a saint, but in another sense he himself managed to achieve the perfection of life that consists in living it to the full. How he would have envied Johnston his wartime experiences, just as he envied the 'affable Irregular' and the 'brown Lieutenant' in 'Meditations in Time of Civil War'![12] He might even have envied him his academic posts, an unfulfilled ambition with Yeats. We cannot deny Denis Johnston 'perfection of the life'; we must also acknowledge 'perfection of the work' in *The Old Lady Says 'No!'*, *The Moon in the Yellow River* – and, I insist, in *Nine Rivers from Jordan*.

NOTES

1 Herbert Howarth, *The Irish Writers 1880–1940: Literature Under Parnell's Star* (London: Rockliff, 1958).

2 Denis Johnston, *Nine Rivers from Jordan: The Chronicle of a Journey and a Search* (London: Derek Verschoyle, 1953), p. 294. All further references to this work appear in the text.

3 Francis Stuart, *Black List, Section H* (Carbondale: Southern Illinois Univ. Press, 1971).

4 Harold Ferrar, *Denis Johnston's Irish Theatre*, The Irish Theatre Series 5 (Dublin: Dolmen Press, 1973), p. 75.

5 Vivian Mercier, 'Dublin Under the Joyces', in *James Joyce: Two Decades of Criticism*, ed. Seon Givens (New York: Vanguard Press, 1948), pp. 297–98.

Denis Johnston: a retrospective

6 Denis Johnston, 'Drama: The Dublin Theatre', *The Bell*, Feb. 1942, pp. 359–60.
7 Johnston, quoted in Ferrar, p. 74.
8 Denis Johnston, *The Brazen Horn: A Non-Book for Those Who, in Revolt Today, Could be in Command Tomorrow,* Dolmen Editions XXII (Dublin: Dolmen Press, 1976), p. 202.
9 William Butler Yeats, *The Collected Poems of W.B. Yeats*, 2nd ed. (London: Macmillan, 1950), p. 267.
10 This and the four following quotations are from Hilton Edwards, 'Denis Johnston', *The Bell*, Oct. 1946, pp. 7–18; see especially pp. 9, 10, 17.
11 Yeats, p. 278.
12 Yeats, p. 229.

CHECK-LIST

DENIS JOHNSTON'S WRITINGS

Books of plays:

'The Moon in the Yellow River' and 'The Old Lady Says "No!" ':
  Two Plays, London, Jonathan Cape, 1932. Includes 'Foreword'
  by C. P. Curran and 'Author's Note.'
The Moon in the Yellow River, London, Jonathan Cape, 1934.
  Includes 'Foreword' by C. P. Curran.
'Storm Song' and 'A Bride for the Unicorn': Two Plays, London,
  Jonathan Cape, 1935.
Blind Man's Buff, London, Jonathan Cape, 1938.
Pastor Hall and Blind Man's Buff (the former by Ernst Toller, the
  latter by Denis Johnston in collaboration with Toller but dis-
  claimed by Johnston), New York, Random House, 1939.
'The Golden Cuckoo' and Other Plays, London, Jonathan Cape,
  1954. Includes 'Introduction,' 'The Golden Cuckoo,' 'The
  Dreaming Dust,' 'A Fourth for Bridge.'
Six Characters in Search of An Author, by Luigi Pirandello, trans-
  lated and adapted for opera by Denis Johnston, Bryn Mawr,
  Pennsylvania, Merion Music, 1957. (With musical score, same
  publisher, 1960.)
Collected Plays, 2 vols., London, Jonathan Cape, 1960. Vol. I:
  general 'Preface', 'The Old Lady Says "No!"' with preface 'Opus
  One', 'The Scythe and the Sunset' with preface 'Up the Rebels!',
  'A Fourth for Bridge' with preface 'Arma Virumque.' Vol. II:
  'The Moon in the Yellow River' with preface 'Let There Be
  Light', 'The Dreaming Dust' with preface 'Period Piece',
  'Strange Occurrence on Ireland's Eye' with preface 'The Scales
  of Solomon'.
'The Old Lady Says "No!"' and Other Plays, Boston, Toronto,
  Atlantic, Little, Brown, 1960. Same contents as *Collected Plays,*
  above, but contained in one volume.
Nine Rivers from Jordan (libretto), Bryn Mawr, Pennsylvania,
  Theodore Presser, 1968.
The Dramatic Works, Vol. I, Gerrards Cross, Colin Smythe, 1977.
  'General introduction,' 'The Old Lady Says "No!"' with preface

'Opus One' and afterword 'A Note on What Happened', 'The Scythe and the Sunset' with preface 'Up the Rebels!', 'Storm Song', 'The Dreaming Dust' with preface 'Period Piece', 'Strange Occurrence on Ireland's Eye' with preface 'The Scales of Solomon'. Published in N. America by Macmillan of Canada/Maclean Hunter.

The Dramatic Works, Vol. II, Gerrards Cross, Colin Smythe, 1979. 'Introduction', 'A Bride for the Unicorn', 'The Moon in the Yellow River' with preface 'Let There Be Light', 'A Fourth for Bridge' with preface 'Arma Virumque', 'The Golden Cuckoo' with 'Introduction', 'Nine Rivers from Jordan' ('Based upon some sections of the Operatic Libretto *Nine Rivers from Jordan* by the same author'), 'Tain Bo Cuailgne: A pageant of the great Cattle Raid of Cooley and of the high deeds of Cuchulainn, Champion of Ulster'. Published in N. America by Humanities Press Inc. Atlantic Highlands, New Jersey.

Der Mond Im Gelben Fluss, Ins Deutsche übertragen von W.M. Treichlinger, Frankfurt am Main, Walter Ruppert, n.d.

Books other than plays:

Nine Rivers From Jordan: The Chronicle of a Journey and a Search, London, Derek Verschoyle, 1953.

Nine Rivers From Jordan: The Chronicle of a Journey and a Search, Boston, Toronto, Little, Brown, August 1955.

In Search of Swift, Dublin, Hodges Figgis, 1959.

John Millington Synge (Columbia Essays on Modern Writing, No.12, ed. William York Tindall), New York and London, Columbia University Press, 1965.

The Brazen Horn: Lenaea 5: A Non-Book for Those Who, In Revolt Today, Could Be In Command To-morrow, Line drawings by Rory Johnston, Alderney, privately printed, 1968. (Revised as Lenaea 6)

The Brazen Horn: A Non-Book for Those Who, In Revolt Today, Could Be In Command Tomorrow, diagrams by Rory Johnston, 1050 signed copies, Dublin, Dolmen Press, 1976.

Plays and stories included in collections:

'The Old Lady Says "No!"' in *Plays of Changing Ireland,* ed. Curtis Canfield, New York, Macmillan, 1936.

'The Moon in The Yellow River' in *Specimens of Contemporary*

Drama, ed. Edward Rudolph Wood, London, Heineman, 1957.
'The Moon in the Yellow River' in *Three Irish Plays*, ed. E. Martin Brown, Harmondsworth, Penguin, 1959.
La luna en el rio amarillo, in *Teatro Irlandes Contemporáneo*, Madrid, Aguilar, 1963.
'The Call to Arms' in *Tears of the Shamrock*, ed. David Marcus, London, Wolfe, 1972.

Articles:

'Sean O'Casey: An Appreciation', *Living Age*, Vol. 329, No. 4267, April 1926.
'A National Morality Play', (by E. W. Tocher), *Motley,* March [1932].
'The Making of the Theatre', *The Gate Theatre,* ed. Bulmer Hobson, Dublin, The Gate Theatre, 1934.
'Towards a Dynamic Theatre', *The Gownsman*, 8 June 1935.
'Yeats as Dramatist', *Irish Times*, 13 June 1935.
'The Moon in the Yellow River' (letter), *The New English Weekly*, 25 July 1935.
'Theatre or Cinema', *The Listener*, 11 September 1935.
'Starring the Public', *The Listener*, 16 October 1935.
'Cities With a Difference', *The Listener*, 8 January 1936.
'The World We Listen In', *Radio Times*, 23 October 1936.
' "The Young Roscius": A Boy Genius of Regency Days', *Radio Times*, 12 February 1937.
'The Call to Arms', *The Listener*, 17 March 1937.
'The Theatre in Ireland', *One Act Play Magazine*, October 1937.
' "Lillibulero": A Song that Ended a Dynasty', *Radio Times*, 25 March 1938.
'Public Opinion: A National Morality Play', *The Bell*, Vol. 1, No. 6, March 1941.
'The Mysterious Origin of Dean Swift', *Dublin Historical Record,* Vol. III, No. 4, June-August 1941.
'Shaw: The Man and His Work', *Irish Times,* 26 July 1941.
'The Dramatic Revival' (letter to the Editor), *Irish Times*, 8 August 1941.
'In Peaceful Dublin', *The Listener*, 11 September 1941.
'The American Soldier', *The Listener*, 6 March 1942.
'The Night Before', *Trinity Parade*, June 1943.
'The Assault on Flushing', *The Listener,* 9 November 1944. [Part of

'The Battle for the Scheldt' written in collaboration by BBC war correspondents.]

' "Taking Over" in Bonn', *The Listener*, 15 March 1945. [Despatches by BBC war correspondents.]

'A Problem of Uniforms', *The Listener*, 22 March 1945. [Part of 'In Occupied Germany Today', despatches by BBC war correspondents.]

'The Enigma of Jonathan Swift', *Radio Times*, 12 October 1945.

'The Essential Swift', *Manchester Guardian*, 19 October 1945.

'Jonathan Swift: 1667–1745', *Irish Times*, 20 October 1945.

'Irish Neurosis Reflected in Art and Letters', *The Observer*, 13 January 1946.

' "Juno" and O'Casey,' *Radio Times*, 3 May 1946.

'Parnell and Pigott', *Radio Times*, 21 June 1946.

'Mr. Shaw, We Wish You Well', *The Listener*, 1 August 1946.

' "It's So Good There'll be Trouble" ', *Radio Times*, 13 September 1946. [Introduction to broadcast of *The Plough and the Stars*.]

'Behind the Television Cameras', *English Digest*, October 1946. [Condensed from *Television Again*.]

'Sean O'Casey: Realist or Romantic?' *The Listener*, 17 October 1946.

'Sean O'Casey', *Living Writers*, ed. Gilbert Phelps, London, Sylavan Press, 1947.

'Television: The Present and the Future', *Penguin Parade*, Second Series, No. 1, ed. J. E. Morpurgo, West Drayton, Middlesex, Penguin Books, 1947.

'Television and the BBC', *The Spectator*, 22 July 1949.

'A Decade in Retrospect: 1939–49', *The Month*, Vol. 3, No. 2, 1950.

'Meet a Certain Dan Pienaar', *The Bell*, Vol. XVI, No. 2, November 1950.

'Joxer in Totnes', *Irish Writing*, No. 13, December 1950.

'The Aran Islands', *Portraits of Islands*, ed. Eileen Molony, London, Dobson, 1951.

'Man-Sovereign Man', *The Bell*, Vol. XVI, No. 4, January 1951.

'Detour in Illyria', *The Bell*, Vol. XVI, No. 5, February 1951.

'Buchenwald', *The Bell*, Vol. XVI, No. 6, March 1951.

'A Short View of the Progress of Joyceanity', *Envoy*, V, No. 17, April 1951. [Reprinted in *A Bash in the Tunnel*, ed. John Ryan, London, Clifton House, 1970.]

'The Dublin Trams', *Dublin Historical Record*, Vol. XII, No. 4, November 1951.

'God's Gift to the English Departments', *The CEA Critic,* February 1952. [On Joyce, condensed from 'A Short View of the Progress of Joyceanity', *Envoy,* V, No. 17, April 1951.]

'Eastward Ho!' *The Listener,* 20 August 1953.

'Who Coddled Donizetti' (letter to Editor), *Irish Times*, 6 March 1955.

(Letter to Editor), *Irish Times*, 30 August 1955.

(Letter to Editor), *Irish Times*, 4 September 1955.

'Sentence on the Gate' (letter to Editor), *Irish Times*, 6 April 1956.

'Letter to a Young Dramatist', *The Listener,* 30 August 1956. [Part of a series: 'Letters to Beginners' – no. V.]

'Introduction', Mary Manning, *The Voice of Shem: Passages from 'Finnegans Wake';* London, Faber, 1958.

'Cambridge After the First World War', *The Listener,* 14 August 1958.

'Our First Film', *Creation,* November 1958.

'What Has Happened to the Irish', *Theatre Arts,* XLIII, July 1959.

'That's Show Business', *Theatre Arts,* XLIV, February 1960. [Intended title: 'No Business like Show Business.]

'The College Theatre – Why?' *Theatre Arts,* XLIV, August 1960.

'Humor-Hibernian Style', *New York Times,* 5 February 1961.

'Pleasurable Pilgrimages', *Irish Times,* 16 June 1962.

'Needed: New Perspectives for the Theatre', *Theatre Arts,* XLVI, December 1962.

'What's Wrong with the New Theatres', *Theatre Arts,* XLVII, August–September 1963.

'Dream Theatre', *Smith Alumnae Quarterly,* Winter 1963.

'Clarify Begins At: The Non-Information of *Finnegans Wake*', *Massachusetts Review,* Vol. V, No. 2, Winter 1964. Reprinted in *Irish Renaissance: A Gathering of Essays, Memoirs, Letters and Dramatic Poetry from the Massachusetts Review,* ed. Robin Skelton and David Clark, Dublin, Dolmen Press, 1965.

'Sean O'Casey', *The Nation,* CXCIX, 5 October 1964.

'The Trouble With Swift', *The Dublin of Dean Swift* (Swift tercentenary pamphlet. No date, editor, or publisher indicated).

'The Year of Jonathan Swift', *Irish Times,* 22 March 1967.

'Swift of Dublin', *Ireland of the Welcomes,* Bord Fáilte, March-April 1967. Reprinted in *Eire–Ireland,* Vol. 3, No. 3, Autumn 1968.

'Policy for the Abbey Theatre', *Hibernia,* 15 May 1970.

'Policy in Theatre', *Hibernia,* 29 May 1970.

'Did You Know Yeats? And Did You Lunch with Shaw?' *A Paler Shade of Green,* ed. Des Hickey and Gus Smith, London, Leslie Frewin, 1972. American title: *Flight from the Celtic Twilight,* New York, Bobbs-Merrill, 1973.

'Brian Friel and Modern Irish Drama', *Hibernia,* 7 March 1975. Myles Na cGopaleen', *Myth and Reality in Irish Literature,* ed. Joseph Ronsley, Waterloo, Ontario, Wilfrid Laurier University Press, 1977.

'Giants in Those Days of Shaw, De Valera and Sir William Haley', *Irish University Review,* Vol. 8, No. 1, Spring 1978.

[On the Dublin Gate Theatre], *Enter Certain Players: Edwards-MacLiammoir and the Gate 1928–1987,* ed. Peter Luke, Dublin, Dolmen Press, October 1978. [Excerpt from this article in the *Irish Times*, 30 September 1978].

Book reviews:

'Mr Yeats as Dramatist', *The Spectator,* 30 November 1934. [Review of *Wheels and Butterflies* by W. B. Yeats.]

Reviews of *Purple Dust*, by Sean O'Casey, *The Bell*, Vol. 1, No. 4, January 1941.

'Waiting with Beckett', *Irish Writing,* 34, Spring 1956. [Review of *Waiting for Godot* by Samuel Beckett.]

'James Joyce and the New Criticism', *Sunday Times*, 17 June 1956. [Review of *Dublin's Joyce* by Hugh Kenner.]

'If You Like Them Short', *Saturday Review,* 21 September 1957. [Review of *Domestic Relations* by Frank O'Connor.]

'Sean O'Casey: A Biography and an Appraisal', *Modern Drama,* December 1961. [Review of *Sean O'Casey: The Man and His Work* by David Krause, and *The Experiments of Sean O'Casey* by Robert Hogan.]

'The Non-Theatre of Bertolt Brecht', *Massachusetts Review* Vol. 2, No. 4, Summer 1961. [Review of *Seven Plays by Bertolt Brecht*, ed. Eric Bentley.]

'The Trouble with Swift', *The Nation,* Vol. 196, No. 4, 26 January 1963. [Review of *Jonathan Swift and Ireland* by Oliver W. Ferguson, *Swift the Man, His Works, and the Age* by Irwin Ehrenpreis, and *Cadenus* by Sybil Le Brocquy.]

'Somewhat Sinister Laughter', *The Nation,* Vol. 196, No. 20, 18 May 1963. [Review of *The Irish Comic Tradition* by Vivian Mercier.]

'The Goat's Minions', *The Nation,* Vol. 200, No. 11, 15 March 1965. [Review of *The Orgy* by Muriel Rukeyser.]

Review of *The Theatre of Revolt* by Robert Brustein, *Amherst Alumnae News,* Winter 1965.

Review of *Sean O'Casey: The Man Behind the Plays* by Saros Cowasjee, *Modern Drama,* December 1965.

'Books', *Wascana Review,* Vol. 2, No. 2, 1967. [Review of *Sean O'Casey: The Man Behind the Plays* by Saros Cowasjee, *Blasts and Benedictions,* ed. Ronald Ayling, and *The World of Sean O'Casey,* ed. Sean McCann.]

'Deanery', *Irish Press* 11 July 1970. [Review of *Swift: The Critical Heritage* by Kathleen Williams.]

'Plunkett's People', *Irish Press,* 26 April 1969. [Review of *Strumpet City* by James Plunkett.]

'Three Books on Irish Literature', *Wascana Review,* Vol. 4, No. 1, 1969. [Review of *The Backward Look* by Frank O'Connor, *After the Irish Renaissance* by Robert Hogan, and *Seven Irish Plays,* ed. Robert Hogan.]

'Rococo Ros', *Irish Press,* 10 January 1970. [Review of *O Rare Amanda: The Life of Amanda McKittrick Ros* by Jack Loudan.]

'Drama Notes', *Hibernia,* 17 July 1970. [Review of *The Third Theatre* by Robert Brustein.]

'The Green Room Crowd', *Irish Times,* 28 July 1972. [Review of *A Paler Shade of Green,* ed. Des Hickey and Gus Smith.]

'Under Suspicion', *Irish Press,* 5 August 1972. [Review of *The Suspecting Glance* by Conor Cruise O'Brien.]

'Keep the Home Front Burning', *Irish Times,* 2 September 1972. [Review of *Total War* by Peter Calvocoressi and Guy Wint.]

'Tales of Sad Sam', *Irish Times,* 9 December 1972. [Review of *More Pricks Than Kicks* and *How It is* by Samuel Beckett.]

'Jack Yeats the Novelist', *Irish Times,* 14 September 1974. [Review of *Ah Well: A Romance in Perpetuity, And to You Also,* and *The Charmed Life,* by Jack B. Yeats.]

'Orwell's Bad Conscience', *Irish Times,* 29 November 1975. [Review of *The Road to Minilar: George Orwell, the state, and God* by Christopher Small.

'The Voice of Sean', *Irish Times,* 27 September 1975. [Review of *The Letters of Sean O'Casey,* Vol. I, ed. David Krause.]

'An Interview with Denis Johnston: Anti-Melodrama in Dublin' (interview by Rod Taylor and John Wilson), *The Varsity* (University of Toronto), 12 March 1976.

'Irish Theatre', *Irish Times*, 00 March 1975. [Review of *Theatre in Ireland* by Micheál O hAodha.]

'Master of the Unconscious', *Irish Times*, 11 September 1976. [Review of *Jung and the Story of Our Time* by Laurens van der Post.]

'To Be or Not To Be', *Irish Times*, 23 October 1976. [Review of *Death and Eternal Life* by John Hick.]

'Man of the Theatre', *Irish Times*, 27 November 1976. [Review of *Tyrone Guthrie* by James Forsyth.]

'The Hardworking Rich', *Irish Times*, 6 December 1976. [Review of *The Rockefellers: An American Dynasty* by Peter Collier and David Horowitz.]

'Denis Johnston' (interview by Caroline Walsh), *Irish Times*, 12 February 1977.

'Finding Jesus', *Irish Times*, 16 April 1977. [Review of *Jesus* by Michael Grant.]

'The Playwright of the Tinkers', *Times Literary Supplement*, 13 May 1977. [Review of *J.M. Synge: Interviews and Recollections*, ed. E.H. Mikhail.]

'Barnaby Loves Emily', *Irish Times*, 14 May 1977. [Review of *A Hole in the Head: A Novel* by Francis Stuart.]

'Masked Man', *Hibernia*, 24 June 1977. [Review of *Enter a Goldfish* by Micheál MacLiammoir.]

'Behan without the Folklore', *Irish Times*, 9 July 1977. [Review of *The Writings of Brendan Behan* by Colbert Kearney.]

'On the Verge', *Irish Times*, 27 August 1977. [Review of *Lost Gods* by John Allegro.]

'Testing Times', *Hibernia*, 23 February 1978. [Review of *Janus: A Summing Up* by Arthur Koestler.]

'The Message of Methuselah', *Irish Times*, 25 March 1978. [Review of *Back to Methuselah* by Bernard Shaw.]

'George the Great', *Irish Times*, 6 October 1979. [Review of *The Genius of Shaw*, ed. Michael Holroyd.]

'The Year of O'Casey', *The Irish Press*, 19 February 1981. [Review of *Sean O'Casey: Centenary Essays*, ed. David Krause and Robert G. Lowery.]

Drama Reviews:

'Plays of the Quarter', *The Bell*, Vol. 2, No. 1, April 1941. [Reviews of: *Dancing Shadow* by Micheál MacLiammóir, *Thunder Rock* by Robert Ardrey, *The Seagull* by Anton Chekhov, *Pride and Prejudice* by Christine Longford, *The Summit* by George Shiels, *Money Doesn't Matter* by Louis D' Alton, *Heartbreak House* by G.B. Shaw, *Winterset* by Maxwell Anderson.]

'Plays of the Month', *The Bell,* Vol. 2, No. 2, May 1941. [Reviews of: *The Admirable Crichton* by J. M. Barrie, *Marrowbone Lane* by Robert Collis, *The Forced Marriage* by David Sears.]

'The Theatre', *The Bell,* Vol. 2, No. 4, July 1941. [Reviews of: *The Lady in the Twilight* by Mervyn Wall, *The Trial at Green Street Courthouse* by Roger McHugh, *The Money Doesn't Matter* by Denis Ireland.]

'The Theatre', *The Bell,* Vol. 2, No. 5, August 1941. [Reviews of: *Lord Edward* by Christine Longford, *Of Mice and Men* by John Steinbeck, *Storm in a Teacup* by James Bridie.]

'Dublin Theatre', *The Bell,* Vol. 3, No. 2, November 1941. [Reviews of: *Remembered Forever* by Barney McGinn, *The Fire Burns Low* by P. J. Fitzgibbon, *Swans and Geese* by Elizabeth Connor, the *Jimmy O'Dea Review, No Time for Comedy* by S. N. Behrman, *Hedda Gabler* by Henrick Ibsen, *An Italian Straw Hat* by Blake Gifford.]

'Drama; 'The Dublin Theatre', *The Bell,* Vol. 3, No. 5, February 1942. [Reviews of: *Ceasar and Cleopatra* by G. B. Shaw, *The Old Lady Says 'No!'* by Denis Johnston, *The Great God Brown* by Eugene O'Neill.]

'Theatre in Dublin', *The Observer,* 27 January 1946. [Reviews of: *Goody Two Shoes* by T. C. Murray, '*The Major*', a one-man show of Jimmy O'Dea, *Prunella* by Laurence Housman and Granville-Barker.]

'Theatre in Dublin', *The Observer,* 11 February 1946. [Review of vaudeville combined with movies.]

'Critique', *Mt. Holyoke News*, Spring 1951. [Review of *Das Liederliche Kleeplatt* adapted by Joachim Maass.]

Unpublished Plays:

    'Ulysses in Nightown' (produced 1958)
    'Finnegans Wake' (produced 1959)
    'Riders to the Sidhe: A Musical Synge-Song' (produced early 1960s, Poets Theatre, Cambridge, Massachusetts)

Unpublished screenplays:

'Guests of the Nation' (1933)
'River of Unrest' (1937)
'Ourselves Alone' (1937)

Ballet:

'The Indiscreet Goat' (produced 1931, The Gate Theatre)

Broadcasts:

Broadcast records kept by the networks tend to be somewhat incomplete, especially from before and during World War II. The following list, therefore, is as complete and accurate as the records allow. The intention is to include essentially only scripts written by Denis Johnston, but the list may include some adaptations and readings by him as well. Typescripts of many of these programmes are among the Johnston papers at the New University of Ulster, Coleraine, Northern Ireland.

BBC Radio:

[[The following code will apply:
LR – London Regional
N – National
NIHS – Northern Ireland Home Service
HS – Home Service
F – Forces Programme
LP – Light Programme
TP – Third Programme
NA – North American Service
WEHS – West of England Home Service
rec. – recording date]

14 May 1935	The Moon in the Yellow River	LR
15 May 1935	The Moon in the Yellow River	N
3 Sept. 1935	Theatre or Cinema	LR
7 Oct. 1935	Starring the Public (on documentary films)	LR
30 Dec. 1935	Men Talking	N
24 May 1936	Readings of Kipling	N
24 May 1936	Ulster Recollections	NIHS

2 Aug. 1936	Reading of Kipling	N
23 Nov. 1936	Siege of Derry	NIHS
19 Dec. 1936	The Call to Arms (reading)	N
17 Feb. 1937	We Are Six (series)	NIHS
20 Feb. 1937	Young Roscius (adapted)	LR
22 Feb. 1937	We Are Six (series)	NIHS
2 Mar. 1937	We Are Six (series)	NIHS
11 Mar. 1937	We Are Six (series)	NIHS
17 Mar. 1937	We Are Six (series)	NIHS
23 Mar. 1937	Drama in Ulster	NIHS
12 Apr. 1937	The Call to Arms (reading)	N
10 Aug. 1937	Men Talking (with A. Robinson)	N
7 Oct. 1937	Death at Newtownstewart	N
10 Nov. 1937	Poisson d'Avril (reading)	N
23 Nov. 1937	Phillipa's Fox Hunt	NIHS
2 Dec. 1937	Trinket's Colt	NIHS
7 Dec. 1937	A Little Trouble in Court	NIHS
16 Dec. 1937	The White Cockatoo	NIHS

[The above four items are readings from *Some Experiences of An Irish R. M.* by Somerville and Ross.]

17 Dec. 1937	The White Cockatoo (reading)	N
18 Dec. 1937	Birth of a Giant (panorama of N.I. ship-yards)	LR
24 Dec. 1937	Not One Returns to Tell	NIHS
3 Jan. 1938	A Little Trouble in Court (reading)	N
10 Jan. 1938	Trinket's Colt (reading)	N
18 Feb. 1938	Not One Returns to Tell	LR
24 Feb. 1938	The King of Spain's Daughter (producer)	LR
22nd Mar. 1938	Experimental Hour: A Bride for the Unicorn	N
30 Mar. 1938	Lillibulero	LR
25 May 1938	In Search of Valour (adaptor & producer)	N
31 May 1938	The Parnell Commission	LR
11 June 1938	A Bride for the Unicorn	LR
11 June 1938	Children's Hour. Use of 'Birth of a Giant.'	N
18 June 1938	Weep for Polyphemus	LR
24 Nov. 1938	Multiple Studio Blues (with John Cheatle)	LR
31 Dec. 1939	The Face of Courage (with Stephen Potter)	HS
15 Dec. 1940	These Men Were Free, No. 4. Garibaldi.	HS
23 Dec. 1940	Nansen of the Fram	HS
25 Dec. 1940	Christmas Under Fire	HS

2/3 Jan. 1941	Justice	Overseas
13 Feb. 1941	Great Parliamentarians, No. 3. Edmund Burke.	HS
25 Feb. 1941	We Speak for Ourselves: workers of Belfast	HS
1 May 1941	Great Parliamentarians, No. 6. Palmerston.	HS
31 May 1941	Dublin's Air Raid	HS
9 June 1941	The ATC in Northern Ireland	HS
30 June 1941	Invasion of Ulster	HS
11 Aug. 1941	American Technicians in Northern Ireland	HS
21 Aug. 1941	The Gorgeous Lady Blessington	HS
3 Sept. 1941	Today in Dublin	HS & F
6 Oct. 1941	The Parnell Commission	HS
15 Oct. 1941	Abraham Lincoln	HS
15 Oct. 1941	Northern Ireland Command Junior Leaders' School	HS
17 Oct. 1941	A Crash Exercise	HS
14 Dec. 1941	Autobiography of Mark Twain (reading)	HS
1 Jan. 1942	Visit to the Lough Neagh Patrol	HS
27 Jan. 1942	Arrival of American Troops in Northern Ireland	HS
30 Jan. 1942	American Troop Interviews	HS
21 Feb. 1942	The Train to Eire	HS
23 Feb. 1942	Great Americans, No. 4. George Washington	HS
25 Feb. 1942	The American Soldier	HS
9 Mar. 1942	Radio Theatre No. 6. Playboy of the Western World (adaptor)	NIHS
19 Apr. 1942	American Troops in (Ireland)	HS
20 Apr. 1942	An Irish Steward's Escape from the Germans	HS
22 Apr. 1942	Army Discipline and Battle Training	HS
12 May 1942	Report from an East Anglian Aerodrome	HS
5 Mar. 1943	Battle of Egypt, No. 3. The Building of an Army	HS
27 July 1943	Amanda McKittrick Ros	HS
16 Dec. 1943	Mediterranean Convoy	HS
24 Jan. 1944	Mediterranean Convoy	Overseas
9 Aug. 1944	The World Goes By: Partisans and Patriots in Italy and Jugoslavia	HS

19 Aug. 1944	The World Goes By: Partisans and Patriots	
		NIHS
17 May 1945	Atlantic Gateway (with Glyn Lloyd)	NIHS
2/3 July 1945	Atlantic Gateway	overseas
14 Aug. 1945	Atlantic Bridgehead	HS
18 Aug. 1945	Window on Europe	NIHS
18 Oct. 1945	Weep for Polyphemus	NIHS
19 Oct. 1945	Weep for Polyphemus	HS
14 Feb. 1946	Not One Returns to Tell	NIHS
27 Apr. 1946	Death at Newtownstewart	NIHS
6 June 1946	Current Affairs	LP
7 June 1946	In the Train (adaptor)	NIHS
27 June 1946	The Parnell Commission	HS
1 July 1946	Weep for Polyphemus, in Plays of the Season	WEHS
4 July 1946	Eye-Witness. Stories from a Customs House on the Northern Ireland Border	HS
26 July 1946	A Birthday Tribute to Bernard Shaw	HS
5 Oct. 1946	Living Writers, No. 1. Sean O'Casey	TP
13 Oct. 1946	Living Writers, No. 1. Sean O'Casey	WEHS
20/22 Feb. 1947	Television in Britain	NA
17 Mar. 1947	Contribution to Fantasia	LP
3 July 1947	Palestine – Background of Tension	HS
14 July 1947	The Moon in the Yellow River	HS
23 July 1947	Eye-Witness. Behind the Scenes at the Russian Ballet	HS
27 July 1947	Middle East after Three Years	HS
17 Sept. 1947	Eye-Witness. Visit to Dublin	HS
16 Nov. 1947	Television Studio Production	overseas
3 Dec. 1947	Swift/Stella/Vanessa	TP
13 Dec. 1947	The Week in Britain: Anglo-Irish Drama	
		London Calling Europe
14 Dec. 1947	The Red Horse of Hollywood	HS
15 Dec. 1947	Personal Memories of the Arab Legion	HS
25 Dec. 1947	A Bride for the Unicorn	TP
18 Jan. 1948	A Bride for the Unicorn	TP
30 Jan. 1948	The Red Horse of Hollywood	TP
17 Mar. 1948	Lillibulero	NIHS
23 Mar. 1948	The Moon in the Yellow River	TP
13 June 1948	We'll Keep Your Name in Mind	HS
20/27 June 1948	The Critics (theatre reviews)	HS

257

4/11 July 1948	The Critics (theatre reviews)	HS
20 July 1948	It's Good English (about Joyce's *Ulysses*)	Far Easterns
12 Sept. 1948	The Critics (theatre reviews)	HS
14 Sept. 1948	In the Train (adaptor)	NIHS
2 Oct. 1948	The Riddle of Swift (discussion with Frank O'Connor)	TP
26 Oct. 1948	The Riddle of Swift (as above)	NIHS
14 Nov. 1948	Man and Superman, Act III (narrator)	TP
16 Dec. 1948	Not One Returns to Tell	NIHS
1 Jan. 1949	Backward Glance. In the Train	NIHS
16 Jan. 1949	Amanda McKittrick Ros	TP
16 Mar. 1949	Curtain Up: The Moon in the Yellow River	LP
19 Apr. 1949.	Amanda McKittrick Ros	TP
1 July 1949	Travel Talks, No. 10. Green Pastures and Rich Milk	HS
7 Aug. 1949	I Speak for Myself	HS
22 Aug. 1949	Blind Man's Buff (with Ernst Toller)	HS
27 Aug. 1949	British Half Hour for Far East: I Speak for Myself	Far Eastern
23 Oct. 1949	Silver Jubilee: 25 years of broadcasting in Northern Ireland (recordings used)	NIHS
24 Oct. 1949	Death at Newtownstewart	NIHS
27 Oct. 1949	TV Studio Production Technique	overseas
7 Dec. 1949	After Ten Years	NIHS
5 Jan. 1950	After Ten Years	TP
8 Mar. 1950	Death at Newtownstewart	NIHS
25 Dec. 1950	Christmas Journey	HS,LP
16 Jan. 1951	Echoes from the Past. Despatches from Italy (recordings)	HS
13 Feb. 1951	Echoes from the Past. American Parade in Northern Ireland (recordings)	HS
6 Jan. 1952	Man and Superman, Act III (narrator)	TP
17 Jan. 1952	Echoes from the Past. Despatches from Italy (recordings)	HS
4 Mar. 1952	Senior English II. Bernard Shaw	HS
13 Mar. 1952	What Do You Know? (Commentary on American Parade)	NIHS
2 Sept. 1952	contributed to Portrait of Robert Flaherty	TP
11 Dec. 1952	Abbey Theatre	TP
5 Jan. 1953	Abbey Theatre	TP

2 May 1953	contributed to Portrait of Robert Flaherty	TP
19 June 1953	Abbey Theatre	TP
5 July 1953	Personal Story: A Schoolboy in the Rebellion	HS
24 July 1953	Eastward Ho.	HS
27 Aug. 1953	London Forum: Why Do we Travel?	NA
17 Sept. 1953	Personal Story: A Schoolboy in the Rebellion	TP
4 Mar. 1954	Blind Man's Buff	NIHS
20 Sept. 1954	George Bernard Shaw: An Irish Portrait	TP
26 Mar. 1955	George Bernard Shaw: An Irish Portrait	TP
11 Jan. 1956	The Arts in Ulster	NIHS
9 Mar. 1956	Portrait Gallery No. 1 (interviewed)	NIHS
16 Mar. 1956	This Day and Age: With St. Patrick's Day in Mind	Overseas
22 May 1956	contributed to Portrait of Robert Flaherty	TP
9 June 1956 rec.	Ulster Magazine	Overseas
26 Aug. 1956	Letter to a Young Dramatist	HS
7 Aug. 1958	Cambridge in the Early Twenties	HS
13 Aug. 1958	And So To Sea	HS
21 Aug. 1958	Getting Out	HS
14 Nov. 1958rec.	Two Talks for Ulster Magazine (The 'Enterprise')	Overseas
30 Dec. 1958	The First Time I . . .	NIHS
25 Mar. 1959	Weep for Polyphemus	NIHS
14 Apr. 1959	Ulster Magazine	Overseas
17 Apr. 1959	Pick of the Week: Ulster Magazine	Overseas
4 Aug. 1959	Brains Trust	HS
25 Aug. 1959	Brains Trust	HS
28 Aug. 1959	Pick of the Week: Brains Trust	HS
3 Sept. 1959rec.	Who Are We?	Overseas
3 Sept. 1959rec.	Boyne Battlefield	Overseas
3 Sept. 1959rec.	Ulster Players	Overseas
7 Jan. 1960	The Verdict of the Court: The Ireland's Eye Murder	HS
22 May 1960	Alamein to Tunis	HS
18 Apr. 1961	Oliver St. John Gogarty: A Portrait	TP
10 Oct. 1962	The Moon in the Yellow River	NIHS
26 Nov. 1962	The Moon in the Yellow River	HS
8 Apr. 1963	Cambridge in the Early Twenties	HS
1 Oct. 1963	New Comment. The Irish Dramatic	

	Imagination (took part in conversation)	TP
7 Dec. 1967	The Imagination of Swift	Radio 4
9 Nov. 1975	Romantics and Eccentrics	NIHS

War despatches from the Middle East:

12 July 1942	31 Oct. 1942	17 Dec. 1942
4 Aug. 1942	2 Nov. 1942	18 Dec. 1942
10 Aug. 1942	3 Nov. 1942	19 Dec. 1942
21 Aug. 1942	10 Nov. 1942	20 Dec. 1942
1 Sept. 1942	15 Nov. 1942	24 Dec. 1942
3 Sept. 1942	16 Nov. 1942	29 Dec. 1942
4 Sept. 1942	17 Nov. 1942	30 Dec. 1942
5 Sept. 1942	18 Nov. 1942	31 Dec. 1942
6 Sept. 1942	19 Nov. 1942	5 Jan. 1943
9 Sept. 1942	20 Nov. 1942	25 Jan. 1943
30 Sept. 1942	21 Nov. 1942	29 Jan. 1943
3 Oct. 1942	22 Nov. 1942	1 Feb. 1943
12 Oct. 1942	16 Dec. 1942	

War despatches from Italy and the Mediterranean:

9 July 1943	11 Dec. 1943	12 May 1944
27 Oct. 1943	4 Jan. 1944	13 May 1944
2 Nov. 1943	7 Jan. 1944	21 May 1944
6 Nov. 1943	11 Jan. 1944	26 May 1944
12 Nov. 1943	26 Mar. 1944	20 Sept. 1944
14 Nov. 1943	6 May 1944	
21 Nov. 1943	11 May 1944	

War despatches from France and Germany:

12 Feb. 1945	11 Mar. 1945	16 Mar. 1945

BBC television:

1939	The Parnell Commission
4 Aug. 1941	High Command (with Igor Vinogradoff)
18 June 1946	Picture Page (producer)

260

Check-list of Denis Johnston's writings

2 Aug. 1946	Queen of Spades (producer)
21 Aug. 1947	Weep for the Cyclops
16 Oct. 1947	The Moon in the Yellow River
22 Dec. 1947	Viewers' Viewpoint (discussion of TV prod. of Hamlet)
4 Jan. 1948	Death at Newtownstewart
8 July 1948	News Map: Ireland
18 Aug. 1948	The Unthinking Lobster
10 June 1949	The Call to Arms
2 Dec. 1949	Personal Impressions, No. 3. Discussion of English Speaking Nations
1 Sept. 1951	Speaking Personally
12 Sept. 1954	The Moon in the Yellow River
2 Aug. 1959	The Brains Trust
23 Aug. 1959	The Brains Trust
27 Sept. 1959	Monitor: (talk about Sean O'Casey)

Radio Telefis Eireann:

1940	Departure of President Roosevelt from Galway
6 Jan. 1948	Death at Newtownstewart

R.T.E. Drama Review:

4 Oct. 1955	13 Dec. 1955	20 Mar. 1956
11 Oct. 1955	20 Dec. 1955	27 Mar. 1956
18 Oct. 1955	27 Dec. 1955	3 Apr. 1956
25 Oct. 1955	3 Jan. 1956	17 Apr. 1956
1 Nov. 1955	10 Jan. 1956	24 Apr. 1956
8 Nov. 1955	21 Feb. 1956	1 May 1956
22 Nov. 1955	28 Feb. 1956	8 May 1956
29 Nov. 1955	6 Mar. 1956	14 May 1956
6 Dec. 1955	13 Mar. 1956	

5 Nov. 1958	Plays of Stage and Radio
12 Nov. 1958	Plays of Stage and Radio
19 Nov. 1958	Plays of Stage and Radio
25 Nov. 1958	Plays of Stage and Radio
31 Dec. 1959	Hilton and Micheál: The Story of a Famous Theatrical Friendship

5 Feb. 1963	The Glass Murder
30 Nov. 1967	Jonathan Swift (the oration delivered by Hilton Edwards from a script prepared by Denis Johnston on the tercentenary of Swift's birthday in Saint Patrick's Cathedral, Dublin.
2 Jan. 1974	Orders and Desecrations (autobiography): Songs of Araby
3 Jan. 1974	Orders and Desecrations: The Scales of Solomon
8 Jan. 1974	Orders and Desecrations: The Harvest of Dragon's Teeth
9 Jan. 1974	Orders and Desecrations: Buttercups and Blood
15 Jan. 1974	Orders and Desecrations
5 Nov. 1977	School Days
12 Nov. 1977	Shaw, Haley, Yeats
19 Nov. 1977	Going to America
26 Nov. 1977	

American networks:

25 Sept. 1940	Spirit of People in Wartime Ireland	NBC
14 Nov. 1940	Wartime neutrality of Ireland	NBC
30 Mar. 1960	Operations at Killyfaddy	ABC-TV, Ltd.
June 1965	Yeats Centenary.	

APPENDIX

Addenda and Errata to *The Dramatic Works*

Denis Johnston recently sent me some revisions (and some corrections) to *A Bride for the Unicorn*, as he was dissatisfied with the version published in *The Dramatic Works of Denis Johnston*, Volume 2 (1979) together with some corrections to errors in the text that he had noted elsewhere. It seemed appropriate to include them in this volume. All page and line references are for this edition.

Colin Smythe

p.29, lines 11–12 read		*'six strokes boom out. The woman has dropped her shoes, which remain midway on the ramp, before'*
8 lines up		delete words 'All we need is a Boat.'
p.31, line 8		delete line
3 lines up read		'And bachelors must shiver in the Hall, While dreams are put to bed.
p.32, line 22 read		'Cinderella – twice over. Get the girls to try them'
line 32 read		'JAY. If only I had seen her face!'
line 33 read		'ORPHEUS. Very careless of you! (*He opens*'
p.33, line 18 read		'mooning around in a cornfield. I'd be glad to come along only I'
p.35, line 25 read		'BARNEY (*off*). Go on! Answer her!'
p.46, line 8 read		'JAY. Since bound together by a yellow band, they feed upon'
p.54, line 24 read		'(*He runs below. But* MEEDY *has vanished.*)'
p.55, lines 16–18 read		'HERA. They are your own Sins. I watched you with cat's eyes. When you went out and when you went in. I wrote it all down in a tradesman's note-book with cash columns,'
p.56, 6 lines up read		'Decay! Only if only I could love without sight or sound –'

p.57, line 18   read   'And Cleopatra's charms to keep you quiet? Why must you'

      line 26   read   'JAY. Stop, Thief! I am being robbed! Stop thief! I am robbed! Robbed!'

p.58, 14 lines up   read   'LONGBOTTOM, K.C. That is a most improper remark.'

      9 lines up   for 'PROSECUTOR' read 'LONGBOT-TOM'

  bottom two lines are in the wrong order. Transpose.

p.59, line 23   read   'HAROLD. M'lud, if I argue that A is B I have said nothing of any'

      line 28   read   'LONGBOTTOM. Kindly keep your piffle in your pants!'

p.64, line 4   read   'send for. I am a Leader once more.'

      line 10   read   'drums! So we can get on with the War, so that I can'

      line 16   read   'Preservation of Peace.'

      lines 21–6   read   'ALIX. Possibly, Private Foss. One can never tell. But kindly remember that whatever we may be called upon to undertake, we are a Peace-Keeping Force. Remember that,'

      4–5 lines up   read   'JAY (*fixing his bayonet*). Up the Pole! – Up the Peace Keeping! (*For a little while the two figures stalk each other on the upper level until they*'

p.65, line 1   read   'BARNEY. Fighting. That's funny isn't it!'

      line 3   read   'BARNEY. Oh I wouldn't have hurt *you*. I'm the Enemy you know.'

      lines 8–9   read   'BARNEY. That's right. Would you mind doing it now?'

      lines 11–13   read   'BARNEY. But you were going to. JAY. I didn't know that you were anybody in particular.'

      lines 22–24   read   'JAY. Don't be absurd. Sensible people don't want to get bayoneted. BARNEY. Oh, everybody wants that. Only they don't usually know it.

p.65 bottom 5 lines to p.69 line 23 are replaced by the following.

264

BARNEY. Then I saw that there was a lot to be said for the law, when the very act of suicide prevents one from giving proper expression to one's point of view. Besides it has no psychological importance, unless one can be aware of it. And how can you be aware of it once one is dead? You see my difficulty?

JAY. Yes. I mean No, I don't.

ALIX (*appearing below*). Look here – what about these Operations?

JAY. Well, what about them?

ALIX. Aren't your going to stick him with your bayonet?

JAY. Why?

ALIX. Why? I never heard of such a thing! Stick him with your bayonet at once!

JAY. Oh, go away please.

BARNEY. We're only trying to work to rule.

ALIX. I don't care what you're working to! This is a Peace-Keeping Force. So it's your business to stick him with your bayonet. Otherwise what are we here for? (*He hurries off, grumbling.*)

BARNEY. He's right, you know. That's why war is such a good thing.

JAY. Who says it's a good thing? Look at those fields, sown with Dragon's Teeth, where only the fortunate are still and silent, and where the luckless lie, crying with crooked mouths for sleep. This is a sorry harvest home to mark the Autumn of the Year.

BARNEY. Autumn is a good thing. Sunset is the best time. For soon we shall all go to sleep. And in sleep we will each have our own World. Here we have only a World in common. And what a World!

JAY. To sleep? Perhaps never to wake!

BARNEY. You are against sleep?

JAY. Who isn't – when it may mean Eternity?

BARNEY. You want a Life without Death – a Joy without Pain – a Heaven without Hell?

JAY. Who doesn't?

BARNEY. But that's nonsense. You should cultivate a Sanity like mine, and maybe you wouldn't contradict yourself so much.

ALIX (*re-appearing below in a rage*). Sitting up there – working to rule while everything that matters in the world is breaking down! Bring in that Table! Send for the Government! We'll have to have this out!

(*A long Table and Chairs are brought on and set upstage right while almost the entire Cast assemble, ad-libbing and greeting each other.* JAY *and* BARNEY *come down form the upper level, and greet*

265

many friends, as the upper curtains close behind them.)
POLLUX. Ladies and Gentlemen, pray silence for the Right Honourable Harold Castor – the Prime Incumbent!'

p.70, line 24 read	'properly chosen intervals, and everybody will be happy.'
line 27 read	'of the times are due to the Sunday Papers.'
p.173, line 13 read	'HUSSAR (*lighting up*). You don't say GERMAN. It is an Italian aeroplane. There is always danger that it'
p.205, 9 lines up read	GINNETTE WADDELL
p.212, bottom line read	'at all. (*Shouting*) Take that beast out of my kitchen!'
p.293, 3 lines up read	'Is that what you mean by Jerusalem!'
p.294, line 13 read	'It's only Sodom and Gemorrah.'
p.330, 2 lines up read	'SOUDER. I am Hanwell, of the Royal West Kents.'
p.337, 2 lines up read	'Will the will ass bray, while he has grass?'
p.361, line 14 read	'MAEV. Your Mother never owned a pigsty, let alone all'

Volume 1 (1977)

p.65, bottom line read	YOUNGER MAN. Every hour of the day that you spent filling your'
p.102, 9 lines up	for 'doctors' read 'doctorers'

NOTES ON THE CONTRIBUTORS

John Boyd: playwright, director, author of short stories, verse, and critical articles. Plays include *The Assassin, The Flats, The Farm, Guests, The Street,* and *Facing North.* He has also written many radio plays, and was a radio and television director for the BBC, Belfast, from 1947 to 1972. He has been editor of *Lagan* and *Threshold*, and is now an Honorary Director of the Lyric Players Theatre, Belfast.

Curtis Canfield: retired professor of dramatic arts. He has taught at Amherst College, Yale University, and the University of Pittsburgh, and has held important positions as Director or Trustee in several theatre institutions in the United States. Publications include *Plays of the Irish Renaissance, Plays of Changing Ireland, The Seed and the Sowers,* and *The Craft of Play Directing.*

Richard Allen Cave: lectures in the Department of English at Bedford College, University of London. He is Director of the University's International Summer School for Graduates, and Honorary Secretary of the Consortium for Drama and Media in Higher Education. Publications include *A Study of the Novels of George Moore*, editions of Moore's *Hail and Farewell* and *The Lake*, and *Terence Gray and the Festival Theatre, Cambridge*, the last volume in the series *Theatre in Focus*, of which Dr. Cave is General Editor.

Mark Culme-Seymour: Major in the British Army, World War II, The Rifle Brigade, attached to the Mediterranean H.Q. of Special Operations Executive, where he was a companion of Denis Johnston who was a BBC correspondent at the time. In business life he was mainly in advertising, but later became an amateur engineer and helped build wood processing factories in Sweden, Czechoslovakia and Russia. He is retired and lives in the south of Spain.

Cyril Cusack: actor. He has acted in Ireland, England, Holland, Belgium, France, and the United States. He has played with the Abbey Theatre, the Dublin Gate Theatre, and has directed the

Gaiety. The plays in which he has acted in major roles are too numerous to list, but his work has been especially notable in Shakespeare, Synge, O'Casey and Shaw. He has appeared in *The Moon in the Yellow River, A Bride for the Unicorn, Storm Song* and *The Golden Cuckoo* by Denis Johnston. He has also appeared in several films and television plays, including the television version of Johnston's *The Dreaming Dust*.

Hilton Edwards: actor, director, author. Co-founder and Director of the Dublin Gate Theatre where he has been a principal actor and the major director, having directed over three hundred plays. His acting roles have been very diverse, but have included nearly all of Shakespeare's plays. His productions of Johnston's *The Old Lady Says 'No!'* and *A Bride for the Unicorn* are definitive to date. He has appeared on stage in *The Old Lady Says 'No!'*, *A Bride for the Unicorn,* and *Storm Song*. Publications include *The Mantle of Harlequin*, and several articles on the theatre in Ireland.

Maurice Elliott: teaches at York University, Toronto, where he is Master of Winters College. He has written several critical articles, but is better known for his lectures, especially at the Yeats International Summer School, Sligo, where he has appeared regularly for over ten years. He is presently working on a biography of Coleridge's middle age.

Harold Ferrar: teaches at the New School for Social Research, New York. Publications include *Denis Johnston's Irish Theatre, John Osborne,* and *The Dublin Drama League 1918—1941*.

Robert Hogan: teaches at the University of Delaware and is Editor of *The Journal of Irish Literature* and *The Dictionary of Irish Literature*. He is the author of *Dion Boucicault, Eimar O'Duffy, The Experiments of Sean O'Casey, Arthur Miller, The Independence of Elmer Rice, Saint Jane* (play), *Betty and the Beast* (play), and *After the Irish Renaissance*, and has edited *Feathers from the Green Crow: Sean O'Casey 1905—1925, Drama: The Major Genres, Joseph Holloway's Abbey Theatre, Seven Irish Plays, The Plain Style,* and *Lost Plays of the Irish Renaissance*.

Thomas Kilroy: novelist, playwright, and Professor of Modern English, University College, Galway. Publications include *The

Death and Resurrection of Mr. Roche, The O'Neill, The Big Chapel, Tea and Sex and Shakespeare, and *Talbot's Box*. He is Editor of the Sean O'Casey 20th Century Views Series. Professor Kilroy is a Member of the Irish Academy of Letters and a Fellow of the Royal Society of Literature; he has been awarded the Guardian Fiction Prize, the Heinemann Award for Literature, the Irish Academy of Letters Prize for Literature, and the American-Irish Foundation Award for Literature.

Micheál MacLiammóir: actor, designer, director, author. Co-founder and Director of the Dublin Gate Theatre, he is famous for his designs of sets, lighting and costumes, and has appeared in too wide a range of stage roles to be listed here. He created the part, definitively to date, of The Speaker/Robert Emmet in Johnston's *The Old Lady Says 'No!'* and has also appeared in *A Bride for the Unicorn*. Publications include *All for Hecuba, Put Money in My Purse, Two Lights on Actors, Each Actor On His Ass, Theatre in Ireland, Enter a Goldfish, Ceo Meala Là Seaca*, and *Bláth Agus Taibhse*. He has adapted several literary works for the stage and has translated plays into Irish. He has also written plays: *Diarmuid and Gráinne, Easter 1916, The Ford of the Hurdles, Where Stars Walk, Lúlú, Ill Met By Moonlight, Prelude in Kazbek Street, Dancing Shadows, Portrait of Miriam, The Mountains Look Different, Home for Christmas, A Slipper for the Moon, St. Patrick,* and three one-man shows in which he toured several countries, *The Importance of Being Oscar, I Must Be Talking To My Friends*, and *Talking About Yeats*. Mr. MacLiammóir died in 1978.

D. E. S. Maxwell: teaches as York University, Toronto, former Master of Winters College. Publications include *The Poetry of T. S. Eliot, American Fiction, Poets of the Thirties, Brian Friel*, and he has edited *W. B. Yeats: Centenary Essays* and *English Poems of the Twentieth Century*.

Roger McHugh: recently retired from teaching at University College, Dublin. Publications include *Henry Grattan, Trial at Green Street Courthouse* (play), *Rossa* (play), and *Universities and European Unity*. Books he has edited include *Ballads of Irish Bravery, Newman on University Education*, three other Newman collections, *An Anthology of English Prose, An Anthology of English and Anglo-Irish Poetry, Carlow in '98: The Autobiography of William*

Farrell, W. B. Yeats: Letters to Katharine Tynan, Dublin 1916, Jonathan Swift, 1667—1967: A Dublin Tercentenary Tribute, The Celtic Twilight and the Nineties by Austin Clarke, *Ah Sweet Dancer! W. B. Yeats and Margot Ruddock: A Correspondence, Davis, Mangan and Ferguson: Articles* by W. B. Yeats, *Jack B. Yeats: A Centenary Gathering* by Samuel Beckett and Others, *Our Irish Theatre: A Chapter of Autobiography* by Lady Gregory.

Vivian Mercier: teaches at the University of California, Santa Barbara. Publications include *The Irish Comic Tradition, The New Novel from Queneau to Pinget*, and *Beckett/Beckett*. He is now working on a two-volume critical history of Anglo-Irish literature, 1878 to the present.

Christopher Murray: teaches at University College, Dublin. He is the author of *Robert William Elliston, Manager: A Theatrical Biography*, and has edited an Irish Restoration comedy, *St. Stephen's Green*, by William Philips, and a special issue of *Irish University Review*, entitled *Sean O'Casey: Roots and Branches*.

B.L. Reid: teaches at Mount Holyoke College, Massachusetts. Publications include small amounts of fiction and poetry and larger amounts of criticism and biography: *William Butler Yeats: The Lyric of Tragedy, The Man from New York: John Quinn and His Friends* (Pulitzer Prize for biography) and *The Lives of Roger Casement*.

Joseph Ronsley: teaches at McGill University, Montreal. He is the author of *Yeats's Autobiography: Life as Symbolic Pattern* and has edited *Myth and Reality in Irish Literature*. He is co-general-editor of the series, *Irish Drama Selections* and is President of the Canadian Association for Irish Studies.

Christine St. Peter: has recently completed a doctoral dissertation at the University of Toronto, entitled 'Denis Johnston's *The Old Lady Says "No!"*: The Gloriable Nationvoice.'

INDEX

Note: this index does not cover either the Checklist or the Illustrations

271

Index

Homer, *Odyssey*, 230

Howarth, Herbert, *The Irish Writers*, 228

Hughes, Mrs. Isa, 4

Hull, Henry, 63

Huntington, Catherine, 29

Hunt, Leigh, 123

Ibsen, Henrik, 27, 38, 61, 114, 115; *Emperor and Galilean*, 165; *Peer Gynt*, 28, 178, 208, 228

Inge, William, *Picnic*, 208

I.R.A., vii, 113

Iremonger, Valentin, 24

Irish Bar, 1, 203

Irish Independent, The, 28, 134

Irish Literary Theatre, 178

Irish Review, The, 24

Irish Statesman, The, 22

James, Henry, *The Innocents* (from *The Turn of the Screw*), 211

Jessner, Leopold, 81

Job, Book of, 238, 241

Johnson, Fred, ix, 103

Johnson, Hester (Stella), 120, 125, 128, 180, 181

Johnston, Betty (née Chancellor), 187, 188, 189

Johnston, Denis, *Works*: *The Brazen Horn*, viii, 3, 116, 155, 175, 228, 240, 241; *Blind Man's Buff* see under Toller, Ernst; *A Bride for the Unicorn*, viii, 2, 11, 50, 60, 61, 78, 81, 84, 85-8, 103, 154, 157, 164-6, 168, 181, 185, 191, 193-4, 195, 198, 201, 208, 228, 230, 236; *Collected Plays* (Cape, 1960), 30, 78, 106, 120, 138; *Dramatic Works of Denis Johnston* (Smythe, 1977, 1979), viii, 12, 16, 22, 106-7, 183, 240; *The Dreaming Dust*, 2, 60, 61, 67, 100, 120, 126, 128, 131, 157, 168-71, 180, 181, 201; *The Golden Cuckoo*, viii, 53, 60, 61, 100, 105-18, 167-8, 181, 187, 188, 210, 242; *The Golden Cuckoo and Other Plays* (1954), 157; *In Search of Swift*, viii, 119-132, 168, 209; *The Moon in the Yellow River*, 2, 42, 45-8, 49, 50-7, 59, 60, 61-7, 68-77, 106, 137, 151, 152, 157, 161-4, 173, 178, 185, 190, 191, 192, 199, 203-4, 243; *Nine Rivers From Jordan*, vii-viii, 2, 22, 100, 114, 126-7, 135, 137, 138, 141, 175, 181, 182, 191, 199, 200, 201, 203, 209, 227, 228, 229, 230-9, 243; *The Old Lady Says 'No!'*, 1, 3, 4-9, 10-23, 24, 28, 29, 30, 31, 38-45, 50-7, 60, 68, 75, 81, 82, 84, 100, 106, 137, 138, 139, 142, 145, 151, 152, 157-59, 160, 161, 178, 179-80, 185, 189-90, 199, 203, 231, 232, 243; *The Scythe and the Sunset*, 2, 60, 113, 133-156, 157, 172-6, 180, 190, 191, 192, 201, 209, Toronto production (1976), 153; *Shadowdance* see *The Old Lady Says 'No!'*; *Storm Song*, 113, 164, 167, 185; '*Strange Occurrence on Ireland's Eye*', 60, 99, 100, 106, 171-2; *The Tain*, 182

Johnston, Jeremy, 207

Johnston, Rory, 207

Jones, R.E., 80

Jonson, Ben, *Volpone*, 70

Joyce, James, 5, 18, 30, 60, 83, 141, 175, 228, 231; *The Day of the Rabblement*, 178; *Finnegans Wake*, 228, 231, 232, (adapted by Mary Manning), 208; *A Portrait of the Artist as a Young Man*, 231; *Ulysses*, 38, 141, 159, 231, 232, 243; *Work in Progress*, 232

Kaiser, Georg, 30, 79; *From Morn to Midnight*, 29, 31, 87, 159

Kaufman, George S., and Connolly, M., *Beggar on Horseback*, 30, 31, 40, 41, 159

Kennedy, M., and Dean, Basil, *The Constant Nymph*, 206

King, Archbishop William, 126

Lee, Bernard, 103

Leonard, Hugh, 184

Leskor, Nikolai, 170

Lever, Charles, 18

Longford, Countess of, 28

Longford, 6th Earl of, 28, 187, *Yahoo*, 120, 181

273

Index